IMAGES
of America

OREGON STATE PENITENTIARY

On the Cover: Taken in 1888, this photograph shows the Oregon State Penitentiary after an iron fence was installed across the front. The center tower and crenellations on the roof created the look of a medieval castle. The administration building was in the center, while the convicts were housed in the two wings. (Courtesy of the Oregon State Archives.)

IMAGES
of America

Oregon State Penitentiary

Diane L. Goeres-Gardner and John Ritter

ARCADIA
PUBLISHING

ISBN 978-1-4671-3221-3

Published by Arcadia Publishing
Charleston, South Carolina

Printed in the United States of America

Library of Congress Control Number: 2014933090

For all general information, please contact Arcadia Publishing:
Telephone 843-853-2070
Fax 843-853-0044
E-mail sales@arcadiapublishing.com
For customer service and orders:
Toll-Free 1-888-313-2665

Visit us on the Internet at www.arcadiapublishing.com

This book is dedicated to all the corrections officers of OSP who served in the past with loyalty and dedication; especially Mitch Morrow, who during an amazing career rose from corrections officer through every rank to become deputy director of the Department of Corrections. He epitomizes the ideal corrections employee, who rises through the ranks after years of commitment and hard work.

Contents

ACKNOWLEDGMENTS

Unless otherwise noted, all images appear courtesy of the Oregon State Penitentiary. Other organizations that contributed images are as follows:

Oregonian	*Oregonian* newspaper, Portland, Oregon
OSA	Oregon State Archives, Salem, Oregon
OSL	Oregon State Library, Salem, Oregon
SJ	*Statesman Journal* newspaper, Salem, Oregon
SPL	Salem Public Library, Salem, Oregon
WHC	Willamette Heritage Center, Salem, Oregon

Introduction

The early history of the Oregon State Penitentiary (OSP) is shrouded in disagreements, contradictions, and accusations of graft. Superintendents and wardens were appointed according to their party affiliation and not their knowledge of prison administration. The prison was mismanaged, inmates were mistreated, and money was spent unwisely. It was not until the middle of the 20th century that the state began to recognize the necessity of selecting administrators with prison experience to run the OSP.

The first Oregon Territorial Prison was built in Oregon City in 1845. The two-story, 20-foot-square structure was built of new logs and cost $875. It had no doors or windows on the first floor and a set of stairs going up the side of the building to the second story, where the only door opened into a room with a three-foot square hole in the middle. Prisoners were lowered through the hole and only allowed out at the discretion of the jailor. On August 18, 1846, it burned to the ground.

In January 1851, the second territorial prison was opened in Portland. It was 114 feet long, 50 feet wide, and had three tiers of 28 cells each. It was built of brick on the southwest side of Portland, in the vicinity of Front Street between Hall Boulevard and Harrison Street, at a cost of $85,000. Records show that by 1857 warden Joseph Sloan was caring for 17 men and one woman. OSP was not very effective at keeping prisoners, as escapes were reported regularly in the Portland newspapers.

On May 16, 1866, the prisoners were transferred to a temporary wooden building in Salem. Wooden planks were used to erect a 90-foot-by-36-foot building. It had windows that were nine feet by three feet and covered by iron gratings. The cellblock ran down the center of the building, was two tiers high, and consisted of 40 cells. Again, many escapes were reported. On August 27, 1866, about 50 inmates attempted to escape. They could literally walk out or climb over the temporary wooden stockade wall.

In October 1870, the Oregon Legislature allocated $50,000 to erect a permanent penitentiary. On August 1, 1872, the first permanent building (cellblock A) was finished at a cost of $159,693. It was 212 feet long and 45 feet wide. It had cantilevered tiers with electric controls, which raised and lowered an iron bar across the door of each cell or an entire row until the warden could clasp each padlock shut. A creek ran through the center of the prison yard and powered a large waterwheel. In the engine room, a four-horsepower turbine provided power to the prison.

The new prison was an octagonal building with three radiating wings. The center wing housed the administration offices, with the chapel on the first floor and the kitchen in the basement. Two wings radiated off the opposite sides. The chapel was a notorious place because that was where inmate punishment was administered, which was usually a flogging, with the inmate tied to a central post.

Twenty years later, the penitentiary accepted the bid of $6,547 to add 24 double cells and 32 single iron cells. The new addition to the north wing (cellblock B) had a door of thick seasoned fir and an outer grating around the rows of brick cells, with three upper tiers made of iron. It was 80 feet long, 40 feet wide, and 40 feet tall, with a solid concrete floor. Inmates made the 80,000 bricks needed to construct it. New buildings continued going up through the 1950s. Bricks made in the prison brickyard supplied building material for all the state buildings and many of the buildings in downtown Salem.

By 1907, the Oregon State Penitentiary came to be known as a "hard prison," with inmates required to wear striped uniforms, have their heads shaved, receive frequent floggings, be chained to their cell doors, and be hosed with water. Inmates were not allowed to talk in the dining hall or in their cells and were required to walk single file with their arms crossed in front of them as they went to and from the various buildings. Violent convicts were required to walk in a "bull ring," a circle painted in an isolated exercise yard, from daylight to dark and sleep in open-air sheds, regardless of the weather. The men were supervised by "bulls," guards who carried leather saps or truncheons and used them frequently to maintain order. Eventually, the harsh punishment system was abolished.

Industrial activities included brick making, a robust flax industry, a stove foundry, a harness factory, and a farm that produced much of the food needed to feed the people in prison and other state institutions.

In 1927, the penitentiary was placed under the supervision of the board of control, with the governor as head of the board. The board now had the ability to appoint the warden and deputy warden and could also set policy for the prison.

A parole system and part-time parole board were initiated in 1939. By 1965, it had 58 officers supervising 7,700 parolees. In 1965, a newly instituted work-release program was initiated. An Oregon Women's Corrections Center with 84 beds was opened adjacent to the penitentiary that same year. It was supervised by the warden of OSP and staffed with prison corrections officers until 1972, when it acquired its own administrator.

In August 1968, a riot caused an estimated $2.5 million in damages as inmates raged inside the facility, and much of the prison was burned. An investigation revealed numerous reasons for the riot. It initiated a radical shift from a harsh, security-oriented prison to a more thoughtful and safe facility, with policies and procedures designed to maintain control and offer rehabilitation to those inmates who wanted to change. A full-time parole board was created to better handle the inmates waiting for a hearing.

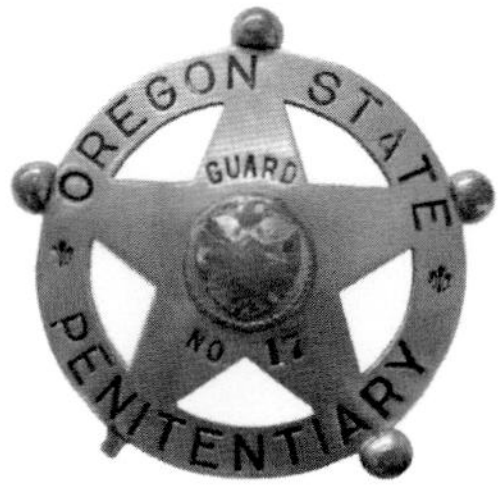

One

Inside the Prison Walls

Oregon's population grew quickly during the last decades of the 19th century and even more so during the first few decades of the 20th century. The Oregon State Penitentiary felt that growth and scrambled desperately to accommodate the resulting overcrowding. In 1929, the inmate population was 710—in a facility with a capacity of 594.

An intense program of modernization began in the 1920s, and a $10 million building program began in the 1950s. A new 22-foot-high concrete stockade wall was built in 1949, which replaced the old 15-foot-high brick wall, and increased the acreage inside the prison walls to 22 acres. Cellblock C was built in 1932, and cellblock D was opened in 1949. OSP celebrated a milestone in 1958 when cellblock B, built in 1871, was finally demolished and replaced with cellblock E. A new cellblock A replaced the original, built in 1901, and was opened in 1957 to house the minimum-security inmates. The Intermediate building, opened in 1953, housed all the support facilities for OSP: education, chapel, hospital, barbershop, library, and so on. Also, a new segregation and isolation building, constructed to house the execution chamber and 90 of the prison's more dangerous inmates, was opened in 1953. This replaced the old "bullpen," or punishment cells, in the basement of cellblock C.

In 1911, OSP initiated a new parole system, helping to reduce the number of inmates. Oregon opened its first all-women's prison next door to OSP in 1965, relieving serious congestion in that program. Beginning in 1907, inmates were allowed to wear cadet gray prison suits, with stripes only used as a form of punishment. A telephone system was installed in 1913 and electricity in 1924. Before the old dining room was built in 1904, inmates were fed with individual trays in their cells. Today, the penitentiary can house 2,100 inmates. This self-contained city now has four cellblocks, two dormitories, several types of industries, vocational training shops, a physical plant with 10 shops, an education department, a library, an infirmary, a kitchen and dining room, and two recreation areas.

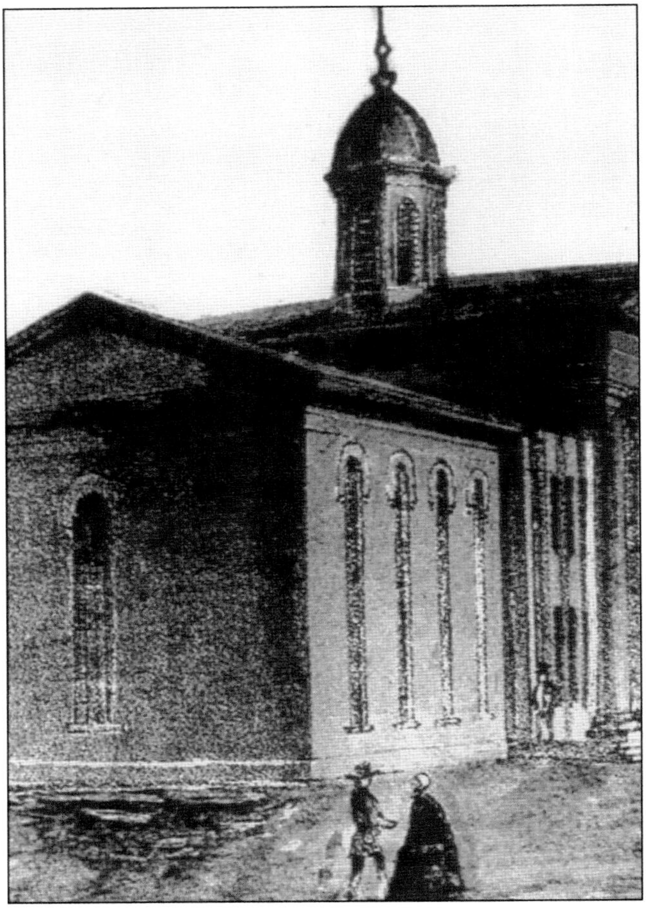

On December 5, 1853, lots were chosen in Portland for a new territorial prison. By February 24, 1857, the exterior walls were up, but no doors had been installed. In July, superintendent Joseph Sloan moved 17 men and one woman, Charity Lamb, into the prison. Difficulties over ownership of the land caused the legislature to move the prison to Salem on May 16, 1866. (Courtesy of OSL.)

OSP was designed by G.W. Rhodes and excavated by the convicts. Prisoners moved into the building in August 1872. At the center was an octagonal building with three radiating wings. The center wing was an administration building. It contained the chapel, a kitchen in the basement, and two wings on opposite sides forming the cellblocks. The final cost was $159,693.

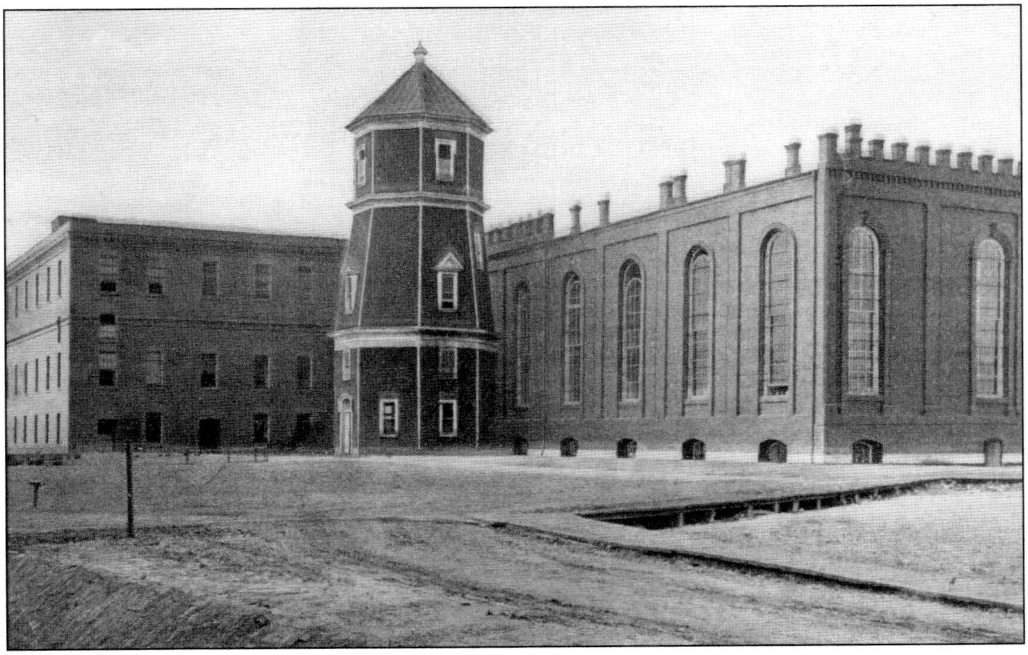

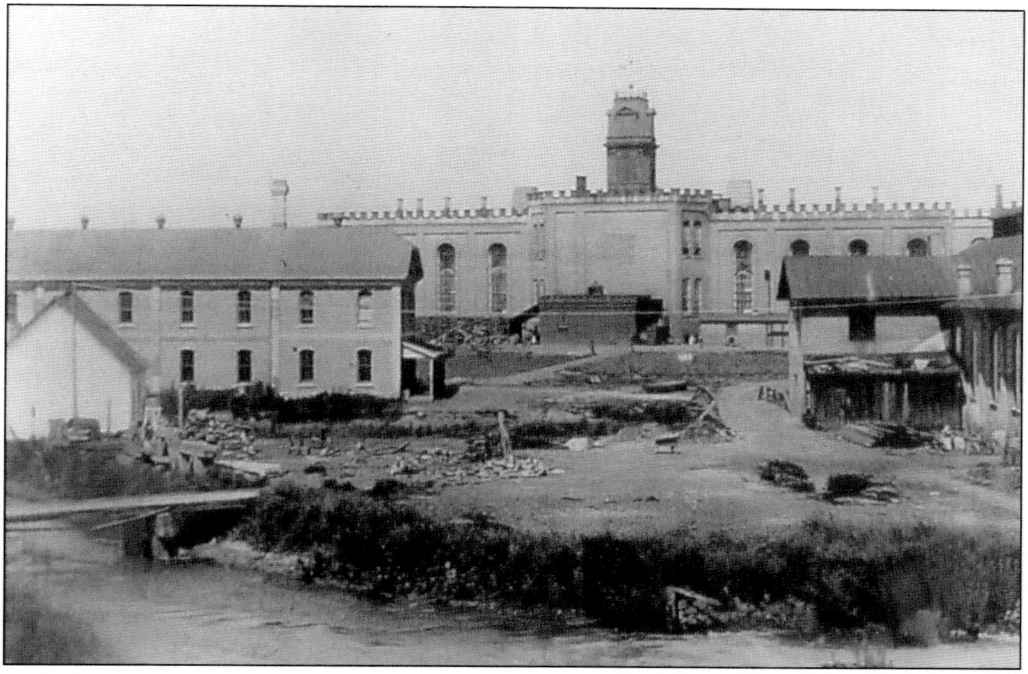

In 1887, improvements costing $21,200 included an iron fence installed across the front of the prison. It connected the corners of the brick walls. Additional upgrades included a two-story brick laundry and workshops. The crenellations across the top of the buildings created a castle-like effect. Convict labor brought in $41,903 to the prison fund.

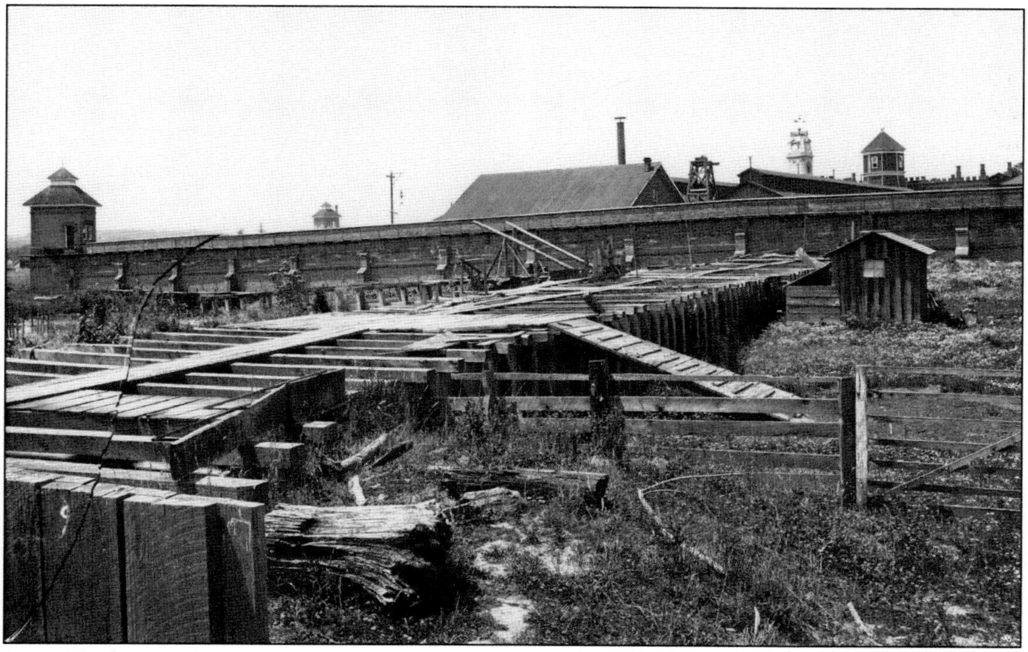

In 1885, the north wing was extended 75 feet. It included three tiers of cells added to those already in use. In 1883, the old 15-foot-high wooden palisade was removed, and a brick wall was built around most of enclosure, with seven sentinel towers on the corners and a guard promenade along the entire stockade. It cost $46,981. (Courtesy of OSL.)

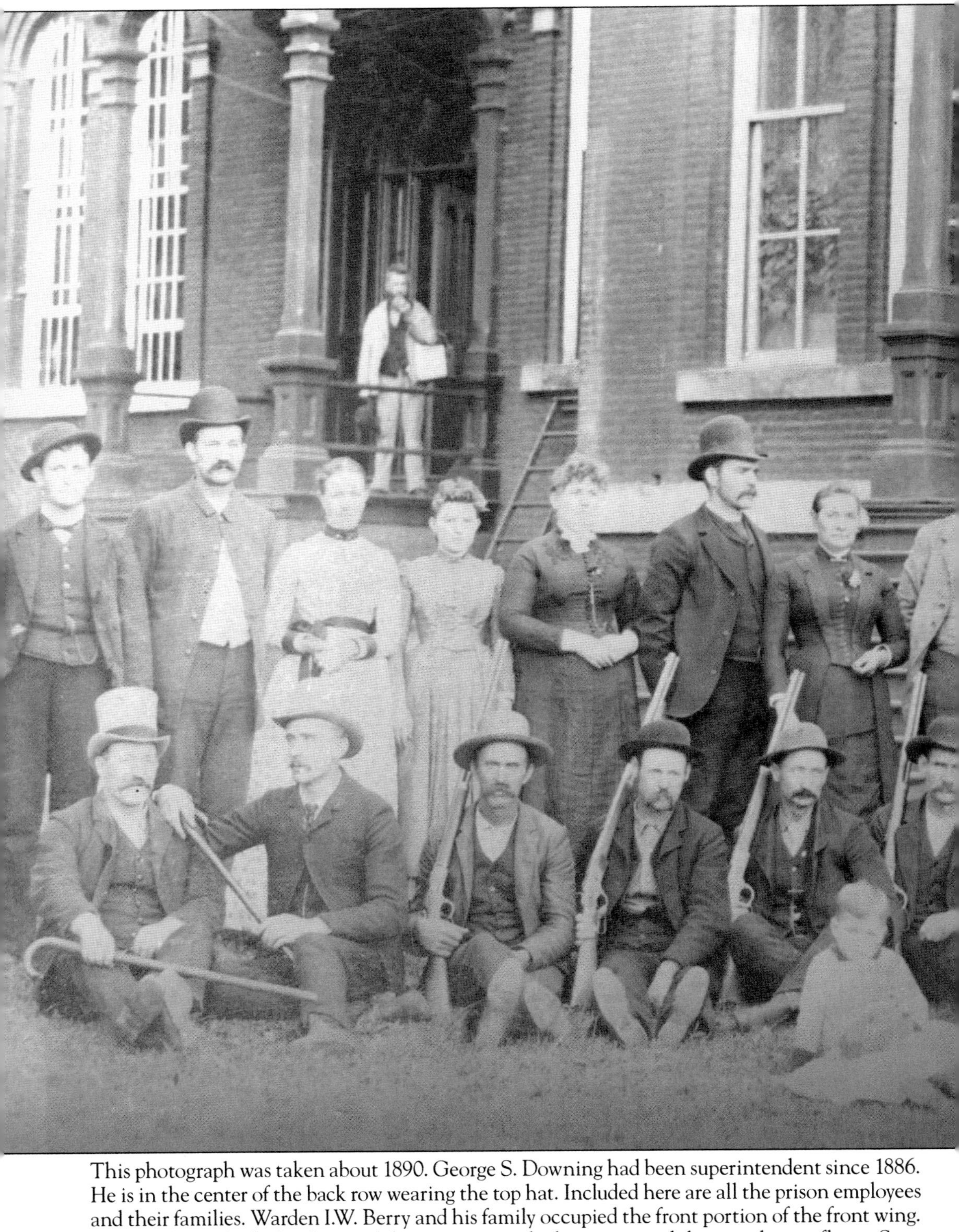

This photograph was taken about 1890. George S. Downing had been superintendent since 1886. He is in the center of the back row wearing the top hat. Included here are all the prison employees and their families. Warden I.W. Berry and his family occupied the front portion of the front wing. The employees had a kitchen and dining room in the basement and slept on the top floors. Sons often followed their fathers' vocations. Guards only carried guns if they patrolled the stockade walls.

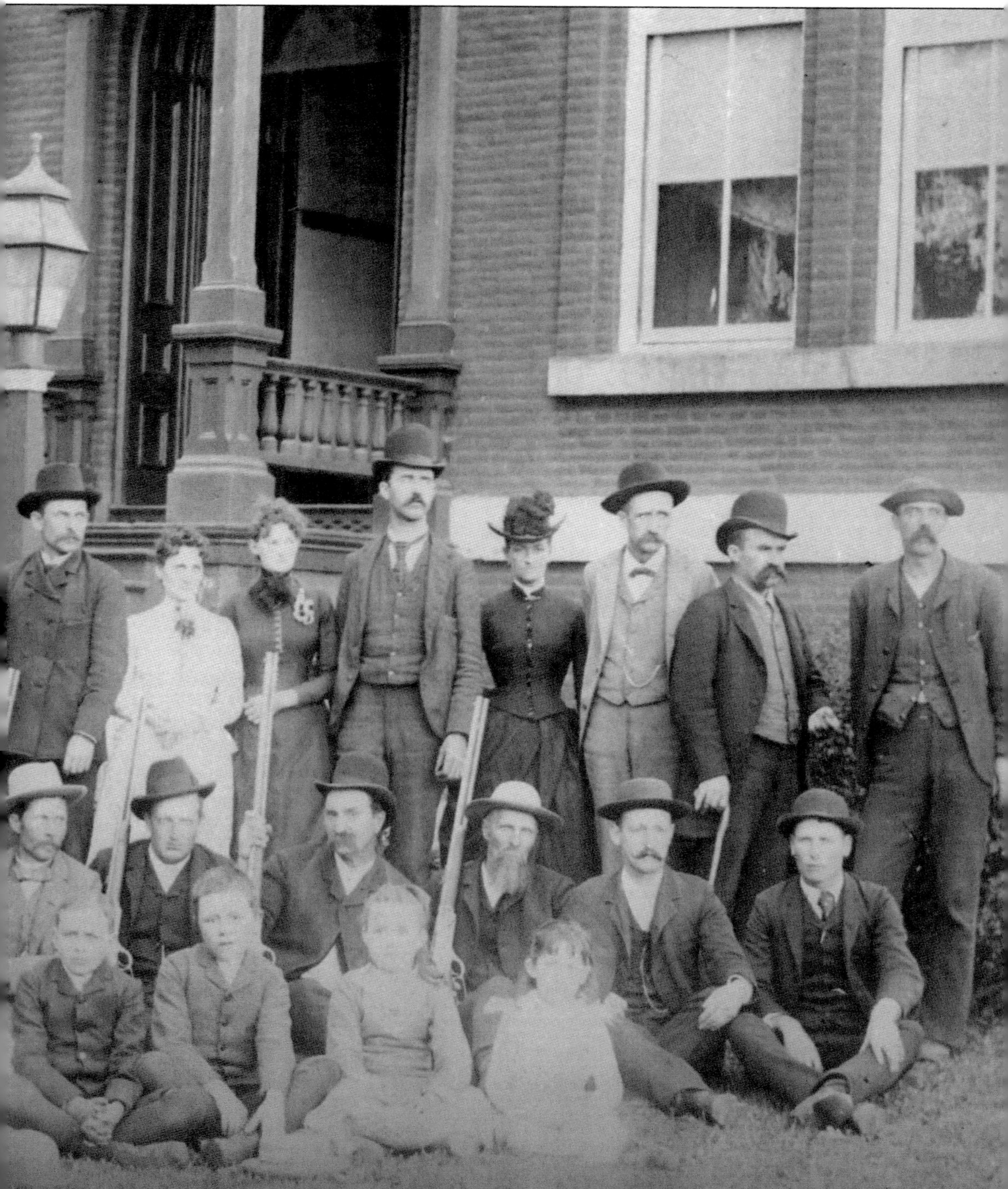

Inside guards carried canes with hooks on one end. OSP averaged between 324 and 421 prisoners a day in 1892. OSP began photographing incoming prisoners that same year. Malaria fever and consumption were the two most common causes of death. Chaplain William Lund disparaged OSP's use of corporal punishment and stated, "Reformation must come from within."

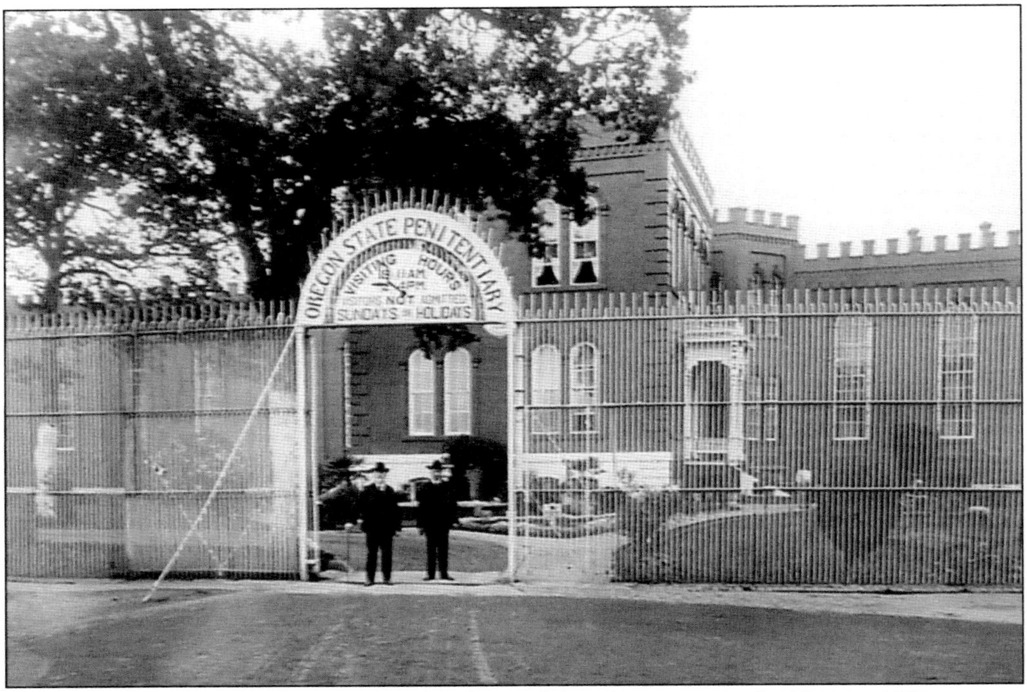

The 432-foot steel bar fence was erected in front of the administration building in 1888 at a cost of $3,715. Each bar was made of three-quarter-inch steel and was 13.5 feet high. The gate was operated by hydraulic water pressure. In 1902, visitors were admitted every day except Sundays and holidays. This photograph shows the entrance in 1890. (Courtesy of SPL.)

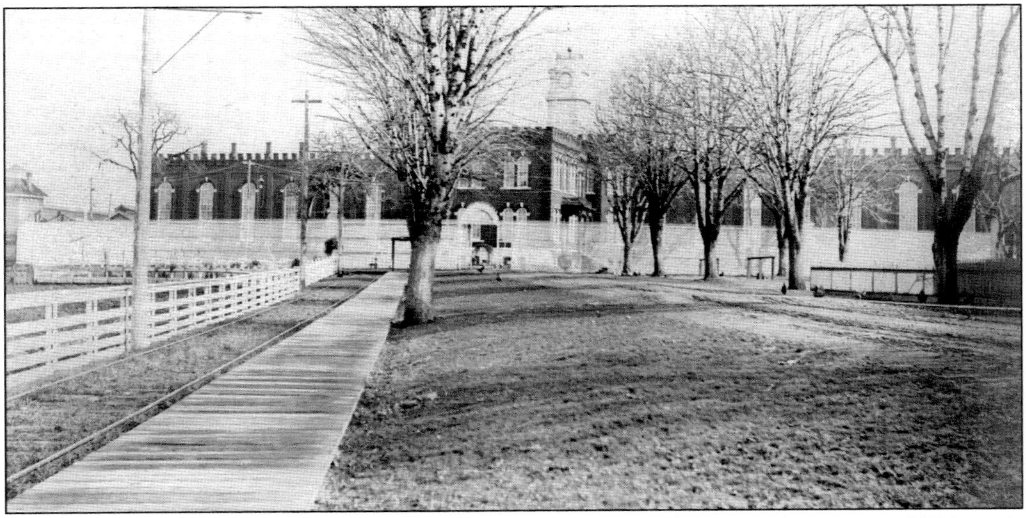

In 1888, the road leading up to the prison gate was graded and improved, requiring 3,780 yards of dirt and 1,160 loads of gravel. A wooden sidewalk protected pedestrians from the mud. All electrical and telephone wires were eventually placed underground, removing the poles around the prison. (Courtesy of OSL.)

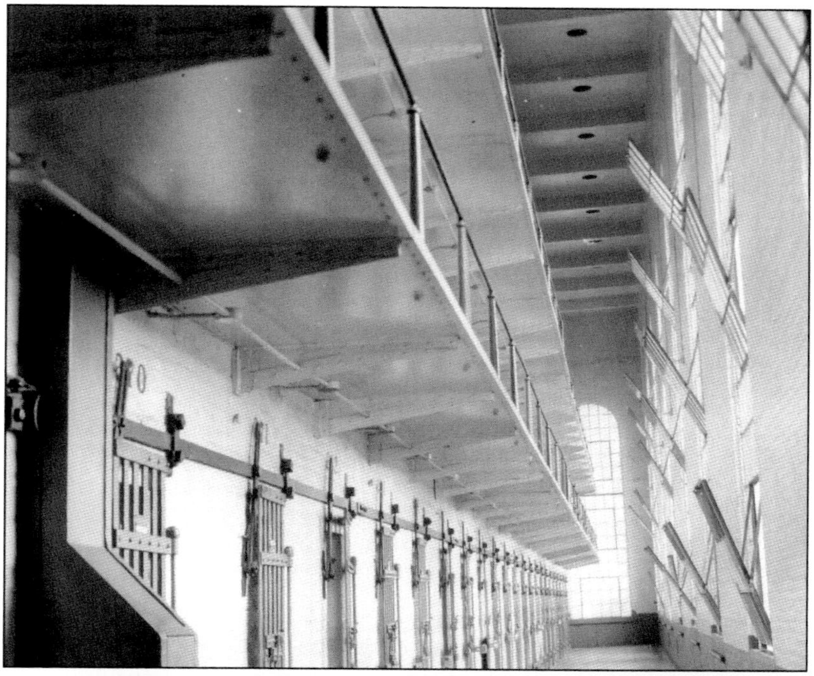

The south wing, or cellblock A, was 22 cells long and three tiers high in two corridors. Each cell had double bunks. In 1894, an addition was built on the south wing that was 80 feet long and 40 feet wide. Steel cells costing $8,000 were finally installed two years later. (Courtesy of OSA.)

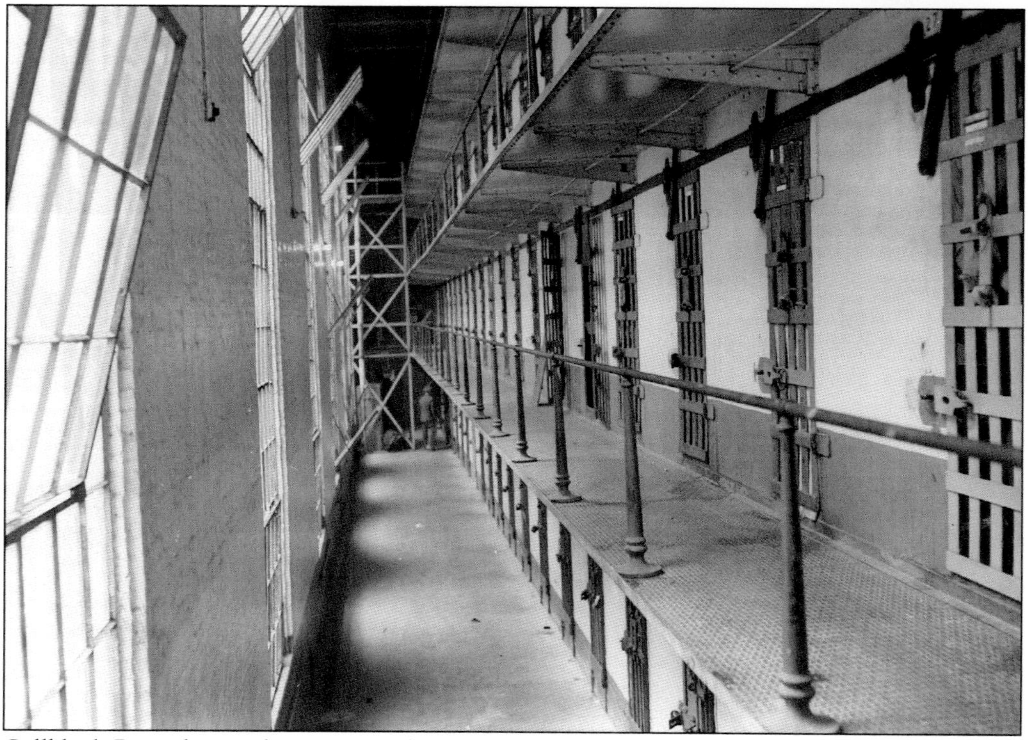

Cellblock B, or the north wing, was the second inmate-housing unit built at the prison. It was constructed in 1871 and eventually demolished when the prison was renovated in 1958. It housed 380 inmates in four cantilevered tiers and was double celled. It was made of brick and was the last part of the old brick prison still standing in 1958. The doors were locked with individual padlocks. (Courtesy of OSA.)

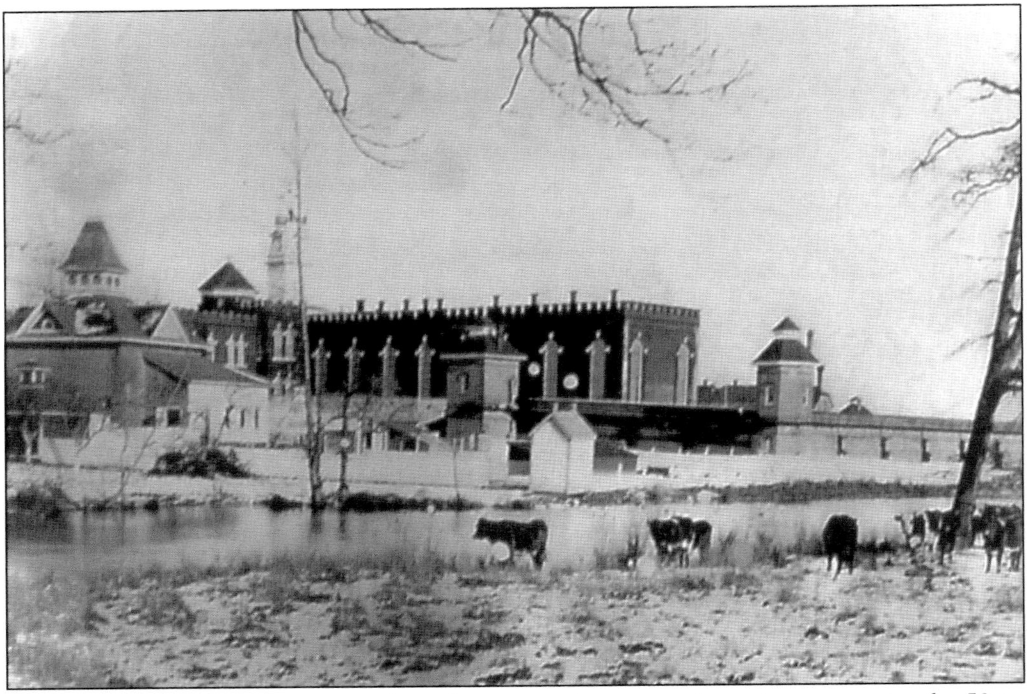

Beginning in 1876, convicts were leased out to various manufacturing companies for 50¢ a day, earning the state nearly $13,500 that year. The prison continued to need improvements. Superintendent George Collins employed 12 guards in 1886 to patrol the new stockade walls. Between 1885 and 1886, the legislature allocated $58,420 to support the prison.

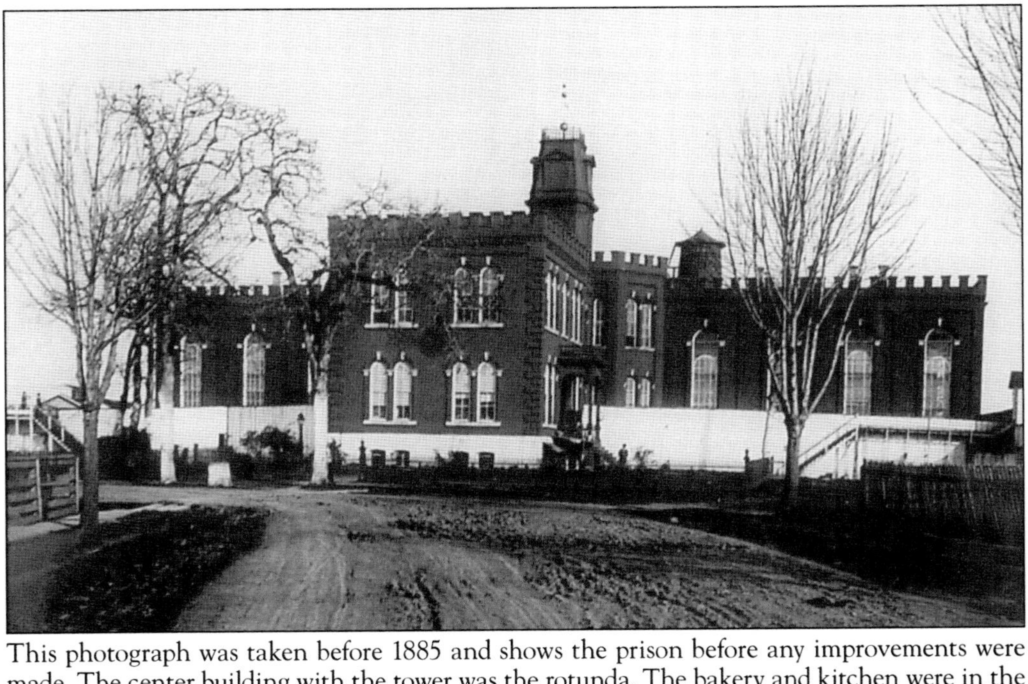

This photograph was taken before 1885 and shows the prison before any improvements were made. The center building with the tower was the rotunda. The bakery and kitchen were in the basement, and the infirmary was on the second floor. One room was reserved for female prisoners during the day, and they were locked in cells at night. (Courtesy of OSA.)

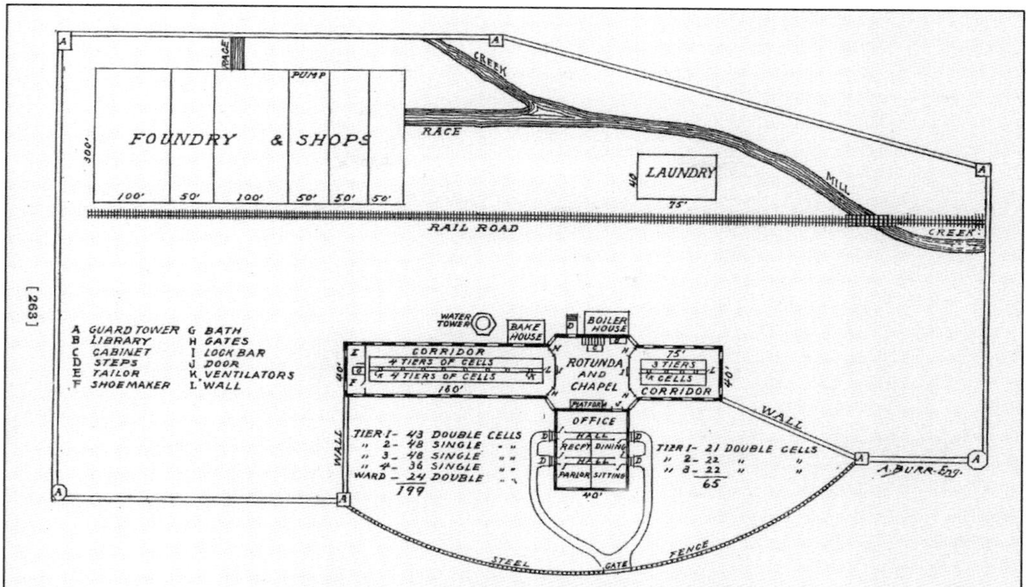

GENERAL PLAN OF THE OREGON STATE PENITENTIARY.

This is a blueprint of the Oregon State Penitentiary as it appeared in 1892, showing a capacity for 264 prisoners. The wing on the left (north) is cellblock B, built in 1871 and including an extension added in 1888. The wing on the right (south) is cellblock A. There was only one bathhouse, with room for nine inmates to take showers. (Courtesy of OSL.)

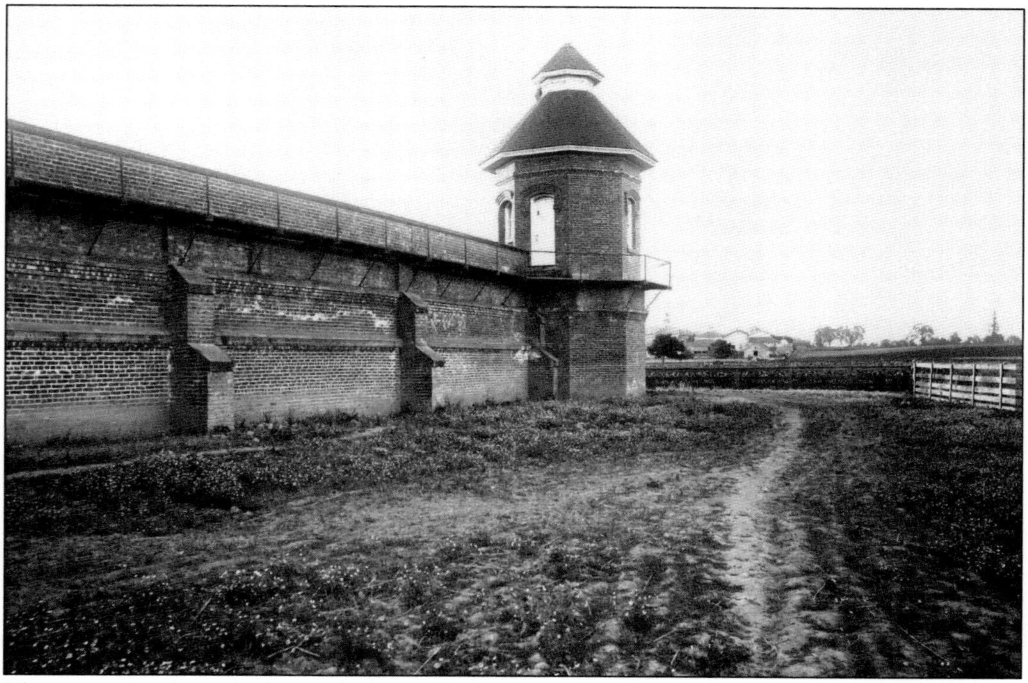

The prison brick stockade was built in 1885 and was four feet wide at its base, 16 feet tall, and extended into the ground over eight feet deep. Three of the seven towers were octagonal in shape and were ready to install Gatling guns; the others were square. Two and a half million bricks were used in the construction of the wall and the first buildings. (Courtesy of OSL.)

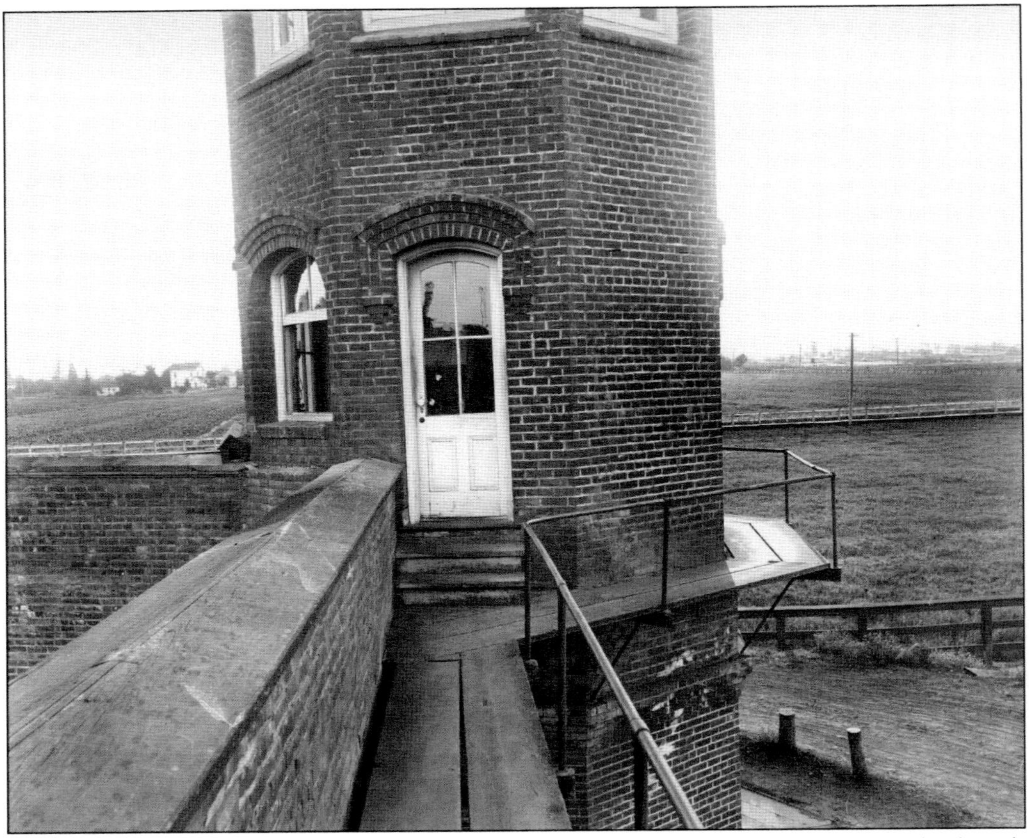

The walkway around the outside of the stockade wall had metal guardrails, and the wooden boards rotted quickly in Oregon's rainy climate. The towers had small stoves inside to keep the guards warm. A deadline is plainly marked both inside and outside. This photograph was taken before 1925, when barbed wire was installed on top of the wall. (Courtesy of OSL.)

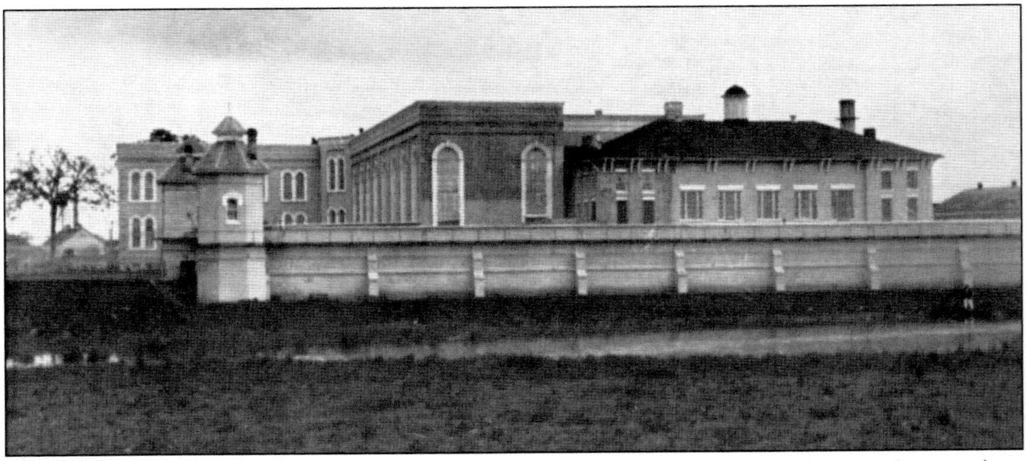

In 1893, a visitor reported that convicts were allowed to decorate their cells according to their individual tastes. Some were uncouth and messy, while others were tidy and attractive. This photograph shows the rear portion of the prison as it looked from the north. Cellblock B and the two-story dining room built in 1900 can be seen inside the walls. (Courtesy of WHC, 2011.006.0619.)

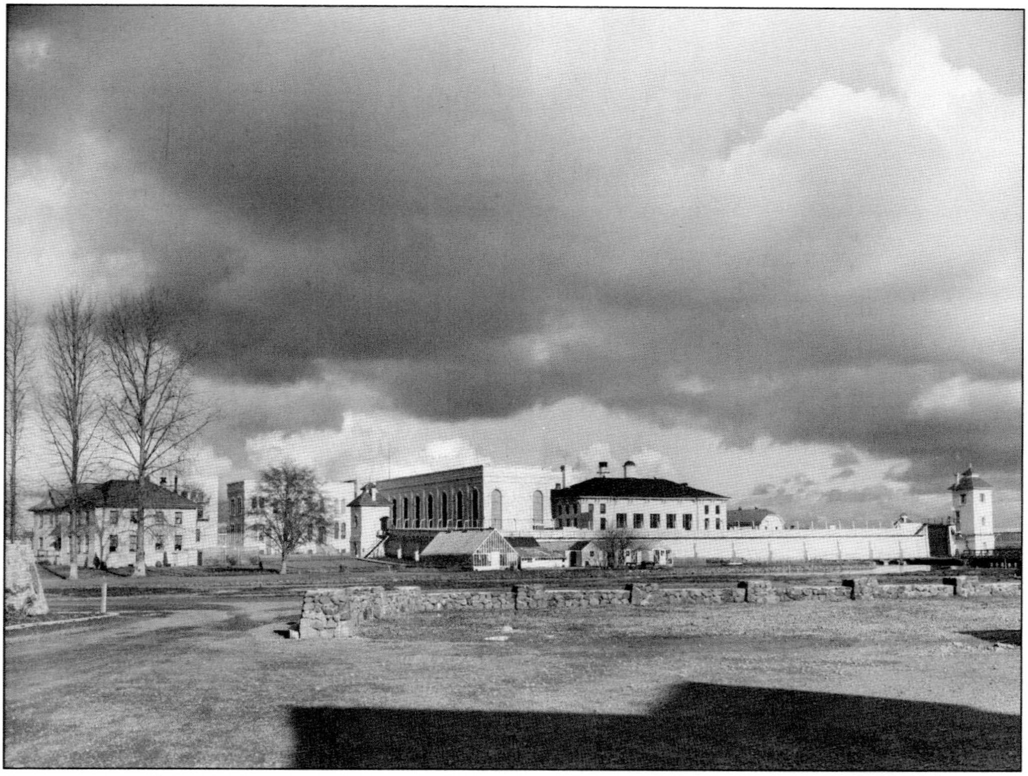

In 1910, new electric lights were mounted in all the cells. In addition, telephones were installed in 1913, connecting the offices with various places in the facility, including the guard towers. On May 30, 1919, Dr. R.E. Lee Steiner became warden and instituted an amazing number of improvements in OSP. He brought order to an institution in chaos before leaving in February 1920. (Courtesy of SPL.)

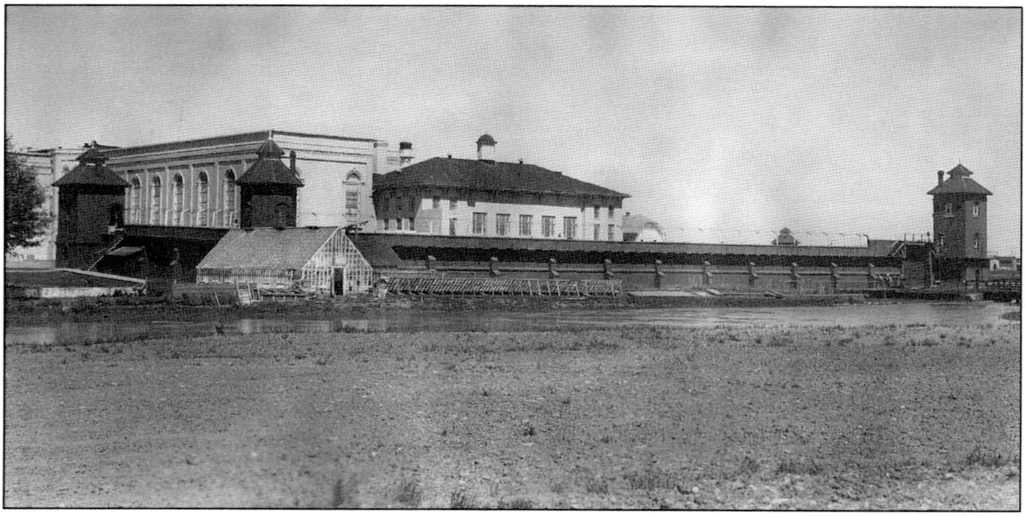

In 1922, a modern greenhouse was constructed on the prison grounds. The street leading from the trolley line on State Street was paved all the way to the main entrance and on to the garage housing the prison vehicles. In addition, many of the buildings were painted. This photograph shows the prison as it looked from the east. (Courtesy of OSL.)

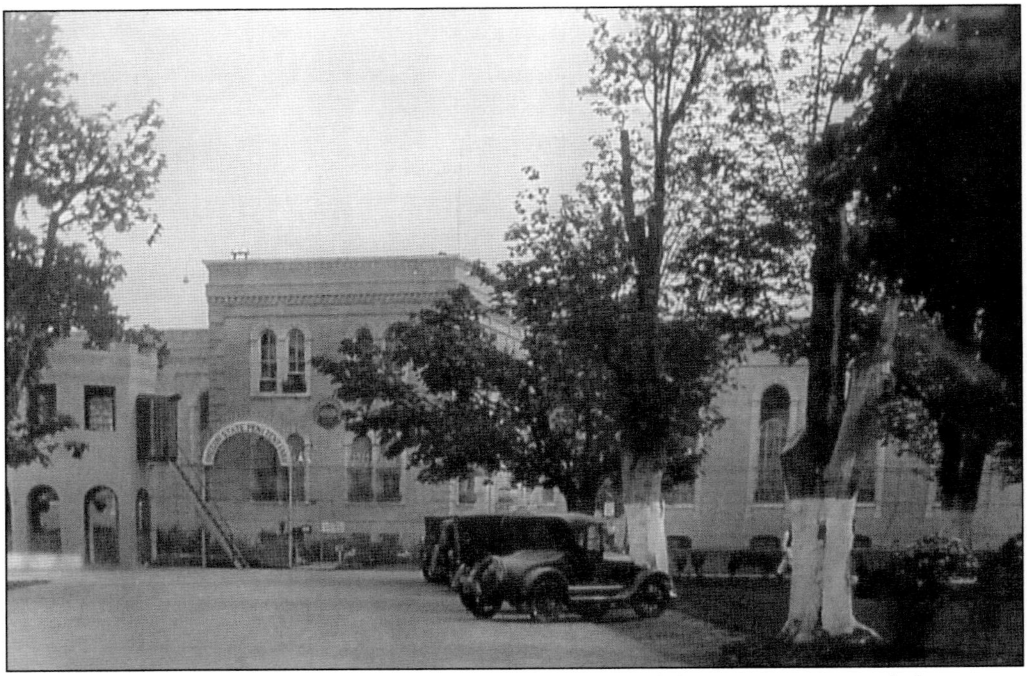

In 1922, warden J.W. Lewis focused repairs on the outside of the prison. He paved the avenue leading from the streetcar line on State Street to the front gate, as well as the roadways inside the walls. He replaced the old wooden sidewalk with cement and planted the trees lining the entrance. The truck entrance was moved to the north side, creating a better impression for visitors.

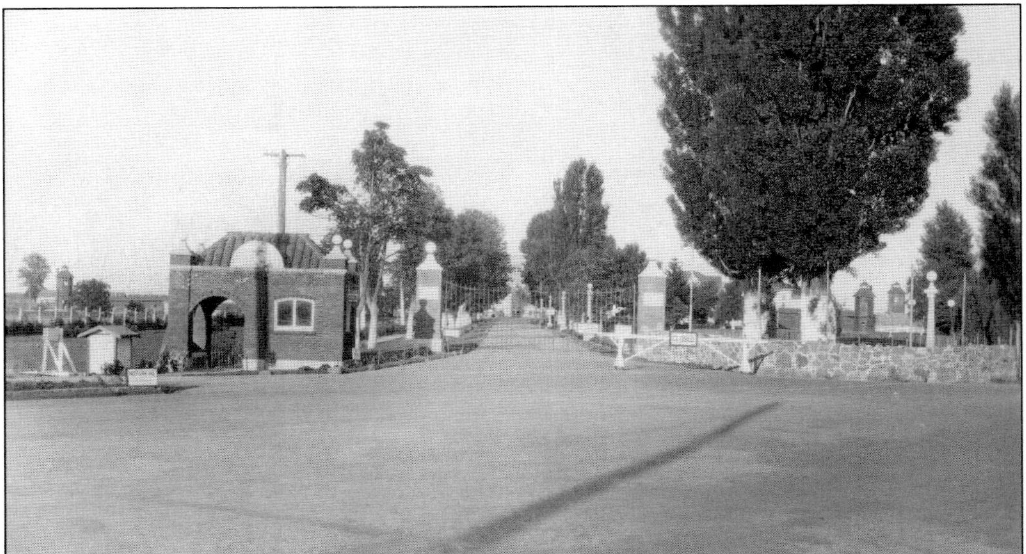

The gatehouse and rock wall were built in 1930 using brick from the prison brickyard. It was later designated a National Historic Structure. The double steel bars at the entrance were added a few years later. The ornamental rock wall cost $875.

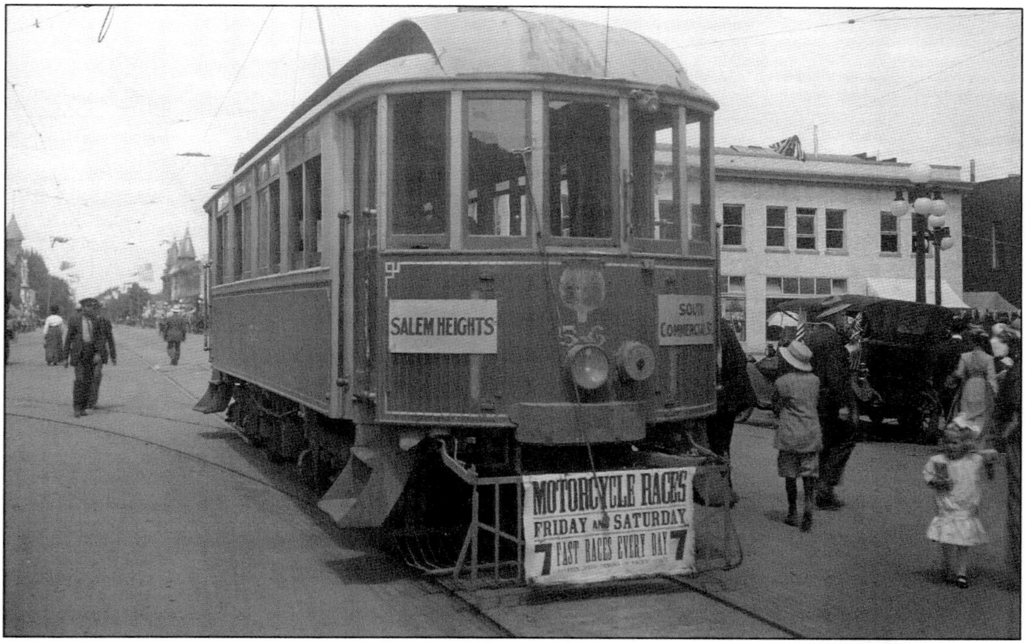

The trolley made it more convenient for relatives and friends to visit inmates. The large increase in personal automobiles finally ended the Salem trolley system, including the line going to the penitentiary. The prison purchased its first automobile in 1918, adding to its fleet of trucks. (Courtesy of OSA.)

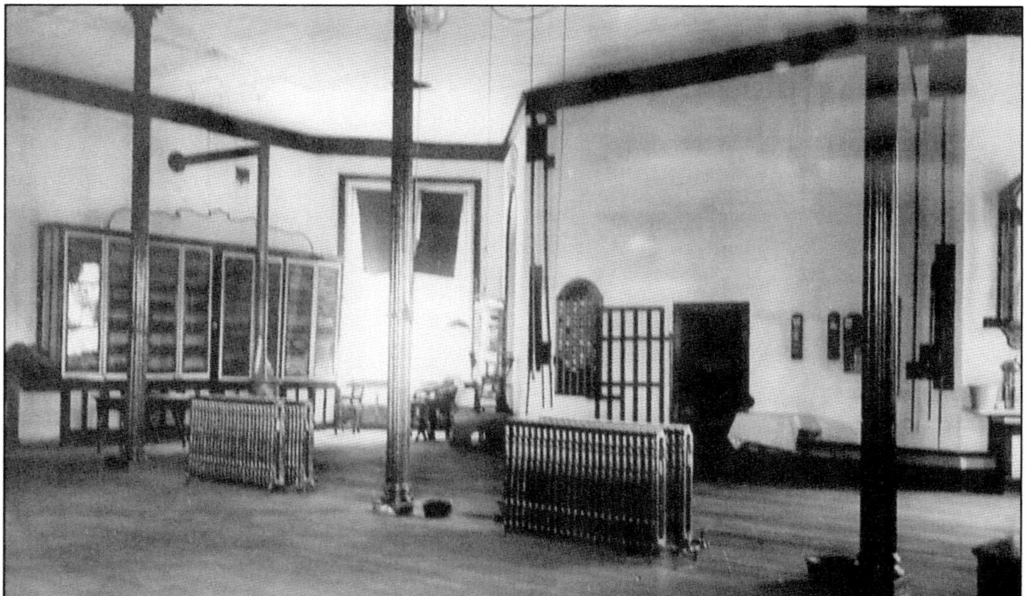

The last flogging took place in this room on August 3, 1907, and the last hosing was on August 21, 1907, until John W. Minto became superintendent on September 28, 1915, and reinstated corporal punishment. Prisoners were tied to pillars in the chapel and flogged. A prisoner was "hosed" when guards took a high-pressure water hose and sprayed a handcuffed prisoner until he was black and blue. (Courtesy of SPL.)

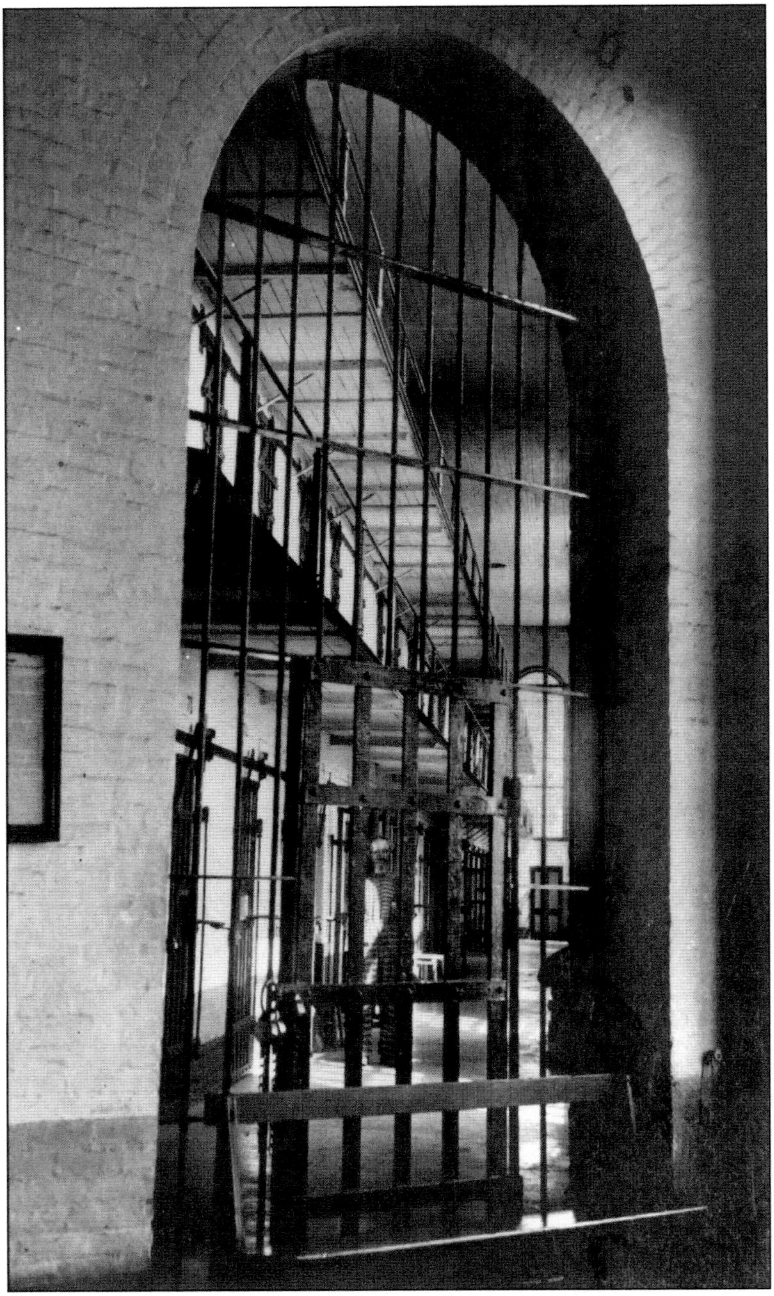

Cellblock B was constructed between 1868 and 1871 and cost $159,000. This was the access from the rotunda into the cellblock. A double-locked door barred the entrance. Guards used a lever to lower an iron bar across the door of each cell located in the row, fastening them until the warden could padlock each one shut. Prisoners moved into it on August 1, 1872. It had 22 double-bunk cells on two corridors and was four tiers high, cantilevered one above the other. Each cell contained an iron bedstead with a mattress and blankets. Three-inch holes in the back of each cell vented into an air space between the walls. Many of the holes were plugged up, cutting off all fresh air. The poor ventilation caused many convicts to become ill and was the greatest defect in the prison planning.

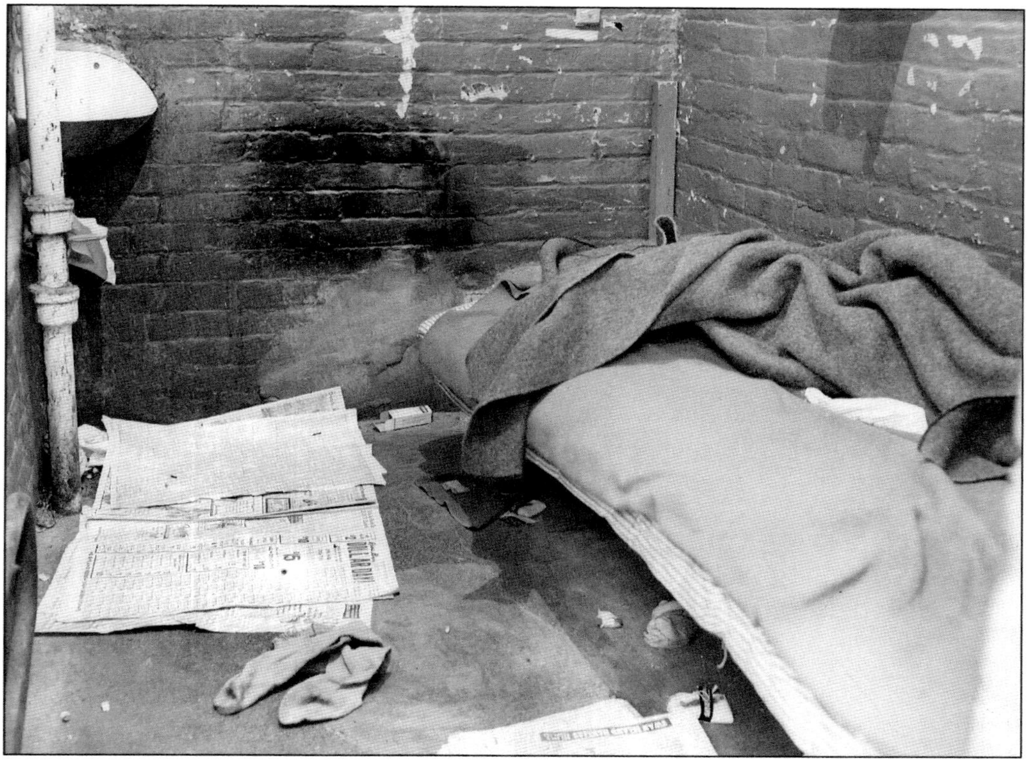

This was a cell in cellblock B, the oldest part of the prison. Most of the cells were nine feet by five feet and housed two men. Each cell had a urinal and a night bucket, which they emptied into Mill Creek in the morning. A faucet provided drinking water. (Courtesy of OSA.)

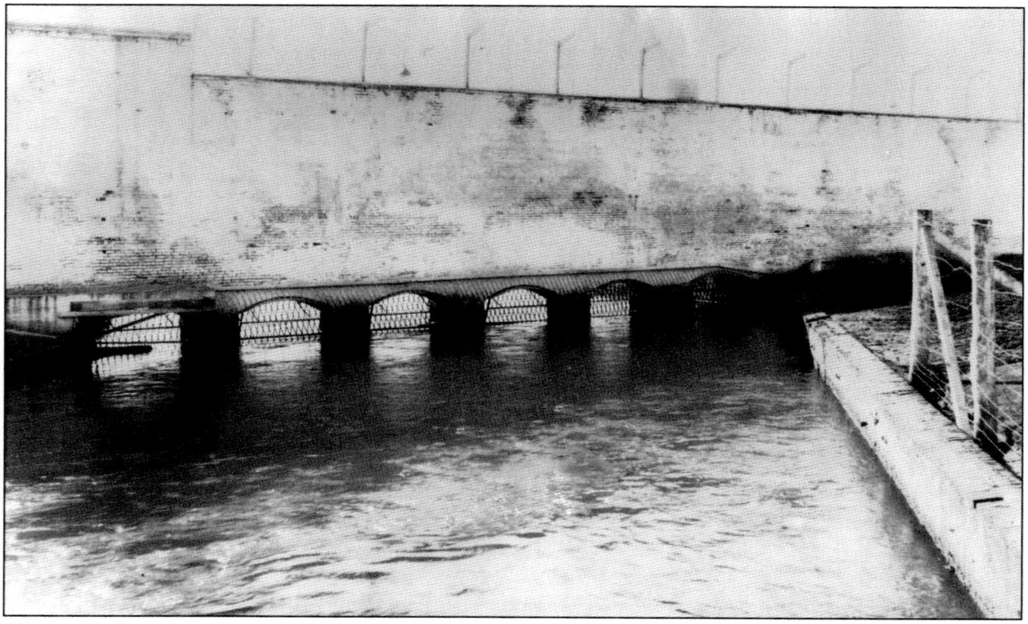

The creek flume and water ditch running through the prison were improved in July 1890. It was again widened the entire length of the ditch in 1892 to 25 feet. It needed constant repairs to keep in good condition. In 1922, the old wooden flume was replaced with a cement flume.

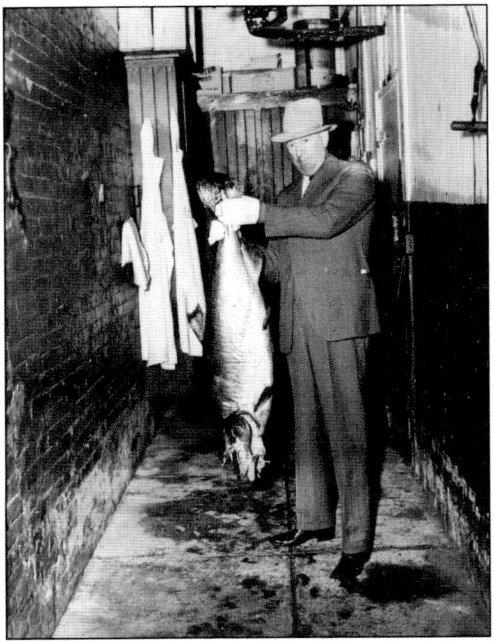

The creek allowed all kinds of fish, turtles, salamanders, and frogs into the prison. Here, James W. Lewis, superintendent from May 1, 1922, to January 15, 1923, is holding a 20- to 30-pound Chinook salmon that swam through the flue gates into the prison. He moved the main yard entrance from the south to tower no. 1 on the north side.

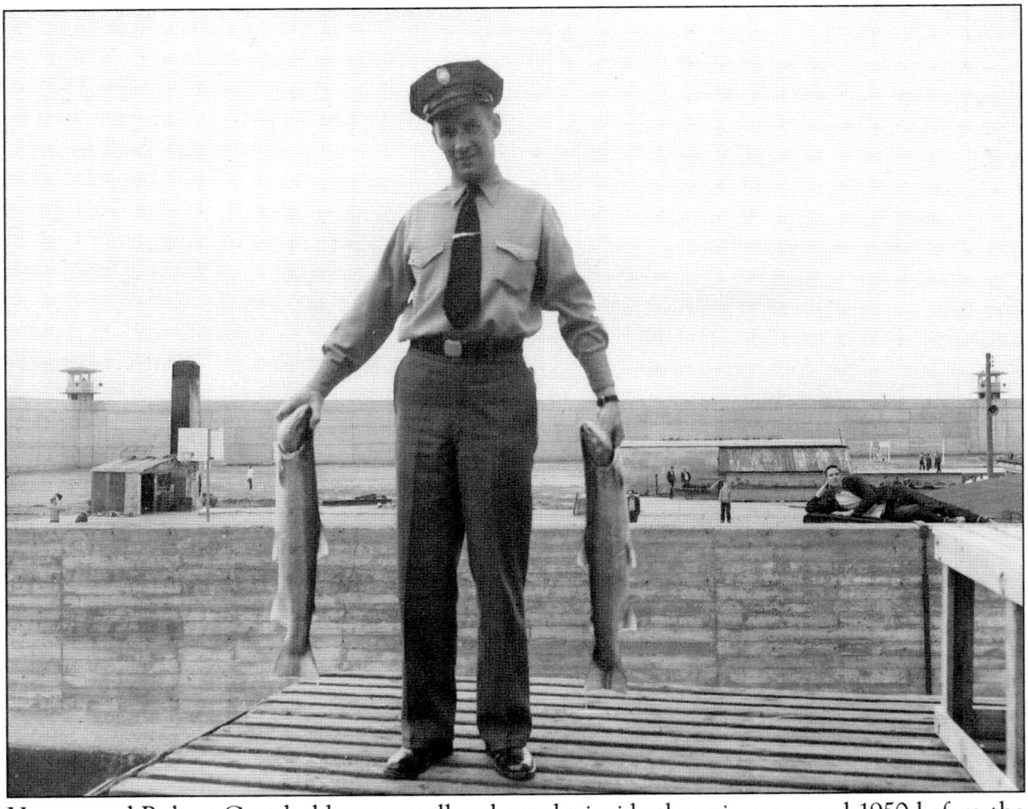

Here, guard Robert Grey holds two steelhead caught inside the prison around 1950 before the creek was diverted outside the walls. A concrete fish ladder and fish rack were built in 1928 on the south side of the main flume from plans and specifications approved by the Oregon Fish and Game Commission at a cost of $373. (Courtesy of OSA.)

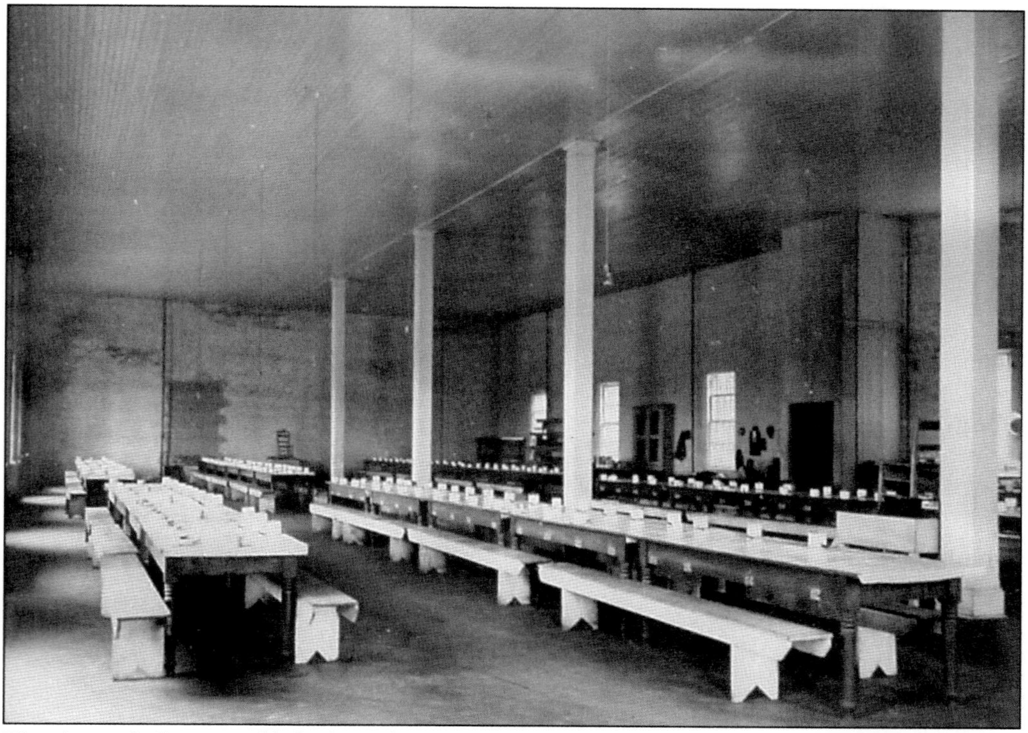

This dining hall was established in July 1904 after the new addition to the south wing was finished. The ceiling was 19.5 feet tall, and a steel guard cage was installed. Prior to this, all prisoners were fed in their cells. Now, everyone ate at tables and received equal service. In 1917, the guard cage was removed.

	Breakfast	Dinner	Supper
Sunday.	**Mush and Milk** Brown Beans Bread Coffee	Vegetable Soup Beef Hash Spaghetti and Cheese Pickles Bread	Baked Beans Peaches Coffee Cake Bread Tea
Monday.	Mush and Milk Brown Beans **Bread** Coffee	Weiners Cabbage Gravy Potatoes Bread and Water	Lima Beans Rice Prunes Bread Tea
Tuesday.	Mush **and Milk** Brown Beans Bread **Coffee**	Beef Stew Carrots Bread Water	Lima Beans Cold Slaw Sago Bread and Tea
Wednesday.	Mush and Milk Brown Beans Bread Coffee	Beef Hash Spaghetti Bread Water	Baked Beans Hominy Stewed Apples Bread and Tea
Thursday.	Mush and Milk **Brown Beans** Bread Coffee	Beef Stew Cabbage Bread Water	Chili Concarne Rice Peaches Bread and Tea
Friday.	Mush and Milk Brown Beans Bread Coffee	Baked Fish Dried Peas Potatoes Gravy Bread and Water	White Beans Cold Slaw Figs Bread Tea
Saturday.	Mush and Milk Brown Beans Bread Coffee	Beef Stew Baked Carrots Bread Water	Lima Beans Hominy Stewed Apples Bread and Tea

—Prisoners employed outside receive the regular ration for dinn

This weekly menu from 1917 shows the kind of food served to prisoners. In 1942, meals were served twice a day in complete silence. Armed guards walked around a wire-protected platform to enforce the rule. It took 600 loaves of bread a day to feed the 1,200 prisoners and cost the state $35 a month to feed and clothe each prisoner. (Courtesy of OSL.)

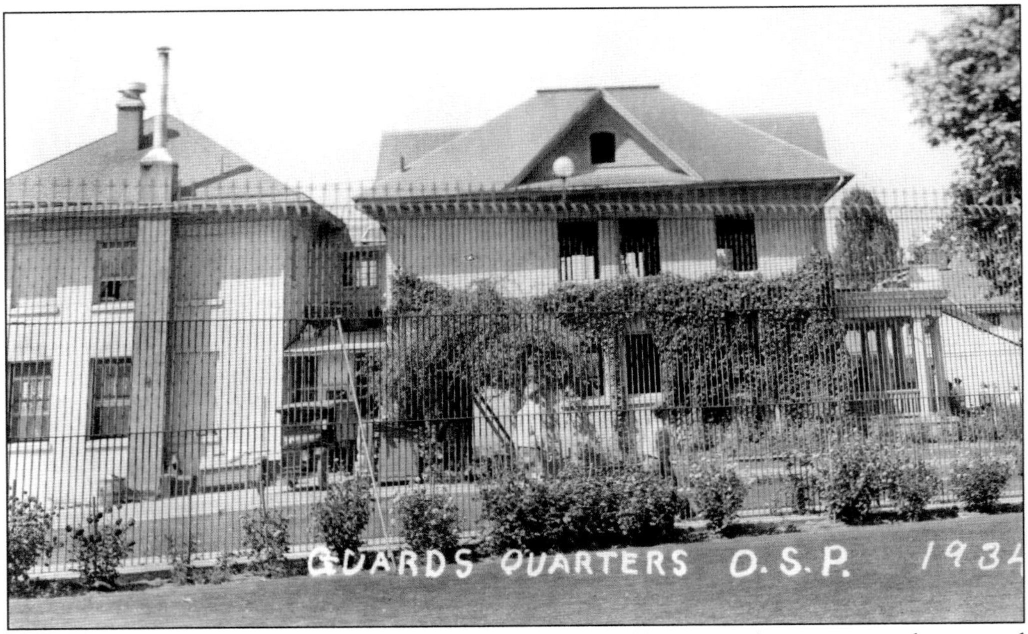

These guards' quarters were constructed in 1913 from an old barn. Single men received room and board here. Guards wore their civilian clothing until 1925, when uniforms were designed. The guards' uniforms were sewn by prisoners and provided to the guards as part of their job.

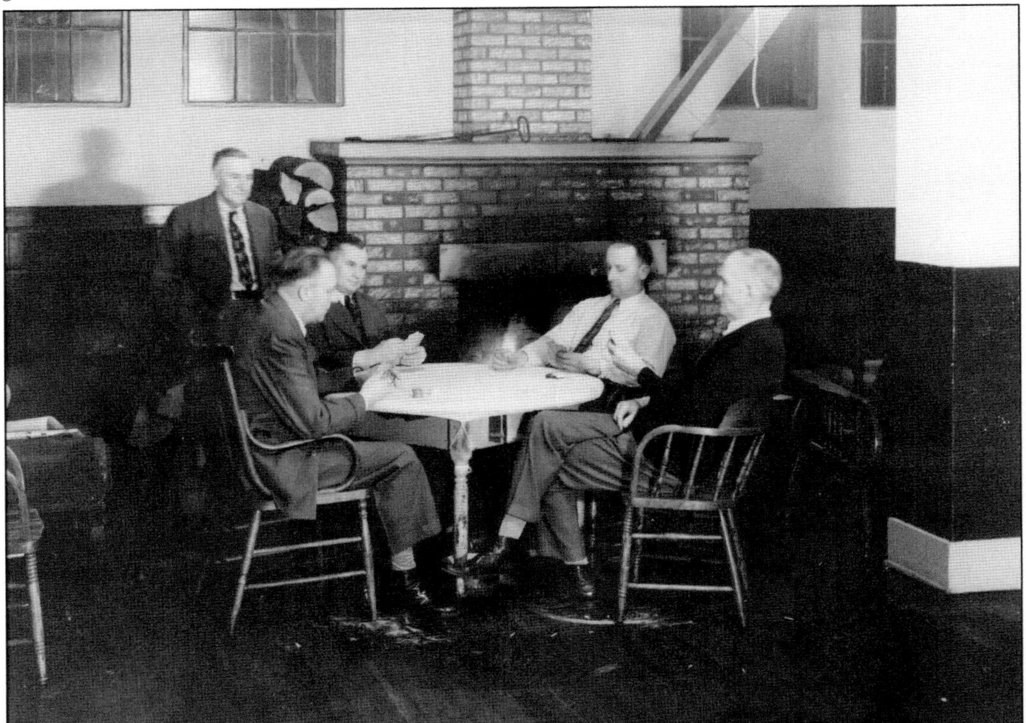

These officials play cards in the officers' club room in the basement of the new administration building, built in 1930. The prison arsenal was housed on the first floor next to the general offices. This room was still used as an official meeting room in 1984.

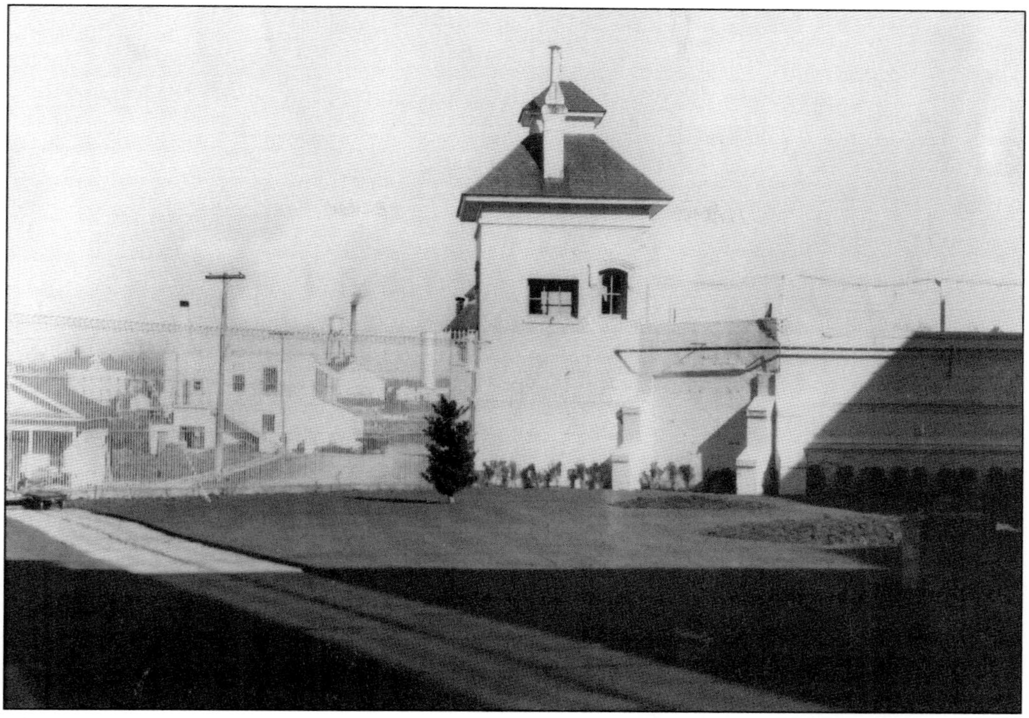

This image of gun tower no. 6 shows the connection between the brick stockade wall and the steel posts making up the fence across the front of the administration building. To the left is the entrance used by trucks and other official vehicles.

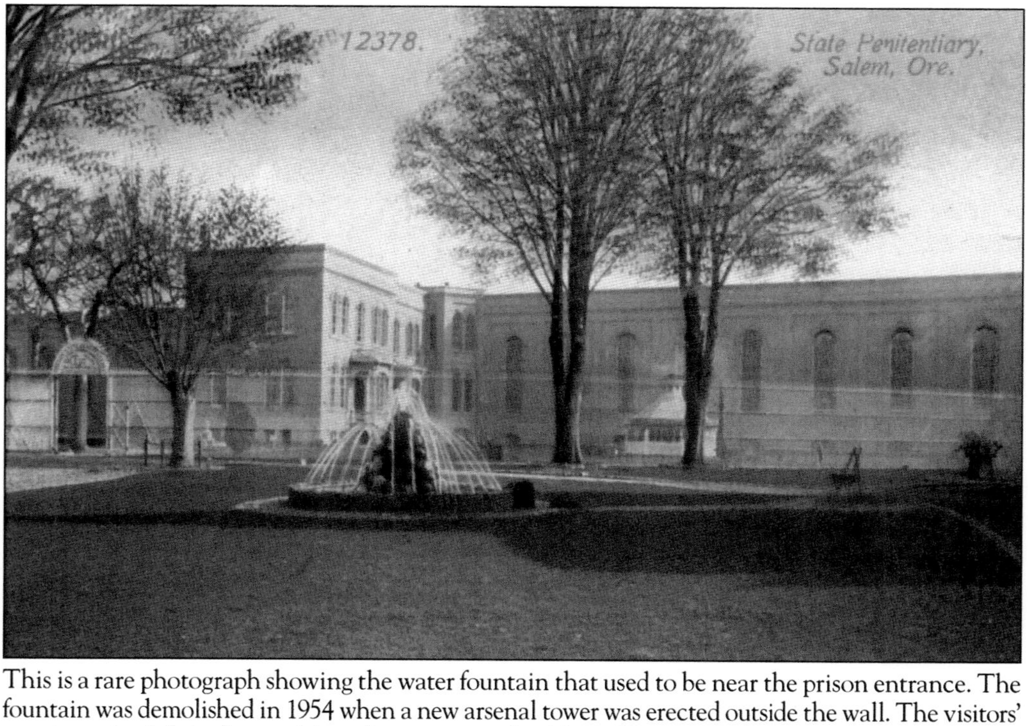

This is a rare photograph showing the water fountain that used to be near the prison entrance. The fountain was demolished in 1954 when a new arsenal tower was erected outside the wall. The visitors' gate is to the left in front of the administration building. (Courtesy of WHC, 2011.006.0616.)

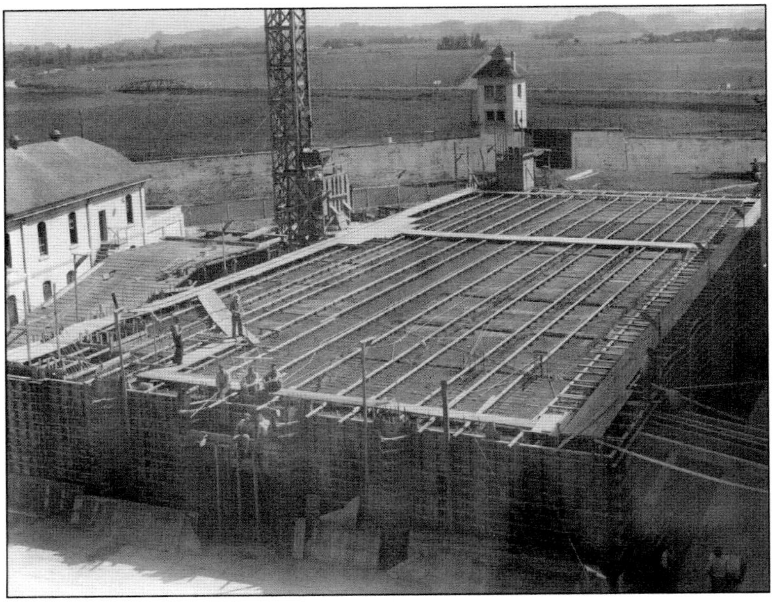

Cellblock C was completed in February 1932 at a cost of $76,000. This increased the prison capacity to 1,000 prisoners. The building housed the "bullpen," a small prison within a prison. It was an enclosure about 100 feet square with a small cell house open to the weather. Violent prisoners housed there were required to walk a dirt track eight hours a day.

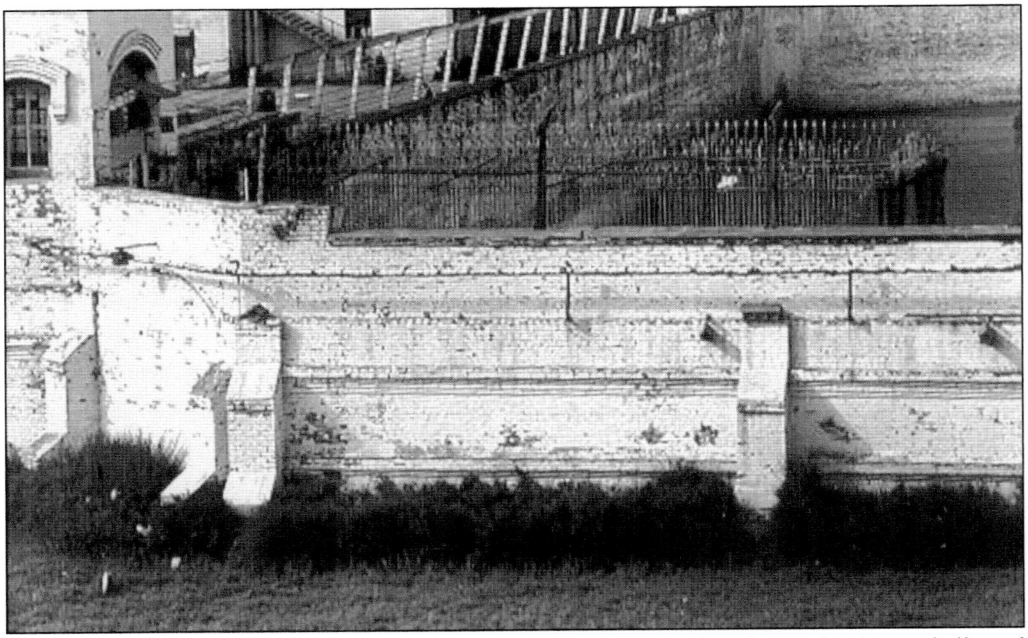

This sally port on the south side of the prison was 25 feet long and 10 feet wide. A guard allowed a team and wagon to enter the outside gate, which was then closed, and the inner gate was opened to permit the wagon to enter the yard. The guards examined the trucks before moving in or out of the prison.

It took three million bricks to make the brick stockade wall around the prison. It was four feet thick at the bottom and 16 inches wide at the top. Spaced around the wall were seven guard houses like the one seen here. This tower is being demolished to make room for a concrete wall.

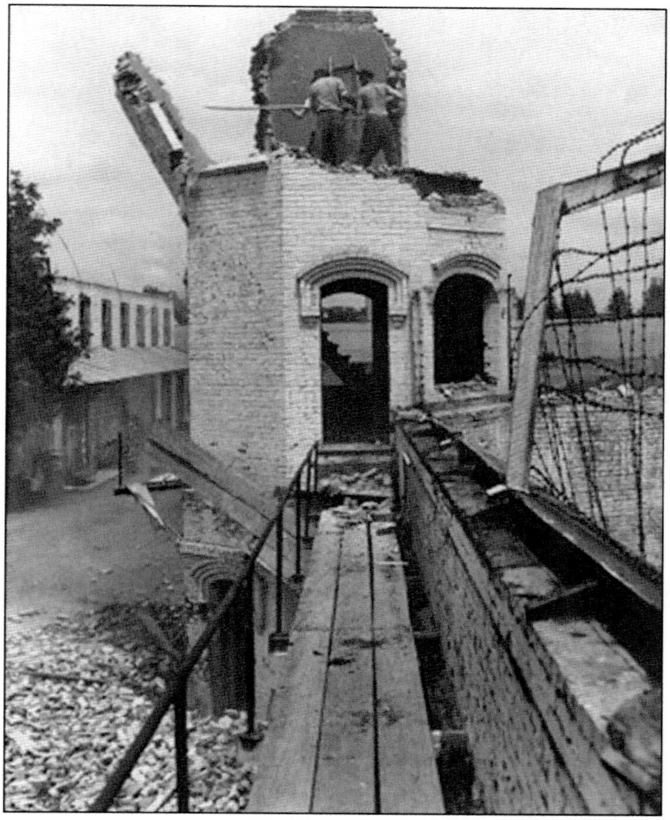

A new concrete stockade was erected in 1949 and cost $180,000. It doubled the acreage inside the prison compound. The wall was 25 feet high and extended 4 to 12 feet below ground to prevent prisoners from tunneling to freedom. It had walkways for guards to patrol, guard towers, and two main entrances with double gates (sally ports).

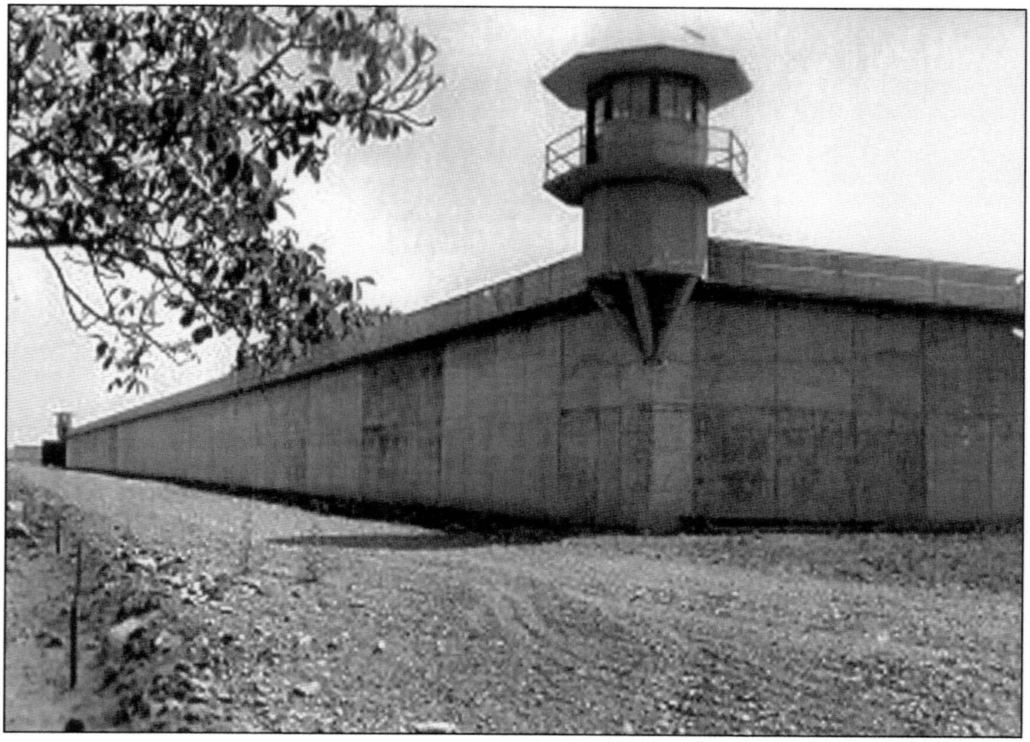

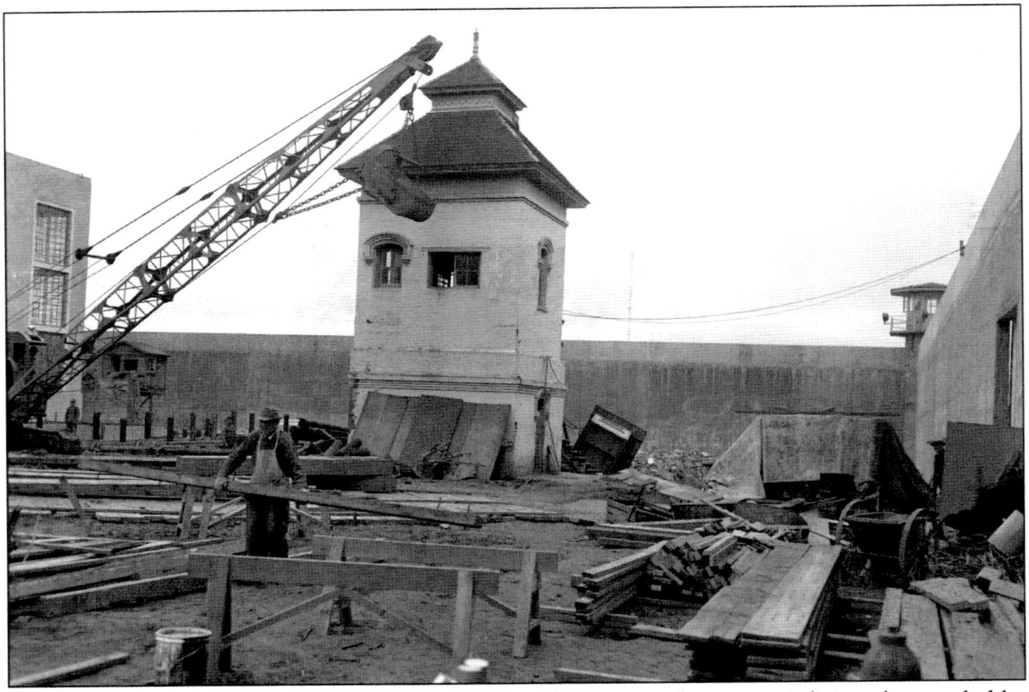

As the wall was built, the old towers were removed. This wooden tower is being dismantled by the E.S. Ritter Construction Company. Every possible effort was made to salvage as much timber and as many bricks as possible. The recycled material was sold to local contractors.

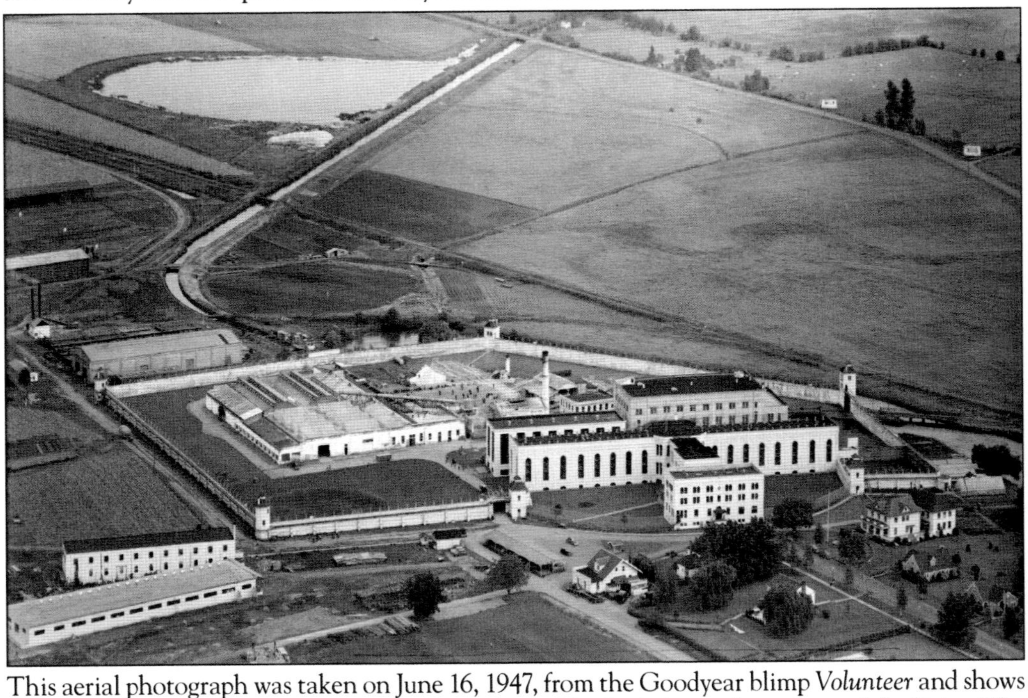

This aerial photograph was taken on June 16, 1947, from the Goodyear blimp *Volunteer* and shows the prison before the new concrete wall was built. To the left are the industrial facilities. The seven towers anchor the corners. Cellblock B is in back to the left, cellblock A is in the left front, cellblock E is in back to the right, and cellblock D is in front to the right. (Courtesy of SPL.)

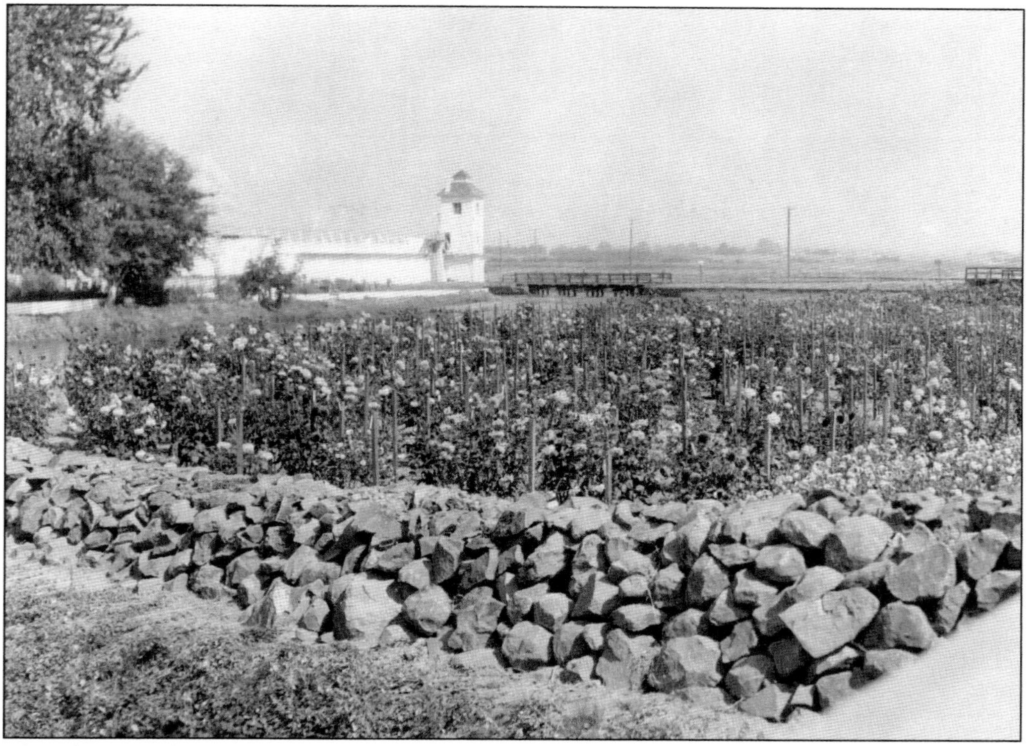

This photograph was taken about 1920 and shows the farmland around the prison before the expansion of Salem grew to surround it. The 15-foot-high brick wall and Gothic-styled center rotunda are both plainly visible. (Courtesy of OSL.)

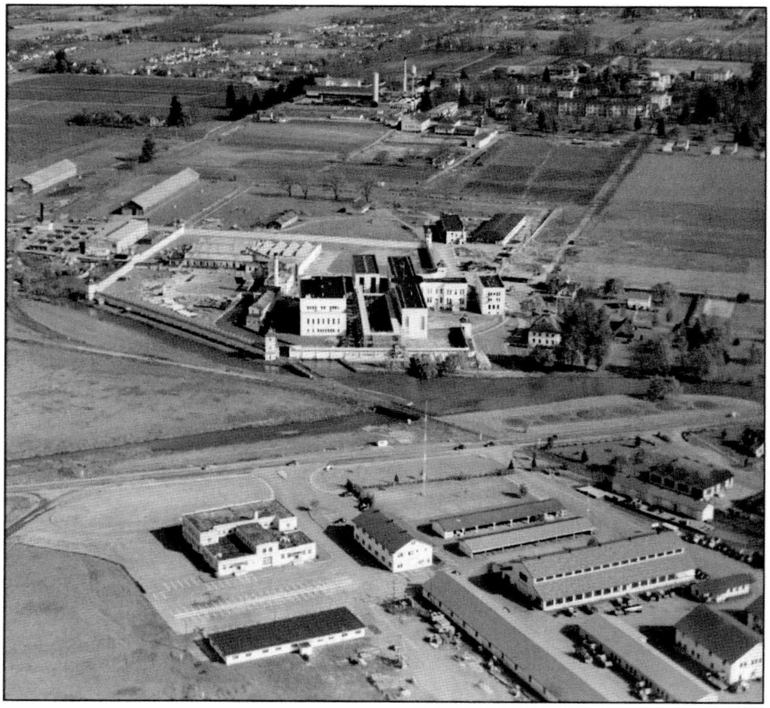

This aerial photograph was taken from the Goodyear blimp in 1948. Near the top (north) of the image, the Oregon State Mental Hospital can be seen. To the south and outside the prison walls, large industrial buildings are located. The administration building and prison entrance face east. (Courtesy of SPL.)

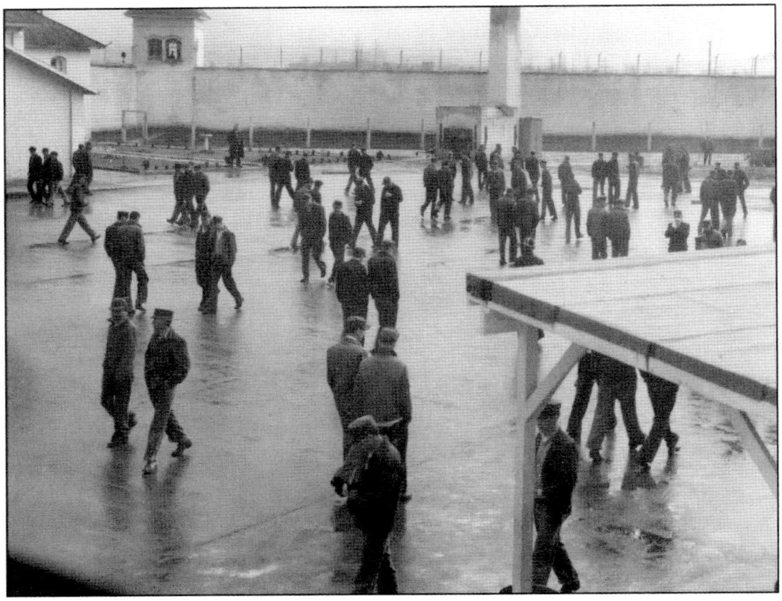

This was "the island" in 1940. Prisoners marched here in silent rows after breakfast. Some went on to work assignments, while others could only walk around in small groups or couples. There was little for the prisoners to do. The only other recreation area was an undersized baseball diamond in the northwest corner of the prison yard.

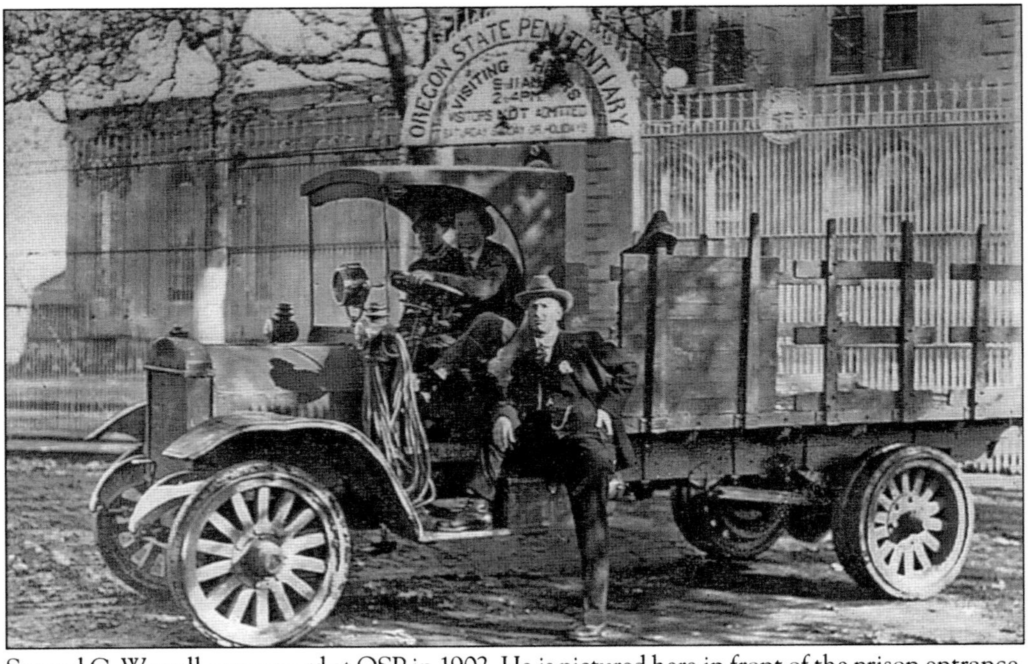

Samuel C. Worrell was a guard at OSP in 1902. He is pictured here in front of the prison entrance. The sign reads, "Visiting Hours, 9–11 AM, 2– 4 PM, Visitors not admitted, Saturday, Sunday or Holidays." The steel posts now have crosses on them—a change since 1888. The prison paid $3,000 for a truck in 1917. (Courtesy of Sue Woodford.)

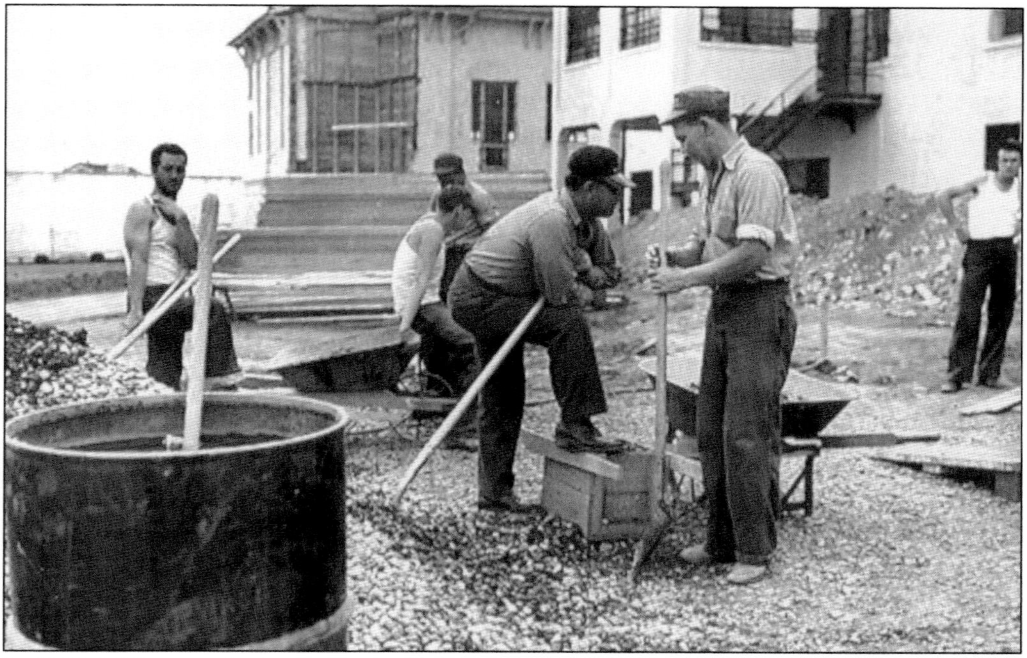

In 1907, OSP stopped requiring prisoners to wear striped suits except as a disciplinary measure. Cadet gray uniforms were substituted for everyday wear, and brown duck cloth was used for work overalls. In 1929, convicts dug 100 double concrete toilets and sewer lines across the prison yard to a new water closet system. These prisoners are repairing water and sewer mains running in and out of the prison in 1940. In 1949, an inmate was allowed one bar of soap a month, one pack of cigarette papers and makings a month, and $6 a month to spend in the commissary. There were only nine shower stalls for 1,300 men.

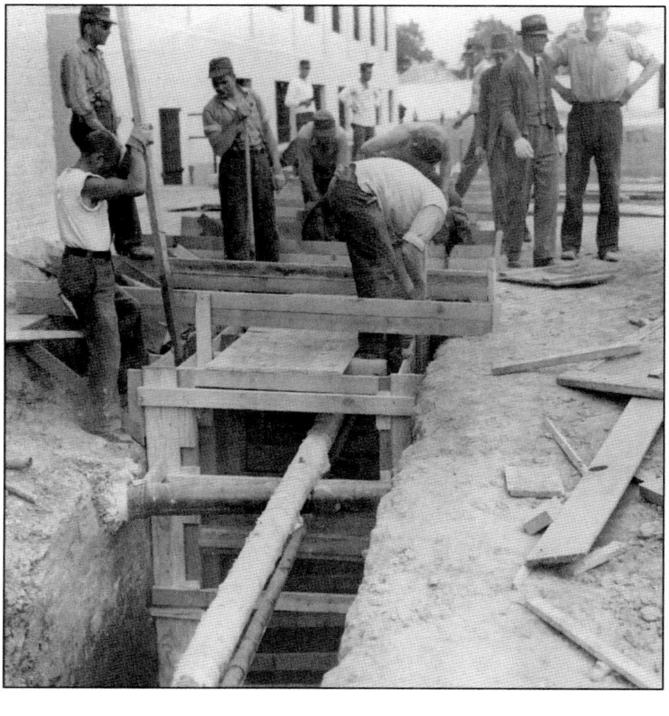

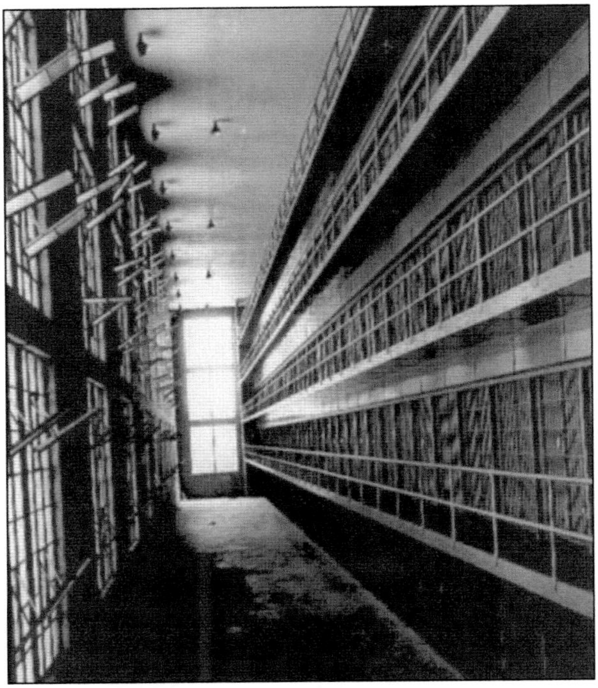

As part of a multimillion-dollar building project, cellblock D was completed in 1950 at a cost of $650,000. It was 60 feet by 254 feet by 52 feet. All cells were provided with air-conditioning and earphones to listen to OSP-approved radio stations. The new building allowed officials to segregate incorrigible convicts and known perverts from young offenders. (Courtesy of SJ.)

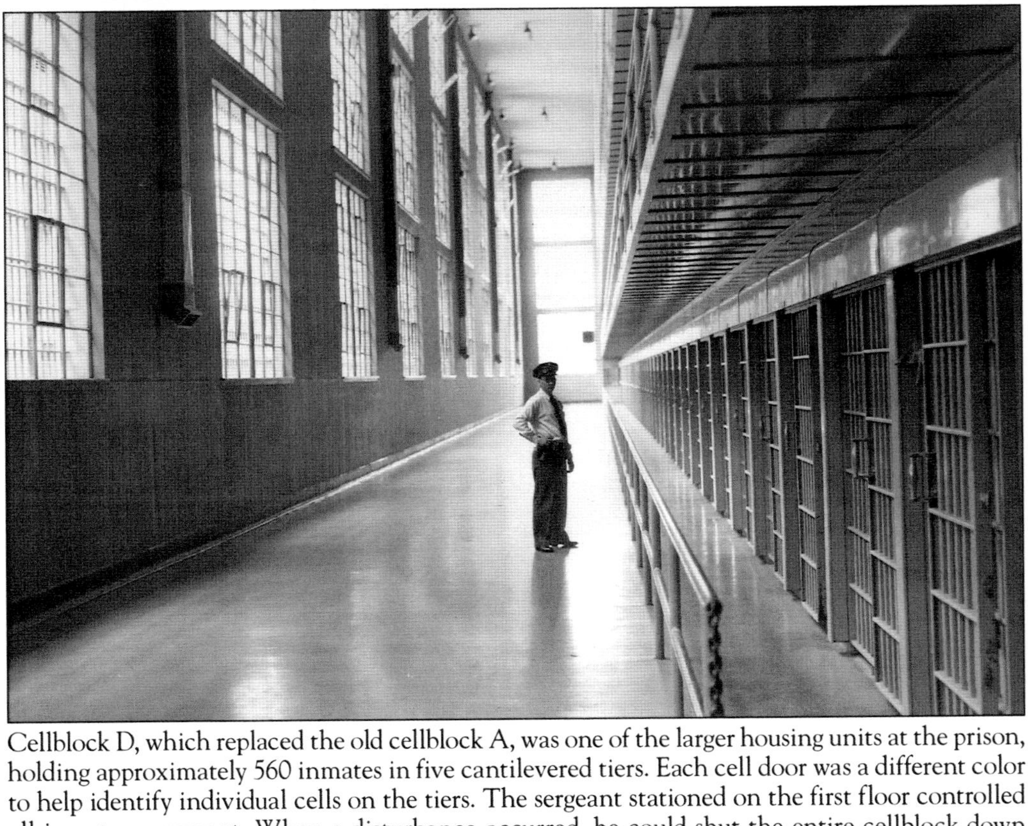

Cellblock D, which replaced the old cellblock A, was one of the larger housing units at the prison, holding approximately 560 inmates in five cantilevered tiers. Each cell door was a different color to help identify individual cells on the tiers. The sergeant stationed on the first floor controlled all inmate movement. When a disturbance occurred, he could shut the entire cellblock down with the flip of a switch. (Courtesy of OSA.)

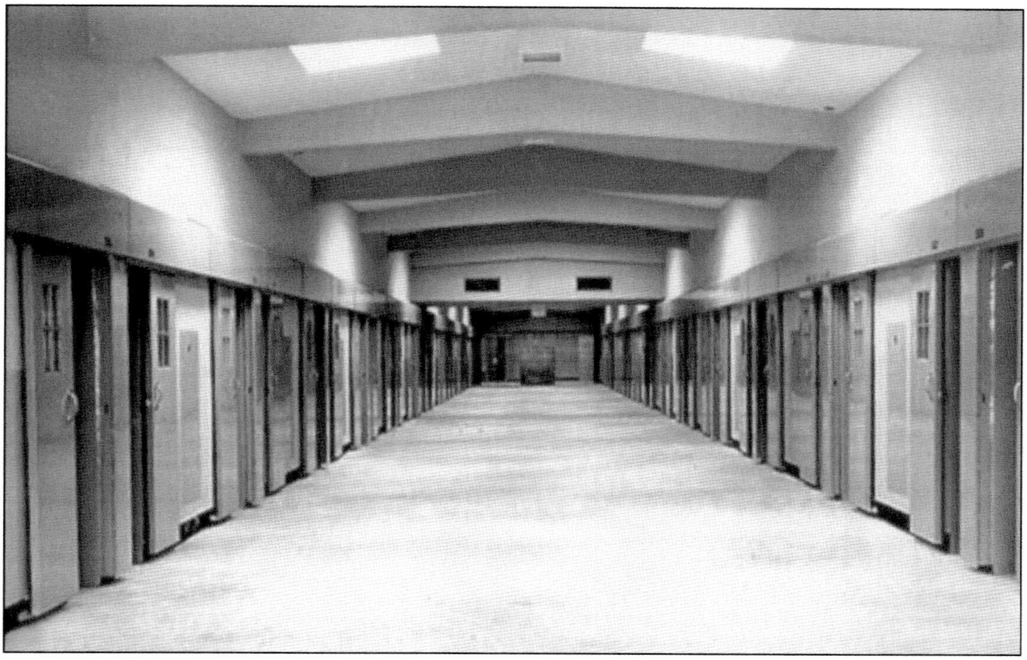

In 1942, prisoners found guilty of disobeying the rules could be sent to the bullpen, the basement correctional cells pictured here, or "the hole." The cells in the bullpen were filthy and so small that inhabitants could barely stand or take more than three steps in any direction. The only clothes allowed were jeans and straw slippers. A single blanket thrown on the cement floor was their bed.

This is the hole, which was located in the basement of the cellblock. Convicts who tried to escape or assaulted a guard were incarcerated here for up to a year. Not only were the individual cells locked, but the cellblock's steel door was also locked to prevent escapes. Two prisoners can be seen in the cell to the right. This photograph was taken on August 30, 1950. (Courtesy of OSA.)

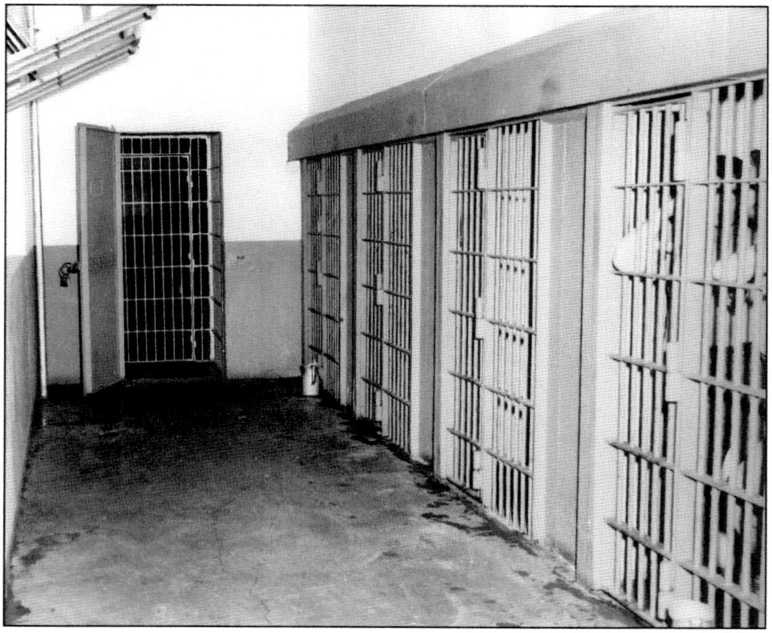

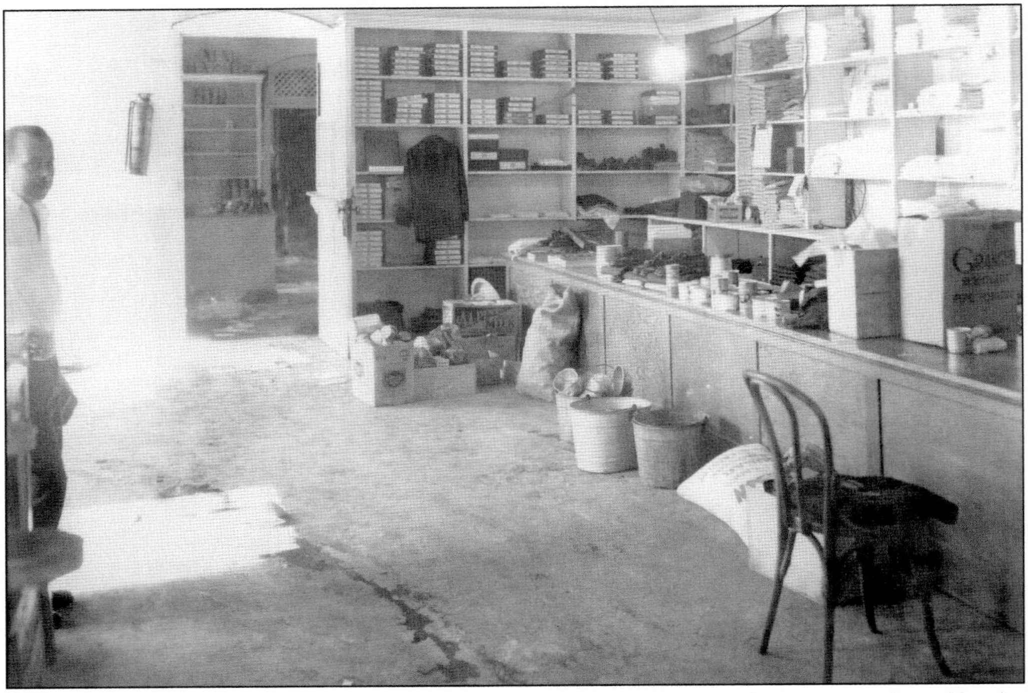

This was the prison storage room in the early 1900s. These extra supplies were purchased by the prison and sold to the prisoners. On the floor is a 50-pound sack of sugar, a box overflowing with canned food, a stainless steel pail full of tin bowls, and a large box of evaporated milk. On the shelves and the counter are other various commodities, shoes, and shirts ready to sell.

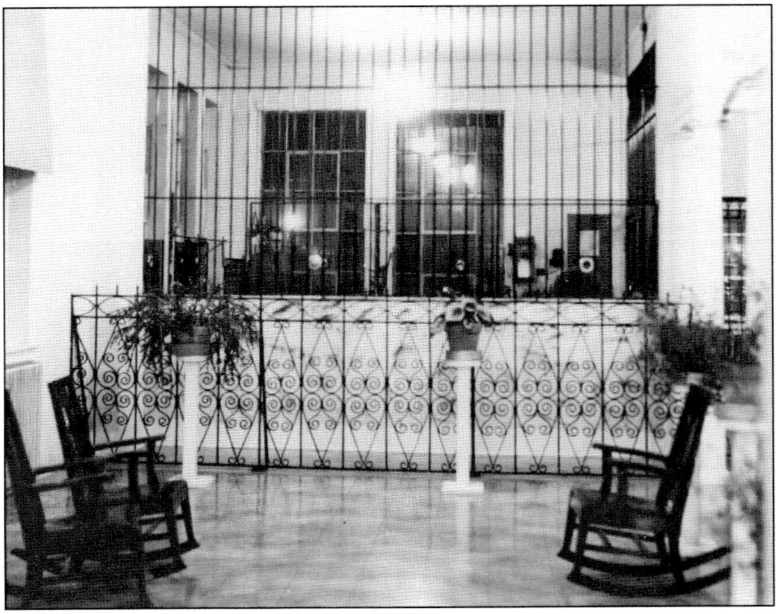

This was the prison entrance before 1950. Prisoners were allowed to send 15 letters a month and receive 30 letters a month from seven approved individuals. Mail was censored and limited to both sides of a single page. Only two visitors a month were allowed. Men in isolation were not allowed to have any cigarettes, receive mail, or see visitors.

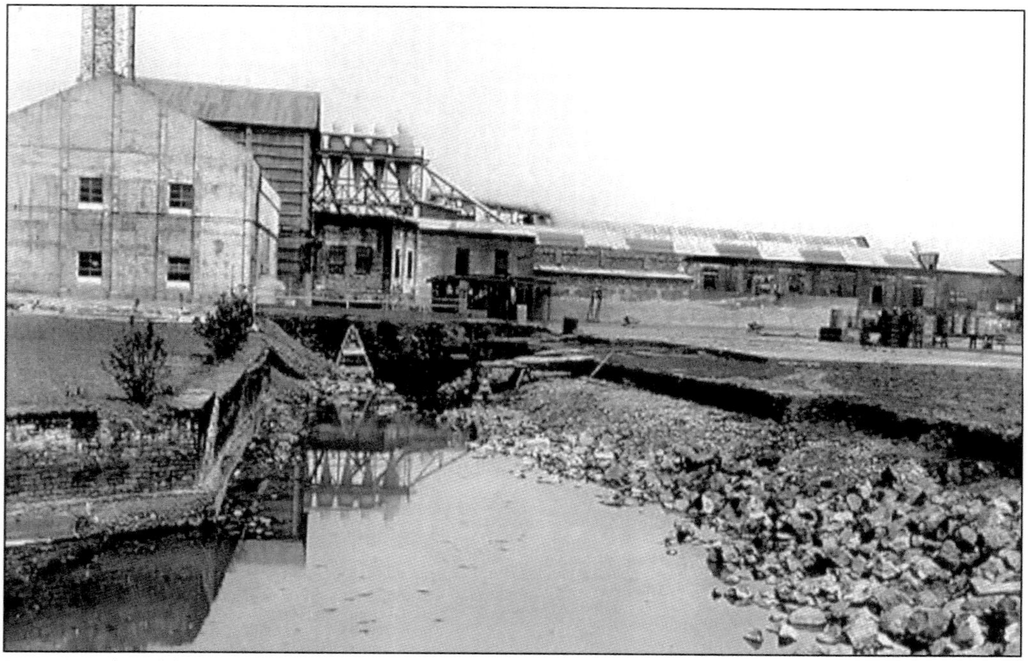

In 1930, the old powerhouse was installed inside the penitentiary. It required a 12-foot water drop to power the turbine, which then sent the generator shaft turning at 900 revolutions per minute and produced 100 kilowatts of electricity. The gear teeth at the top of the turbine shaft were made of maple wood. It was removed in 1956, and a new powerhouse was built outside the walls. (Courtesy of SPL.)

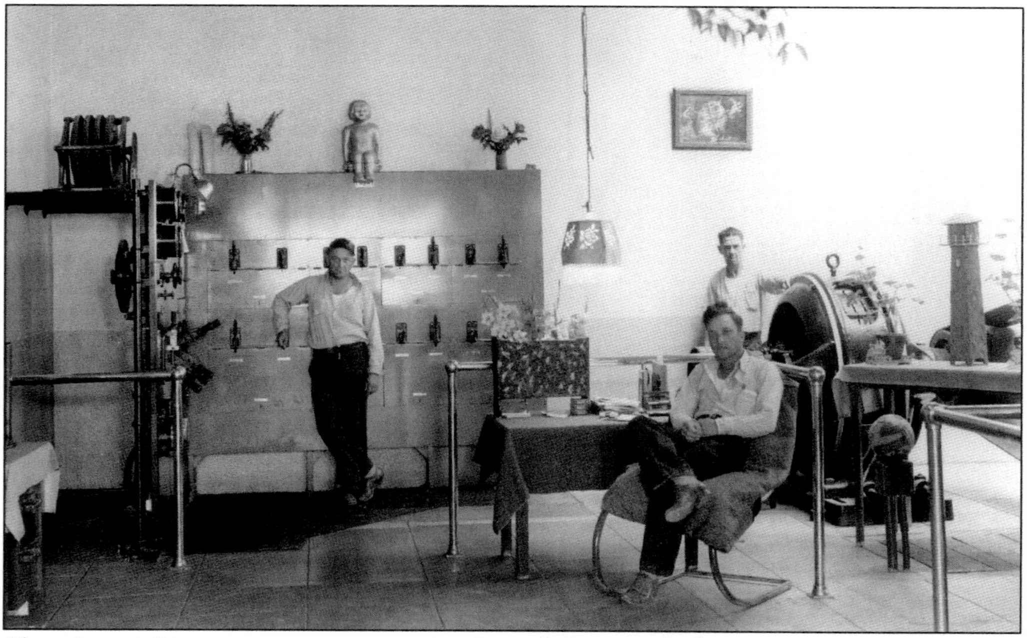

These "trustie" inmates are monitoring the physical plant inside the prison in 1950. This facility controlled the steam pressure heating the prison, and only trustworthy inmates were allowed to work there. The plant was dismantled six years later when a modern facility was built outside the walls of OSP.

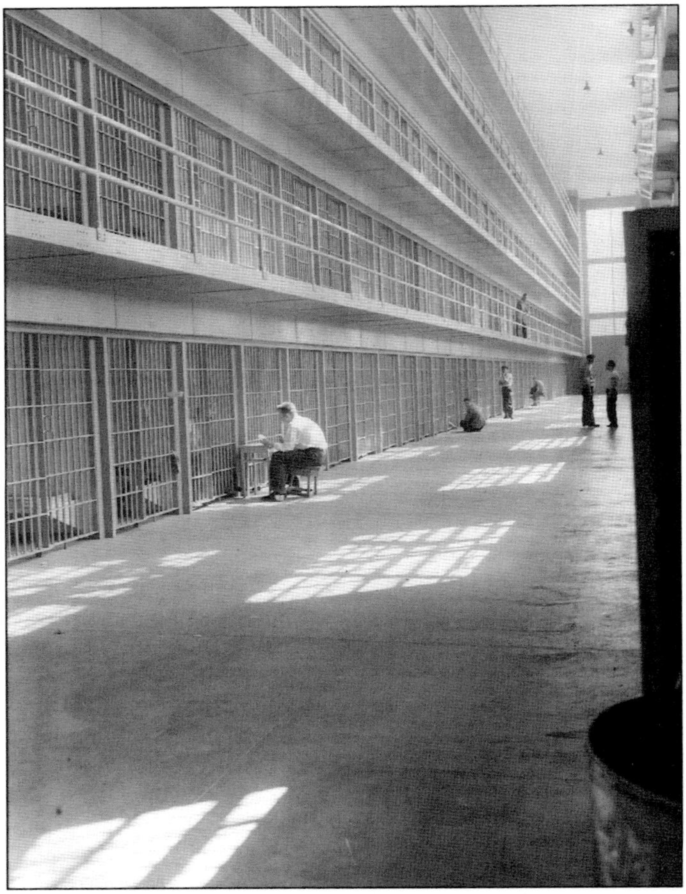

Cellblock E was opened in 1953 and replaced cellblock A, built in 1866. The new cellblock held 400 steel cells painted white and arranged in five tiers. Each cell had a single bunk, a toilet, a sink, a shelf, and a built-in steel table and chair. It was 60 feet by 254 feet by 52 feet and cost $650,000. Cellblock B was torn down after this was opened. (Courtesy of OSA.)

This is the control center for cellblock E. From inside, guards could turn the lights on and off and open or close all the cells at once or individually. The bars around the control panel prevented prisoners from attacking the officer in charge or forcing him to open the cells.

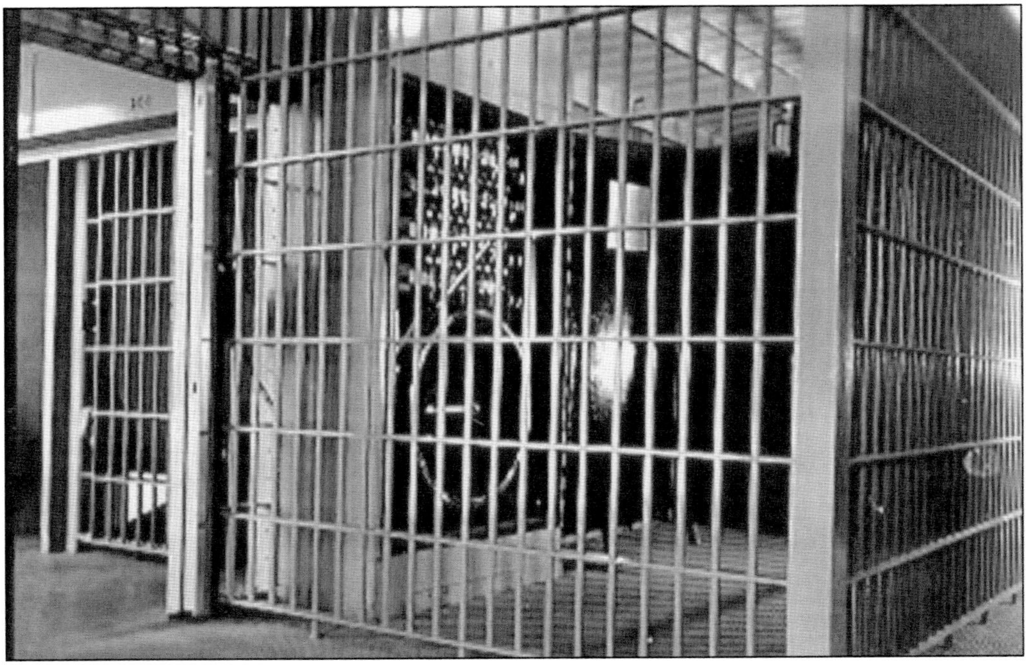

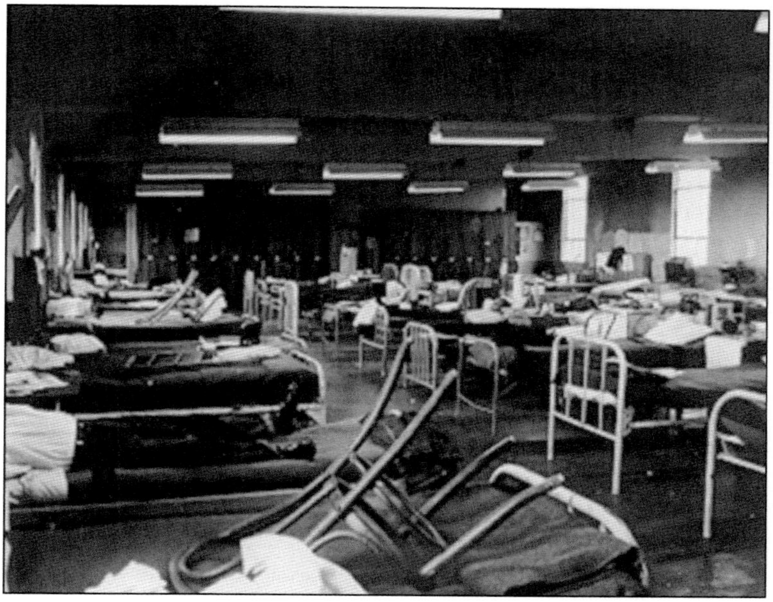

A trustie barracks was built in 1913 for $28,500. In 1930, a large garage was built to house the prison's automobiles and trucks. On the second floor, a dormitory was constructed to house 100 trusties. The "garage dormitory" pictured here cost $14,000 and was a vast improvement over the cells inside the prison.

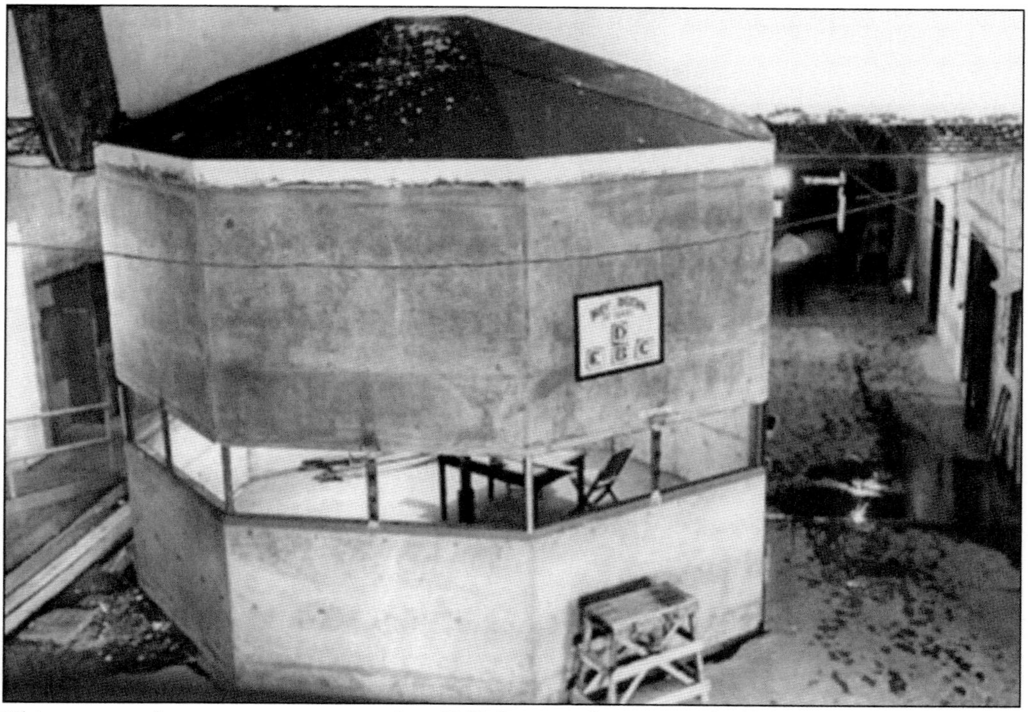

This octagonal center was constructed in 1953. It sat in the center of cellblocks A, C, D, and E. At the same time, the new single-bunk cells helped reduce the rampant homosexual practices reported at OSP. Visiting wardens stated that the degradation, lack of control, and confusion at OSP was without parallel. Clarence Gladden was hired as warden immediately after the wardens' visit.

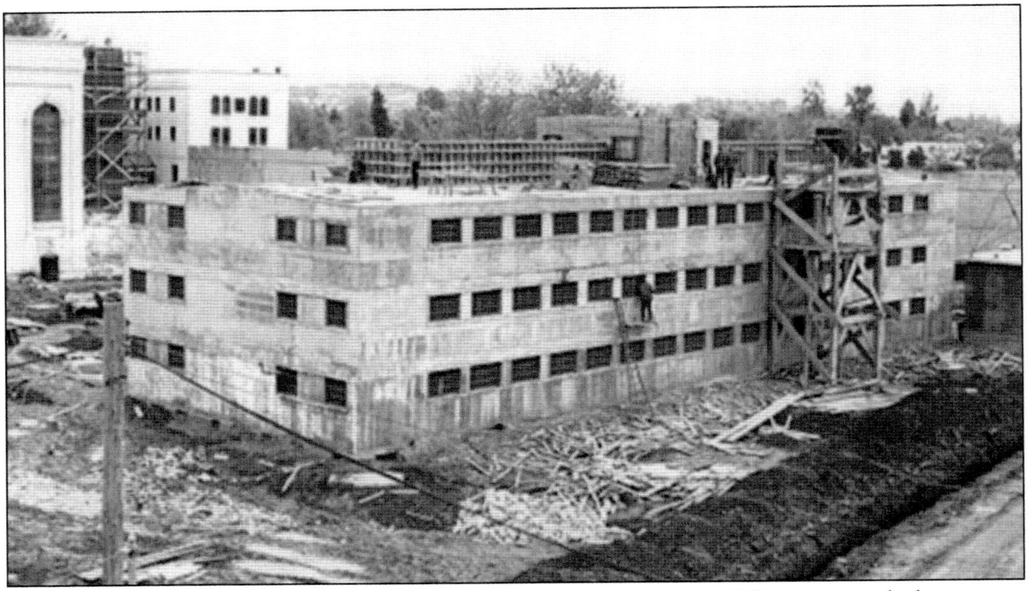

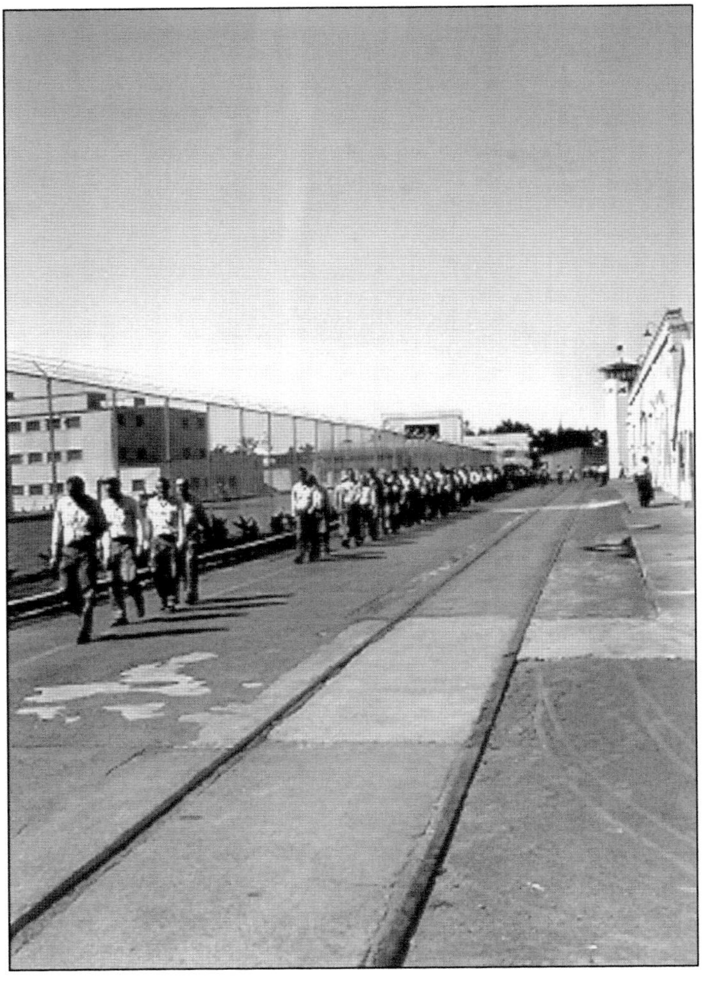

After a particularly expensive riot and fire at the prison, officials hurried to finish the segregation and isolation building by October 1953. It had 90 cells and provided full-time quarters for 84 prisoners. There were six punishment cells with no furnishings other than a hole in the floor for a toilet and four glass bricks to provide light. The execution chamber was located next door.

Before 1970, prisoners were required to walk single file along a white line drawn on the pavement from place to place in the prison. Guards accompanying them could easily examine prisoners for contraband.

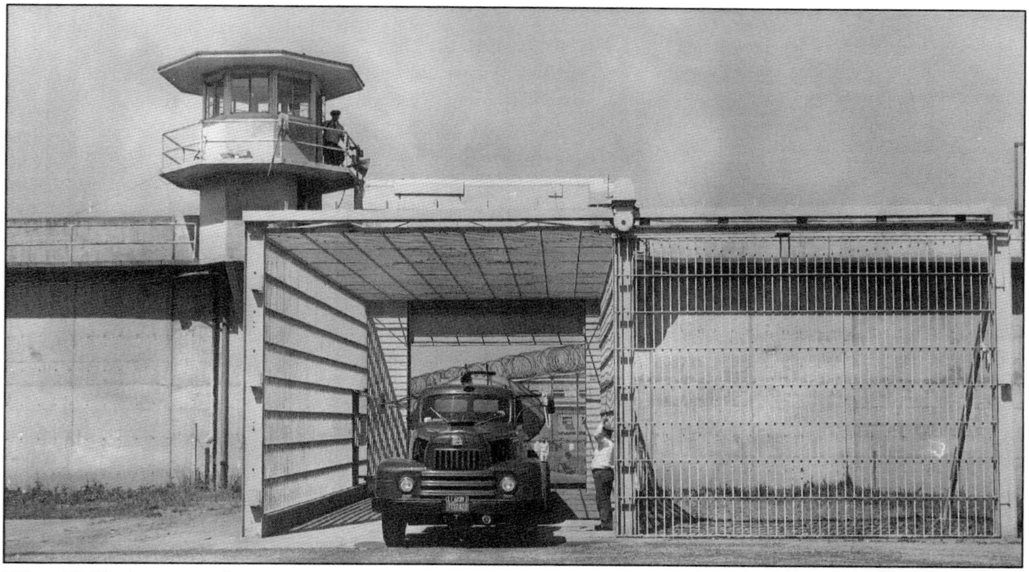

This 1955 photograph shows the completed sally port after the new wall was finished. Concertina wire lines the top of the wall behind the opening, and guards watch above and below. The tower guard controlled the electric gates with a remotely controlled switch. Behind the truck is the yard where inmates could roam freely. (Courtesy of OSA.)

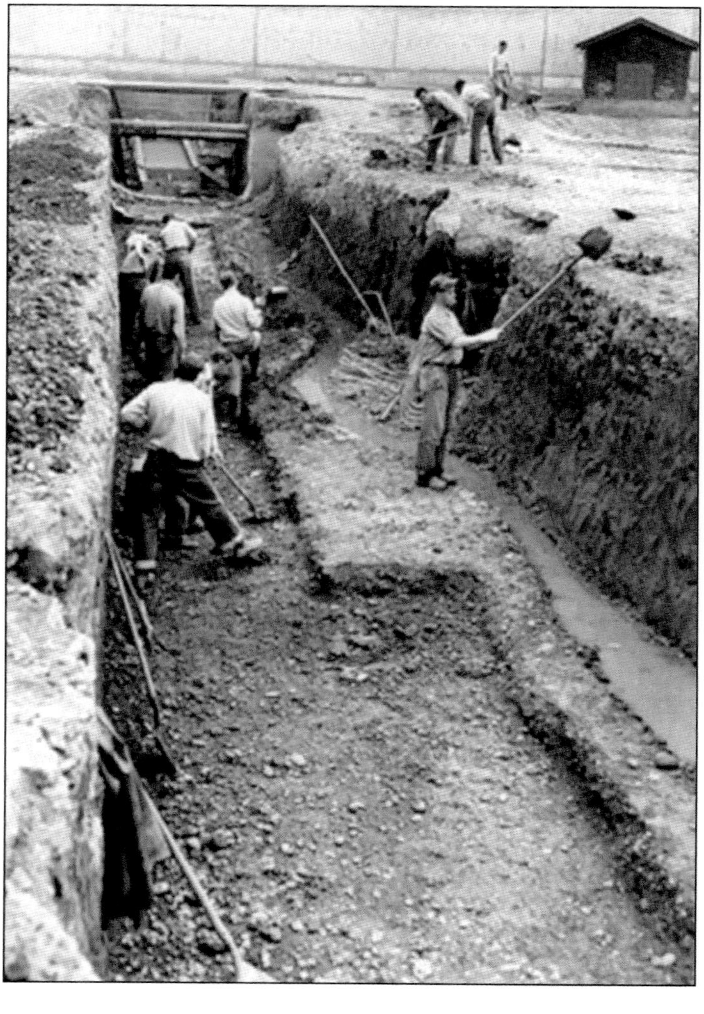

In 1956, the prison diverted Mill Creek outside the prison for the first time since OSP was built. The canal was filled in, and the flume was removed. All the work was done by hand using convict labor. A new power station was installed outside the prison for security reasons, and the water was no longer needed to power the waterwheel.

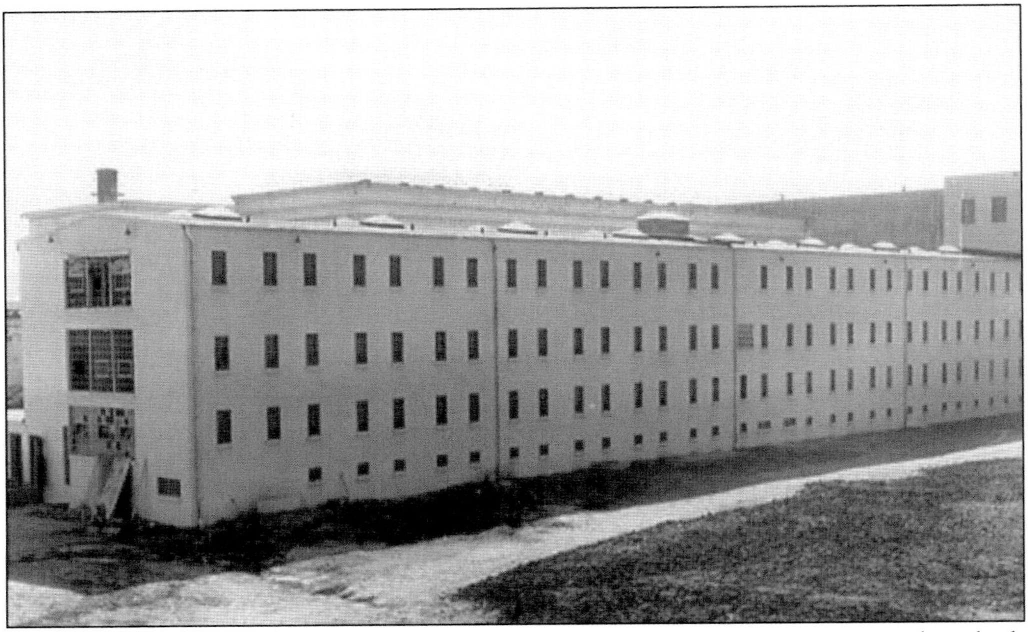

A photograph shows cellblock A in 1956 before it was completed. It had three tiers and was built to house minimum-security inmates. It contained 165 cells with electrically operated locking devices. Each cell had an individual window, a spring bed, a light, a seat and table, a bookshelf, a commode, and a washbasin. The basement contained the central clothing room and 50 inmate showers. It cost about $500,000 to build.

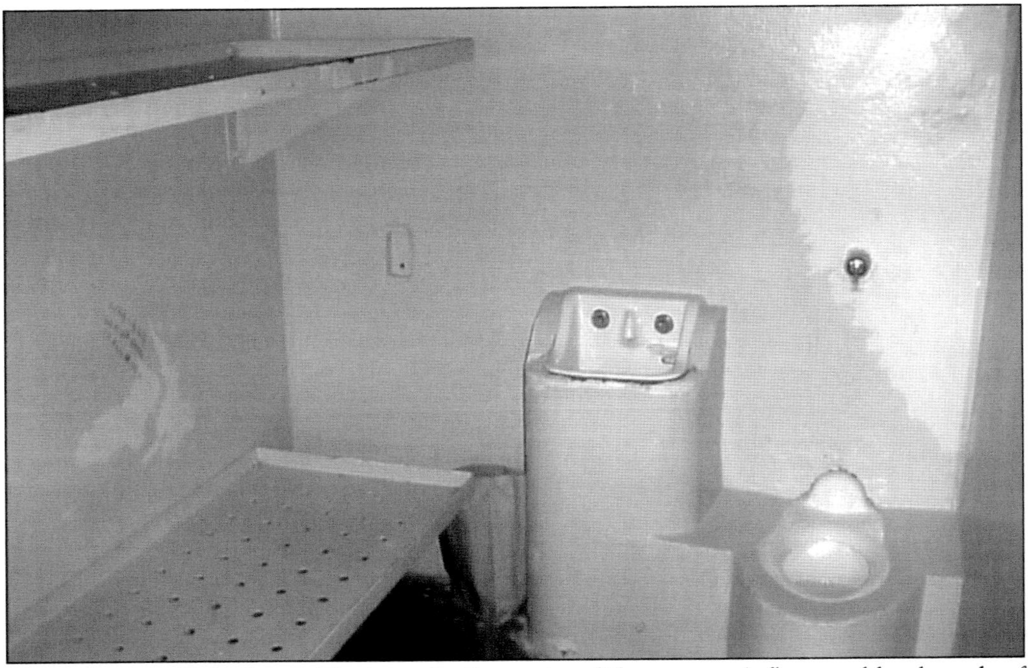

The isolation cells had a washbasin and toilet set in solid concrete. A flat metal bunk made of steel had two inches of lip on the edge. At night, prisoners received a mattress and blankets. Only two meals a day were served. Dinner consisted of rice, cauliflower, lettuce, and two pieces of bread on a paper plate. No meat or salt were included.

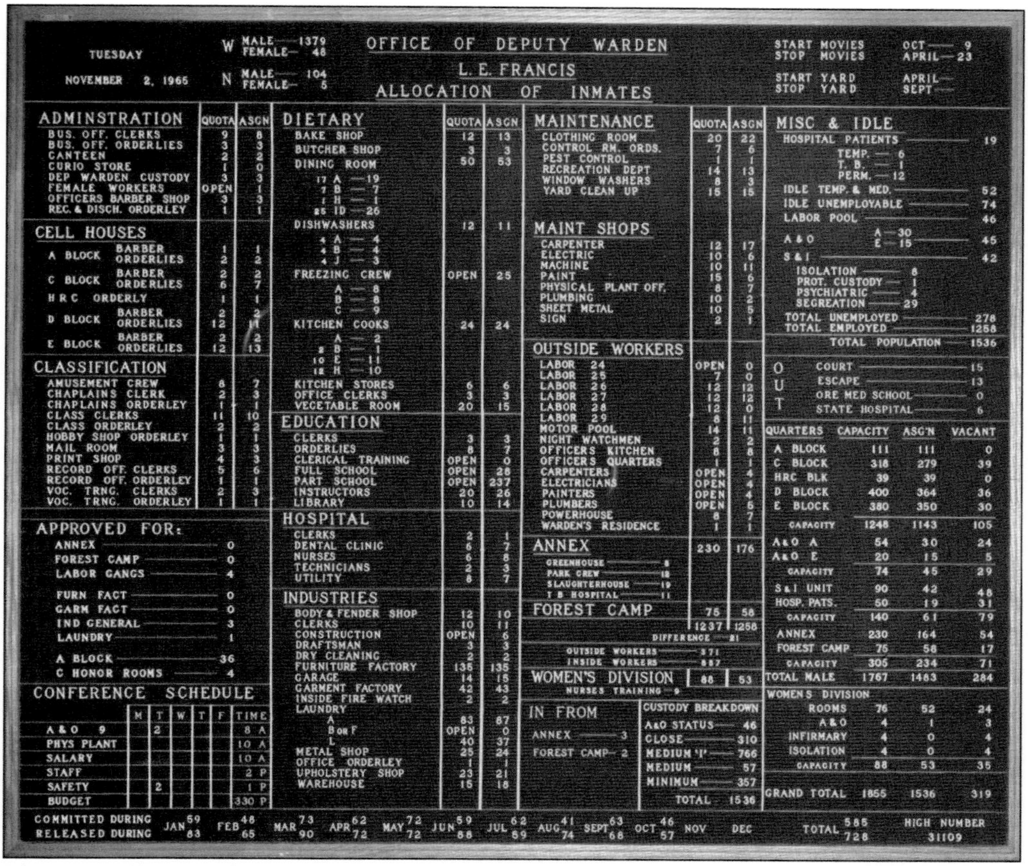

This 1963 allocation board provided comprehensive information about the inmates in OSP. It tells how many men could be assigned to a project and how many were already working there. It even identified how many were black and how many were white. There were eight men in the isolation cells, 53 women, and a total population of 1,536 inmates. The cafeteria, built in 1940, could feed 1,280 at the same time. The silent inmates were only allowed a spoon and a tin cup at the table.

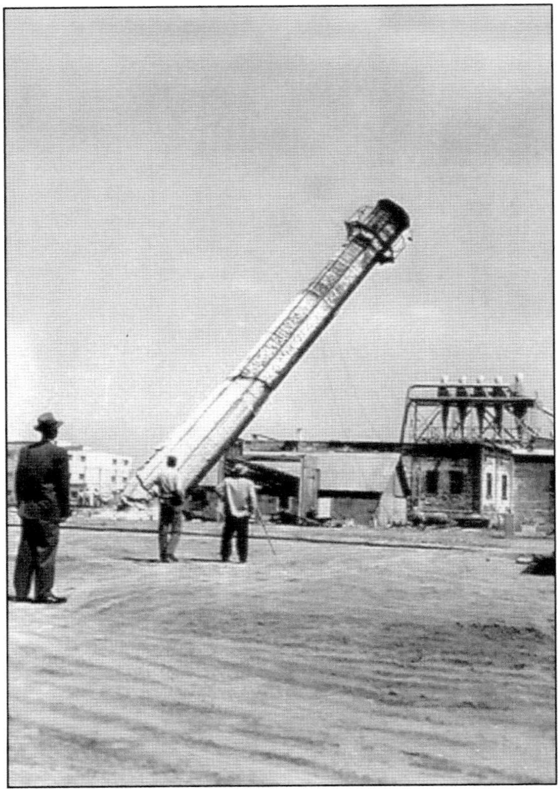

Here is the brick smokestack being pulled down in 1959. It was an iconic symbol at the penitentiary for almost 100 years. Once used to vent smoke from the wood-burning furnaces, the area was now used by the furniture factory.

This four-story administration building was erected in 1930. It cost $36,000, not including the amount for prison labor. The basement held a club room for officers. The first floor was open to the public and used by the warden and his officials as offices. The second and third floors were built to house female prisoners and their necessary facilities.

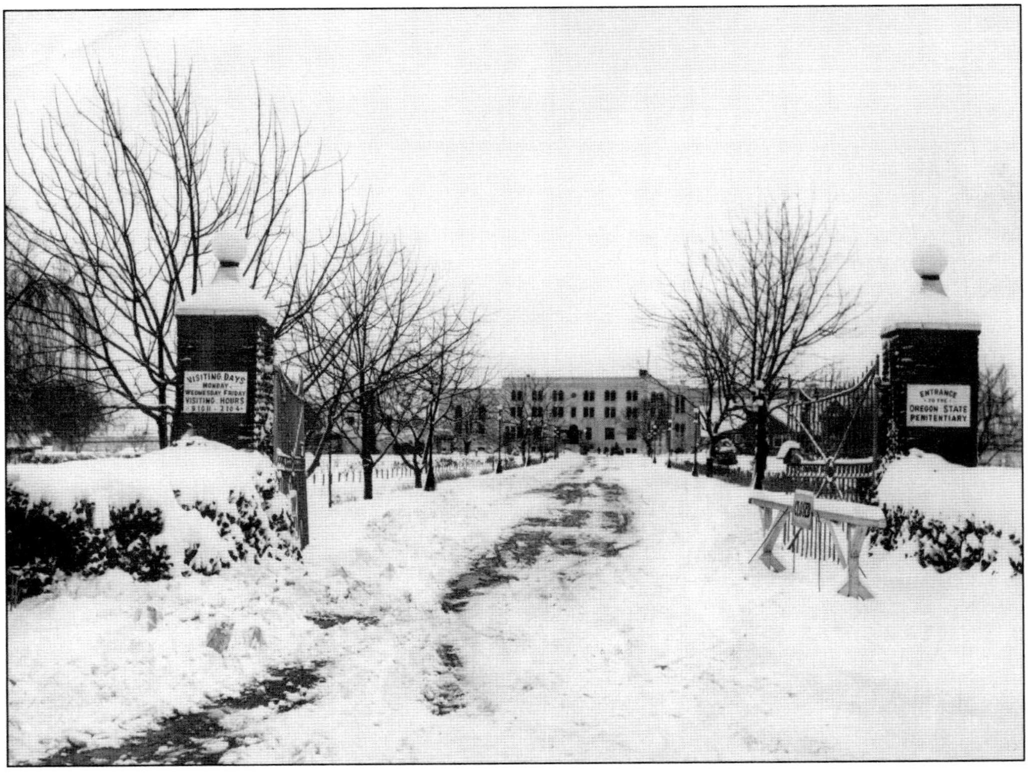

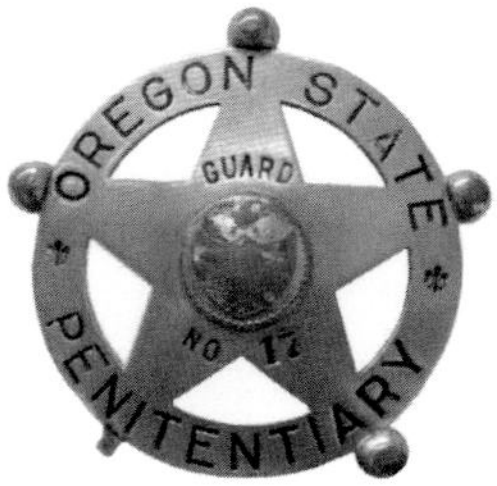

Two

Rehabilitation Programs

Rehabilitation programs provided psychological, educational, religious, medical, and recreational support for prison inmates. From the very beginning of OSP's history, prison authorities recognized the importance of such programs. Entertainment included lectures, musical concerts, boxing matches, and holiday celebrations. Inmates wrote and produced two different magazines until 1967. Sports provided needed exercise for a prison population primarily under the age of 30. The quality of the food was always important. Volunteer ministers provided religious instruction until the 1960s, when the legislature finally allocated money for a salary. An infirmary, manned by a part-time physician, provided medical care in the early years. In 1904, a hospital was built on the third floor of cellblock A. The first full-time physician was hired in 1934. In 1958, authorities began buying modern medical equipment. Hobby classes initiated in 1953 provided articles sold to the public in the prison curio shop.

Various clubs supervised by recreation staff permitted inmates to form groups that fostered special cultural occasions, annual celebrations, and family-centered parties. Clubs included African Americans, Native Americans, Hispanic Americans, motorcycle enthusiasts, automotive fans, and several athletic interest groups. For example, the automotive club built a race car, paid a person to drive the car, and kept up its maintenance. The African American club, called Uhuru Sa Sa, sponsored black-awareness lectures and invited local people to come into the prison and speak on various topics. The Native American Club, called Lakota Oyate Ki, sponsored powwows inside the walls and held an annual salmon feed and dance competition.

Athletic clubs sponsored baseball games with outside teams, boxing matches, and track events. The general education classes grew into a wide range of classes, from English as a second language and General Education Diploma (GED) classes to community college and university classes. The inmate library began as a collection of donated material. It became very popular and included over 10,000 books and a well-stocked legal library.

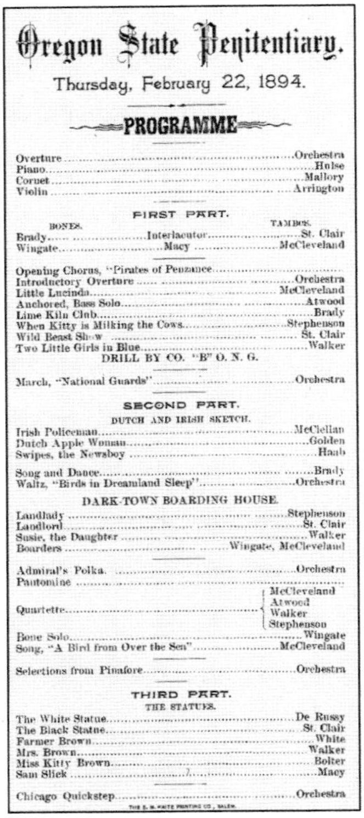

Oregon State Penitentiary.

Thursday, February 22, 1894.

PROGRAMME

Overture .... Orchestra
Piano .... Holse
Cornet .... Mallory
Violin .... Arrington

FIRST PART.

BONES. TAMBOS.
Brady .... Interlacutor .... St. Clair
Wingate .... Macy .... McCleveland

Opening Chorus, "Pirates of Penzance ....
Introductory Overture .... Orchestra
Little Lucinda .... McCleveland
Anchored, Bass Solo .... Atwood
Lime Kiln Club .... Brady
When Kitty is Milking the Cows .... Stephenson
Wild Beast Show .... St. Clair
Two Little Girls in Blue .... Walker
DRILL BY CO. "B" O. N. G.

March, "National Guards" .... Orchestra

SECOND PART.

DUTCH AND IRISH SKETCH.
Irish Policeman .... McClellan
Dutch Apple Woman .... Golden
Swipes, the Newsboy .... Haab

Song and Dance .... Brady
Waltz, "Birds in Dreamland Sleep" .... Orchestra

DARK-TOWN BOARDING HOUSE.
Landlady .... Stephenson
Landlord .... St. Clair
Susie, the Daughter .... Walker
Boarders .... Wingate, McCleveland

Admiral's Polka .... Orchestra
Pantomine ....
Quartette .... McCleveland, Atwood, Walker, Stephenson
Bone Solo .... Wingate
Song, "A Bird from Over the Sea" .... McCleveland

Selections from Pinafore .... Orchestra

THIRD PART.

THE STATUES.
The White Statue .... De Russy
The Black Statue .... St. Clair
Farmer Brown .... White
Mrs. Brown .... Walker
Miss Kitty Brown .... Bolter
Sam Slick .... Macy

Chicago Quickstep .... Orchestra

This photograph shows the entertainment program put on by the inmates on Thursday, February 22, 1894. Minstrel shows were popular, and one was given on July 5, 1907, in the dining room. Nearly 3,000 people attended the nine performances of the 1922 Melody Minstrel show on January 17, 18, 19, 20, and 21. A ticket cost 50¢. (Courtesy of University of Oregon Special Collections.)

In 1893, the prison barber built his own banjo and entertained at special performances. The first band instruments were donated to the prison in 1906. In 1910, the legislature appropriated $600 to buy new band instruments and a piano. A 14-piece orchestra provided music at the prison by 1920.

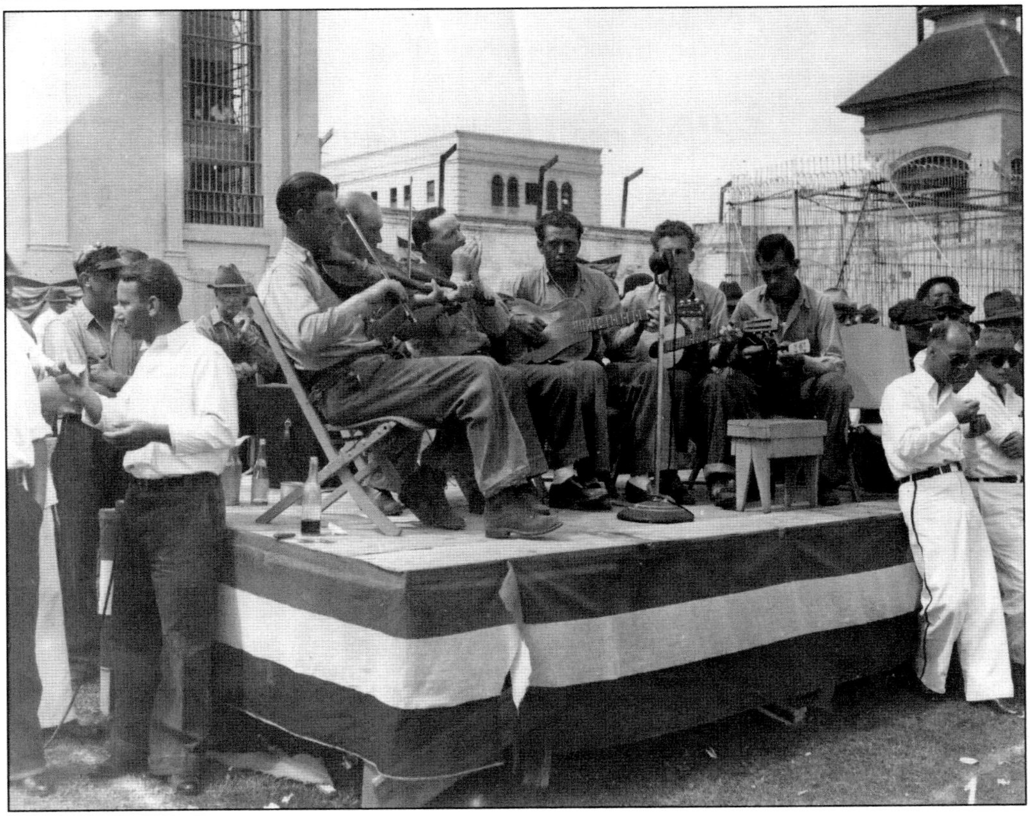

Until 1891, OSP did not permit convicts to read any local newspapers. *Lend a Hand* was first published monthly in 1903 under the direction of chaplain E.W. St. Pierre. It was discontinued in 1920. A subscription cost $1 a year or 10¢ a copy. Eugene O. Smith was the editor in 1917. The magazine reported various events happening inside the prison, as well as comments on social happenings on the outside. The poem "Dreams, Hopes, and Words" was written by prisoner Jack Catron and published in the prison magazine. The magazine was intended "to encourage moral and intellectual improvement among the inmates; to devote its energies along lines calculated to lead recreant ones back to usefulness in society; to acquaint the public with our true status, and to dispel the prejudice which exists against those who have paid the penalty of their transgressions." (Both courtesy of OSL.)

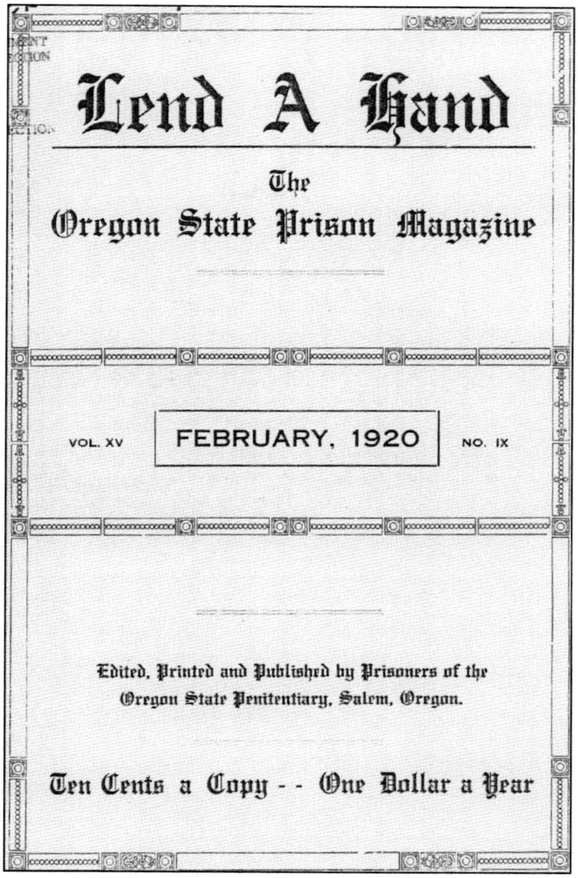

Lend A Hand

The

Oregon State Prison Magazine

VOL. XV FEBRUARY, 1920 NO. IX

Edited, Printed and Published by Prisoners of the Oregon State Penitentiary, Salem, Oregon.

Ten Cents a Copy - - One Dollar a Year

Dreams, Hopes, and Words

Where are all the dreams we dreamed,
That never came to pass?
Where are all the hopes we had
Which, in youth, we knew would last?
What has happened to those words
That we vowed to speak?
We still have every question;
Yet the answers we still seek.

The dreams have died within our hearts,
Grown cold and hard with time.
The fire of our youth's great hopes
Is smothered in the brine.
And all the words we vowed to speak,
When life was young and dear,
Died in silence, for they were
Words no one wished to hear.

JACK CATRON

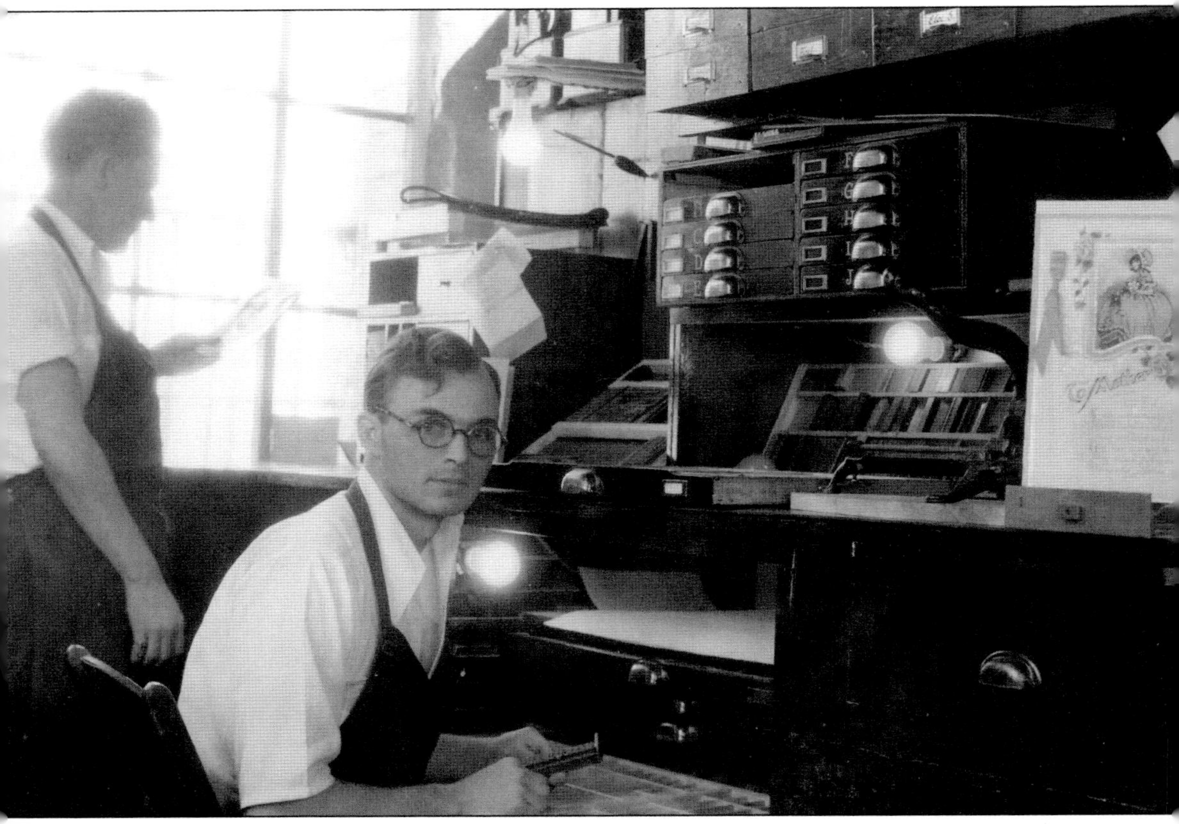

Shadows was a quarterly magazine written and published by the prison inmates between the years 1936 and 1967. "The purpose of *Shadows* was to give the inmates an opportunity for self-expression; to encourage moral and intellectual improvement among the inmates; and to acquaint the public with the true status of the prisoner." From January 1936 to December 1942, Hugh DeAutremont, a convicted train robber and murderer, was the editor. This photograph shows R.G. Witmer, the editor in 1956, working in the *Shadows* office. A subscription cost $1 a year or 10¢ a copy. In 1963, the magazine summed up the industrial program: "All men assigned to industries receive extra good time and pay—benefits which few men received prior to the inception of this new program. Men learn trades—plus good habits and safety rules. They work under conditions that are decent and humane." The magazine addressed all kinds of issues, from capital punishment and crime prevention to poetry and fiction. (Courtesy of OSL.)

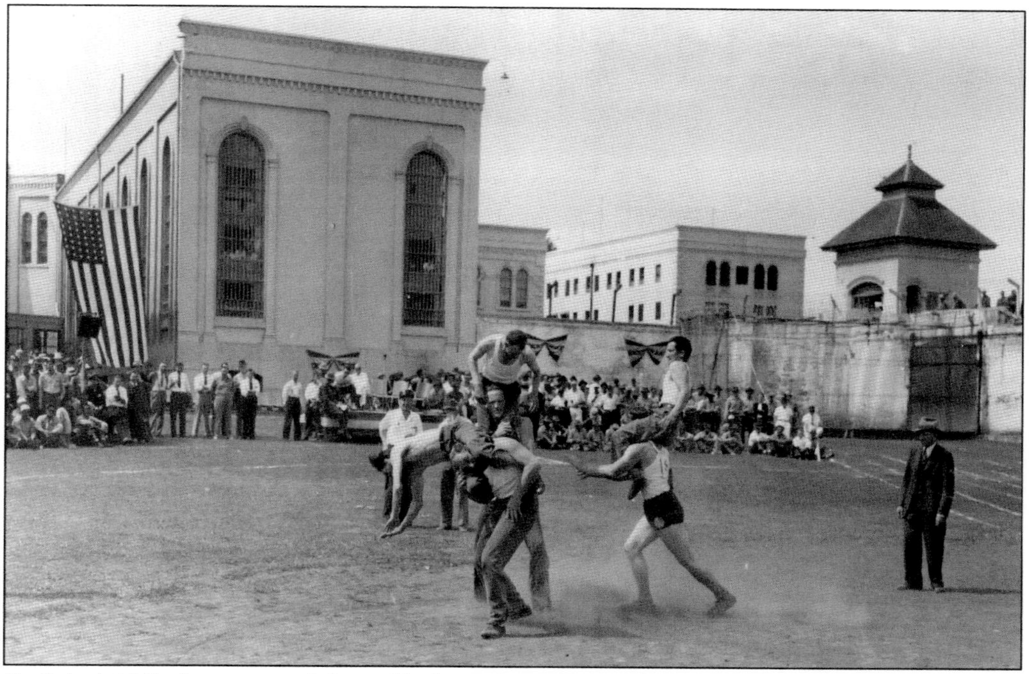

On July 4, 1941, the prison celebrated Independence Day with a series of outdoor activities. Here, inmate roustabout teams compete against each other. Officials and guards line the background, and convicts peer out the windows of cellblock B. Inmates sit on the ground to the left. Field day began at 8:00 a.m., and the boxing began at 12:45 p.m.

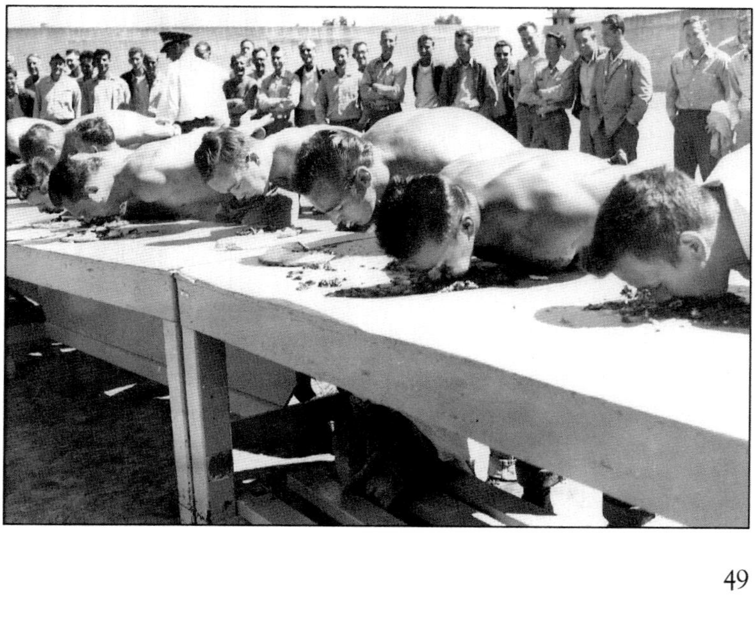

This pie-eating contest took place on July 4, 1959. Prisoners no longer have shaved heads and at the time were allowed to grease their hair back in popular ducktails. The guards are wearing hats, white shirts, and dark pants. The inmates are wearing heavy denim jeans and light-blue work shirts over white T-shirts. (Courtesy of OSA.)

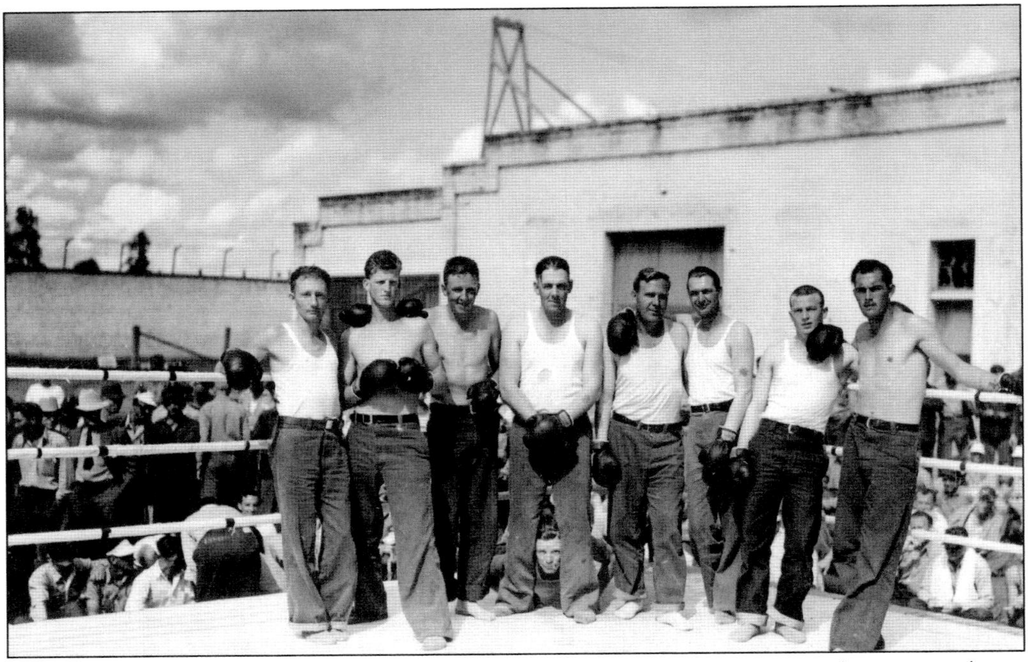

Superintendent L.H. Compton mentioned the occasional boxing tournament of six or more bouts during 1919. By 1936, boxing matches were confined to special holidays like the Fourth of July. When there was boxing, it needed instructors, time to train, and a higher protein diet. "A bad showing," according to warden Clarence Gladden in 1968, "was the cause of its discontinuance."

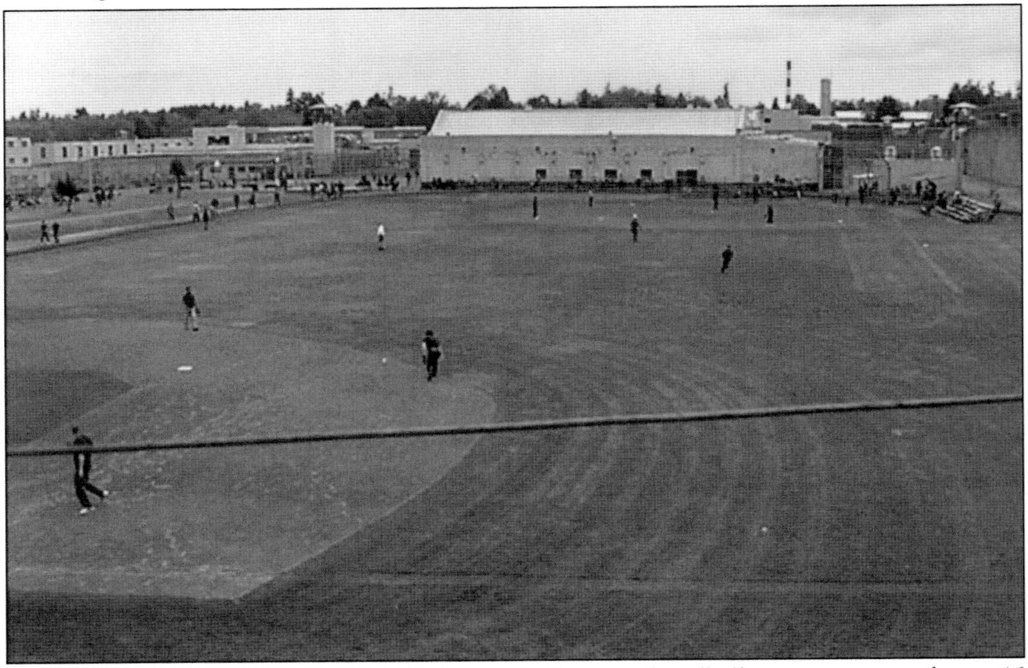

In 1968, the sports program consisted of a baseball area, a handball court accommodating 16 players, a basketball court that handled 10, and a peewee golf course for 72, weather permitting. Four baseball teams in the spring had room for 36 players. This was the only recreation for 1,200 prisoners; it left dominoes, checkers, or chess as the only other options.

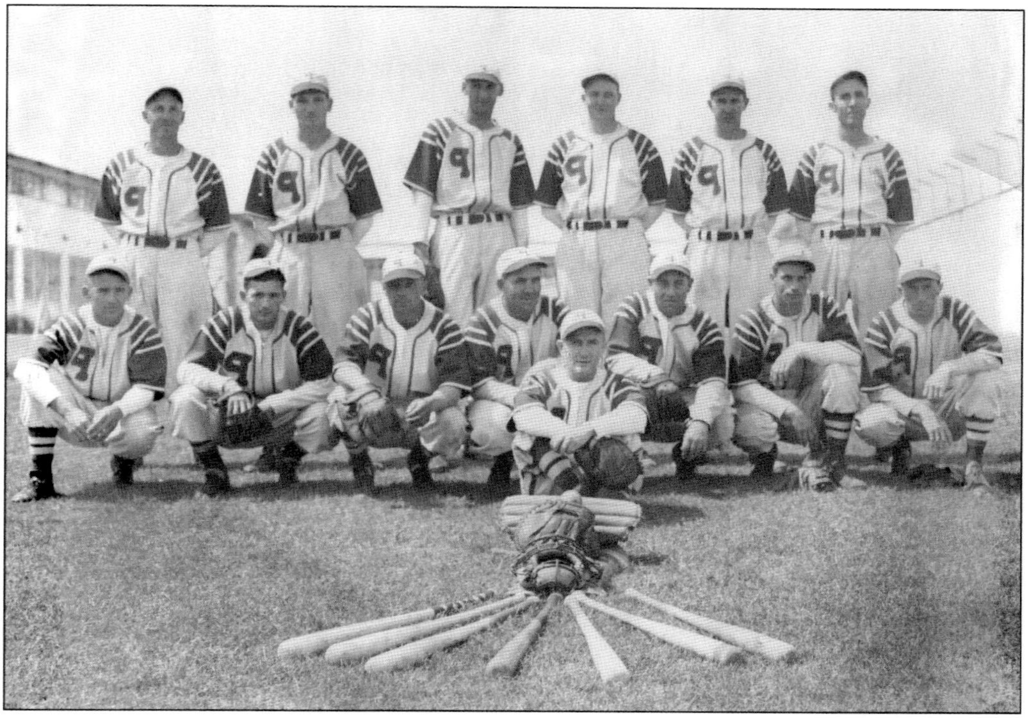

In 1914, recreation consisted of baseball, quoits, and handball. A full-time recreation director was hired in 1951 to supervise and facilitate all kinds of sports activities. Handball courts and horseshoe pitches were added to the facilities. By 1954, recreation consisted of intramural games of baseball, softball, basketball, and handball, as well as boxing, wrestling, horseshoes, miniature golf, and weight lifting.

On April 28, 1917, superintendent Charles Murphy loaded the ball team, the band, and a score of supporters in trucks and autos to play baseball against the Chemawa team. John Devitt pitched, striking out nine, while the Chemawa champion struck out four. In the eighth inning, the game was tied and the prison team was up to bat. In the end, OSP won 5-2. (Courtesy of OSA.)

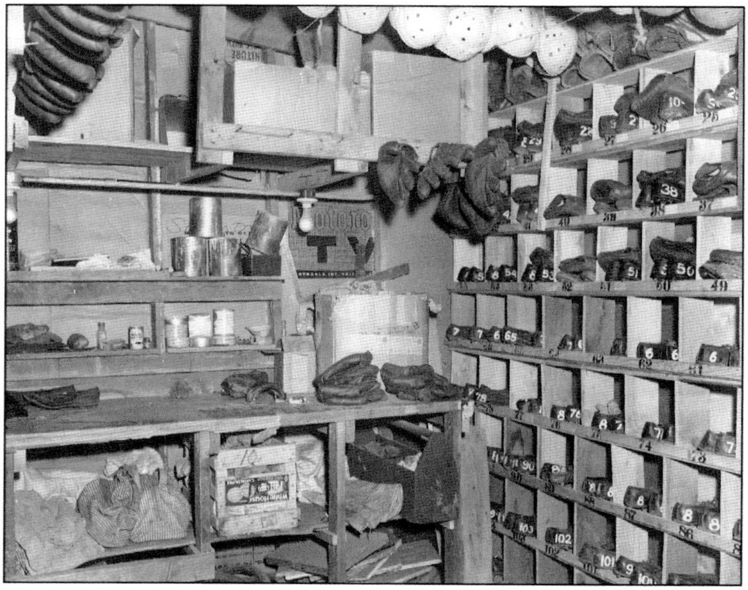

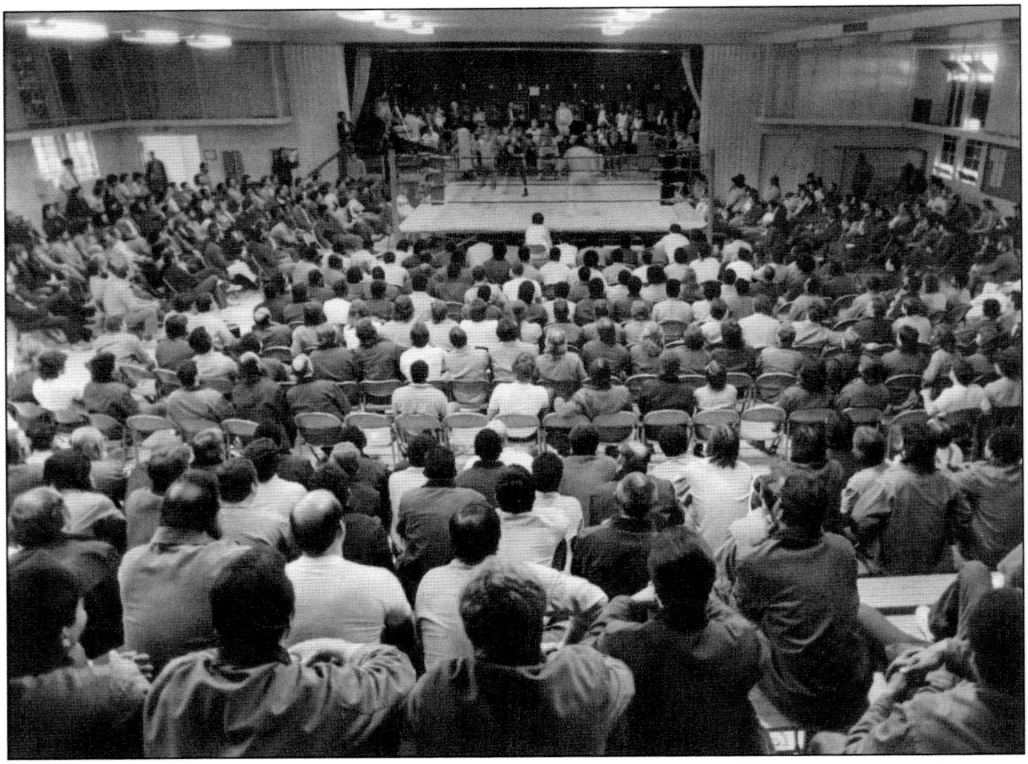

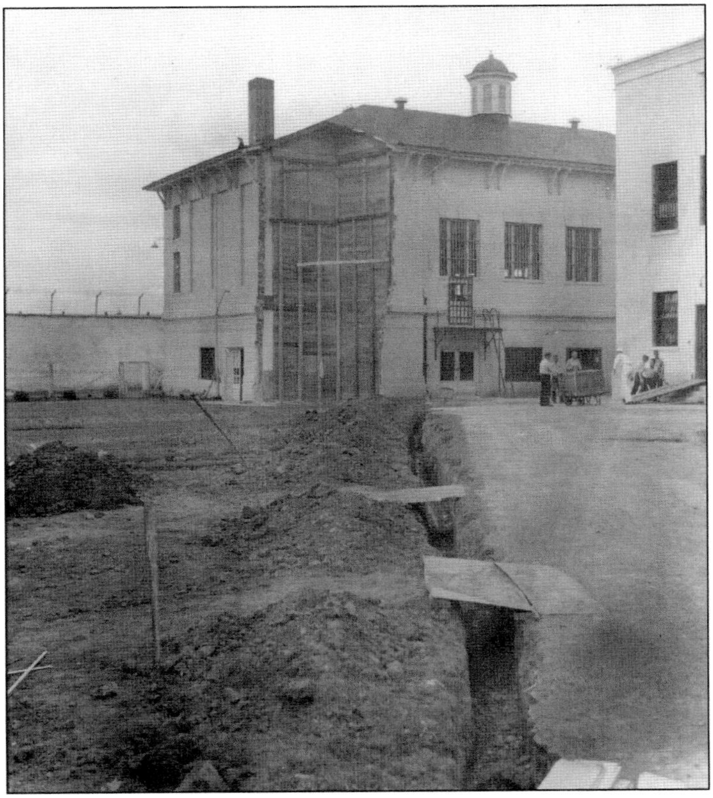

Sometimes, special events were scheduled for prisoners. This photograph shows a boxing exhibition with hundreds of convicts watching. In the center are five men isolated from the crowd by empty chairs. (Courtesy of SJ.)

Repairs and improvements inside the prison were usually done with convict labor, which often created problems for security. A report from April 2, 1953, stated that inmates seemed to roam unsupervised throughout the cellblocks and corridors. There was no uniformity in the inmates' clothing.

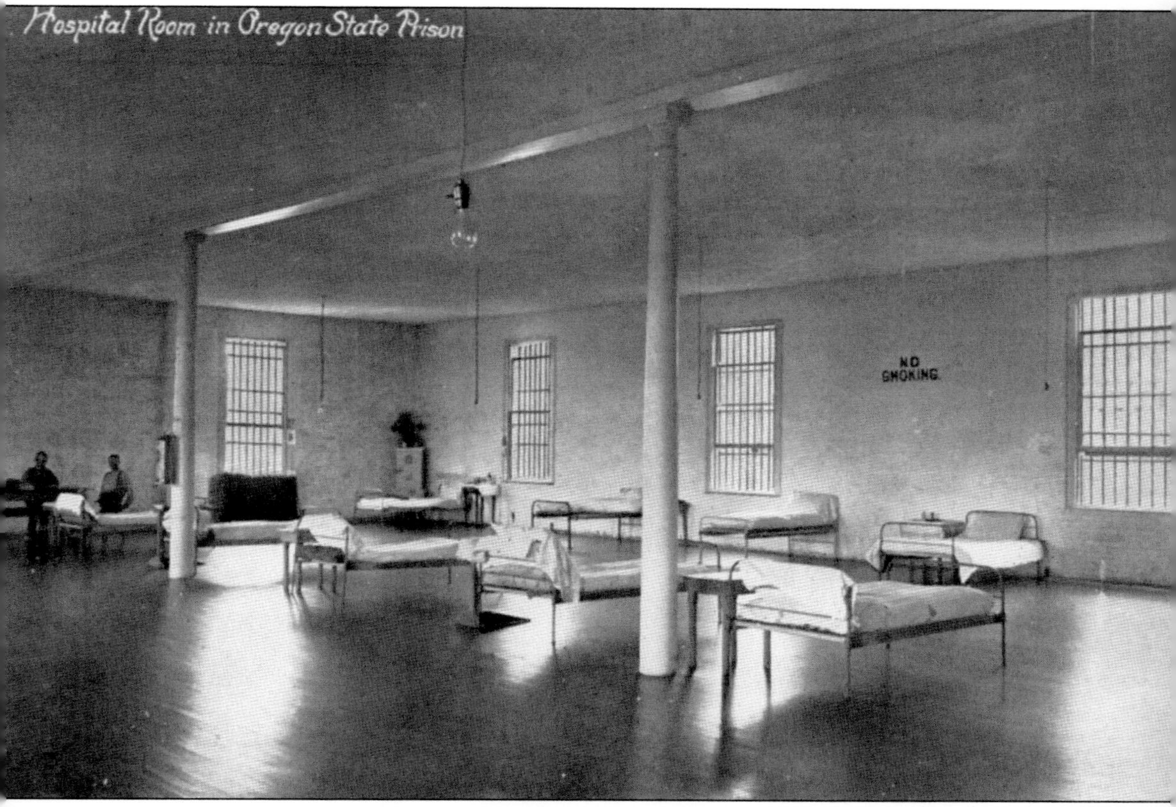

During the winter of 1889–1890, there were 200 cases of influenza—nearly every convict in the prison. All the prisoners recovered. In 1896, the infirmary was supplied with iron hospital bedsteads, spring mattresses, pillows, and sheets. A prison hospital was built on the third story of cellblock A in 1904. It included a druggist's office and a large ward for the patients, pictured here. In 1909, the prison purchased four cases of toilet paper and 1,304 pieces of cutlery. Dr. E.P. Tupker, a full-time physician, was hired in 1934 and paid $174.80 a month. By 1952, the prison added a part-time surgeon and three full-time hospital aides. Chest x-rays reduced the incidence of tuberculosis. (Courtesy of WHC, 2011.006.0635.)

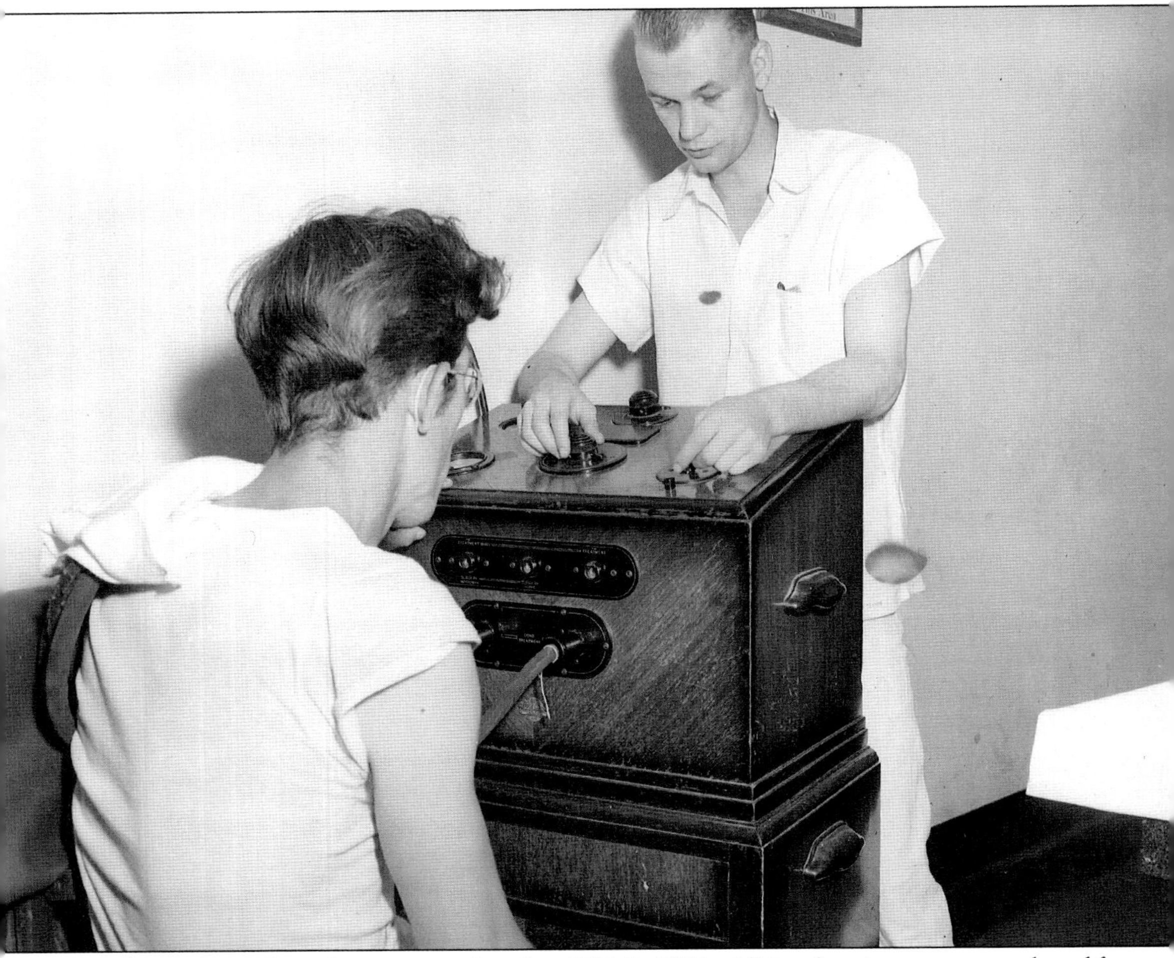

This cardiograph machine was purchased in 1950. By 1958, additional equipment was purchased for the prison hospital, including 10 hospital beds, 30 ward chairs, 50 bedside lockers, and a pressure-dressing sterilizer. Additional equipment for an optometrist included a refractor, an instrument stand, and an examining chair. Max A. Moon, the new part-time prison dentist, reported that he treated 6,000 cases in his first two years working at OSP. He extracted 2,200 teeth and completed 3,783 fillings. The convict dental technician handled most of the work. Dentures and eyeglasses were not available unless paid for by the convict. Dr. Herbert P. Bara, the first full-time dentist, was hired in 1950. (Courtesy of OSA.)

The first hobby class was initiated in 1954. Convicts furnished their own tools and materials. They made purses, wallets, fishing flies, and jewelry. Prisoners were also allowed to paint pictures and produce silver engravings. They were only permitted to visit the hobby shop during their leisure time.

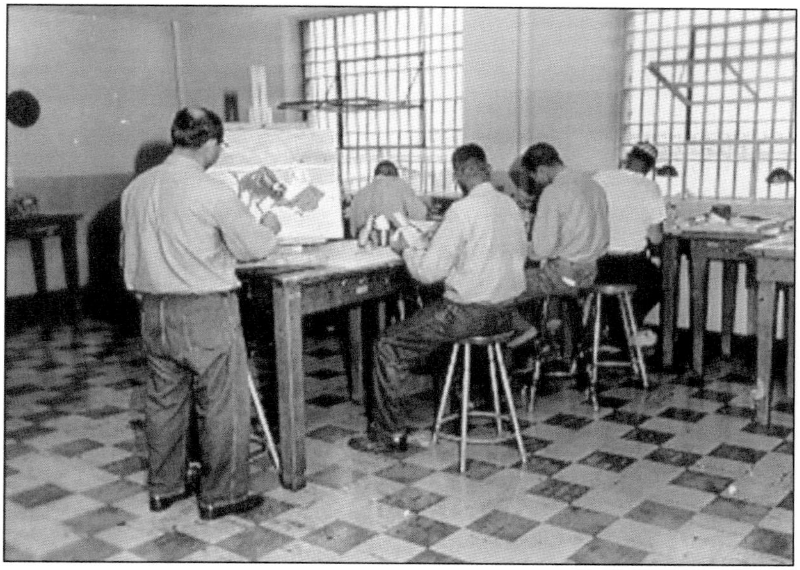

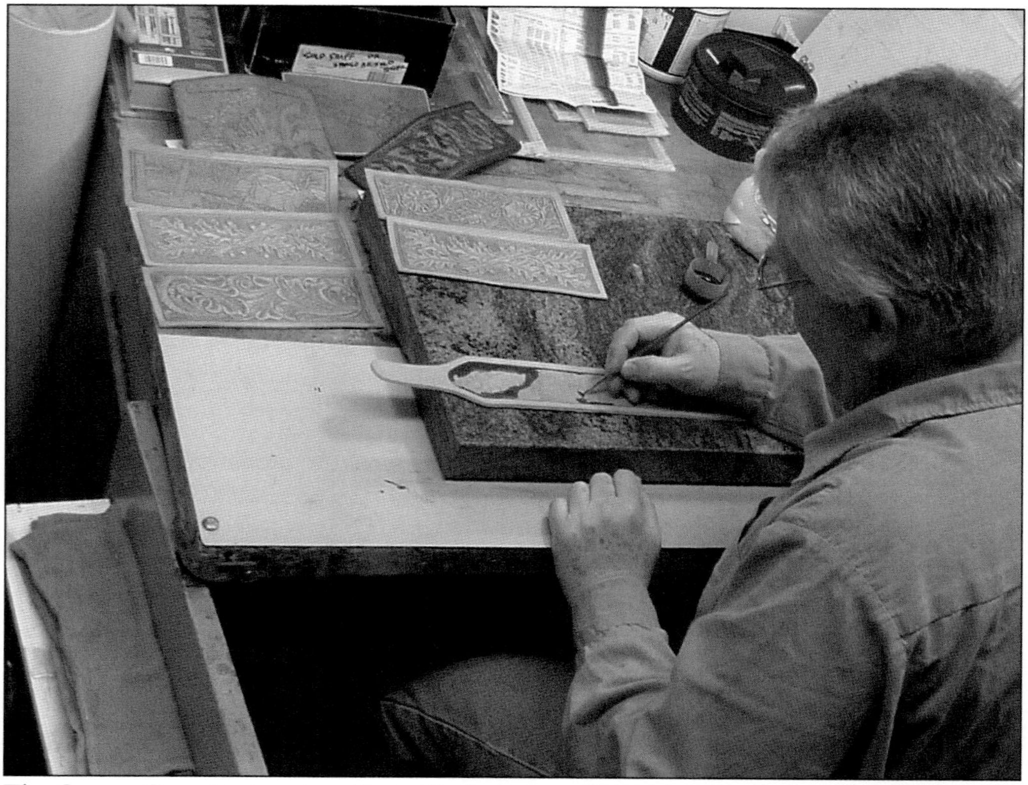

The Oregon State Penitentiary Curio Shop, on State Street, sold inmate-produced articles to the public. In 1960, a total of 63 inmates had earned $53,314 over the previous two years. The proceeds were deposited in their individual institution accounts. The shop was open from 9:00 a.m. to 5:45 p.m. daily, with an hour off for lunch. Because of road construction in 1996, the shop had to be removed.

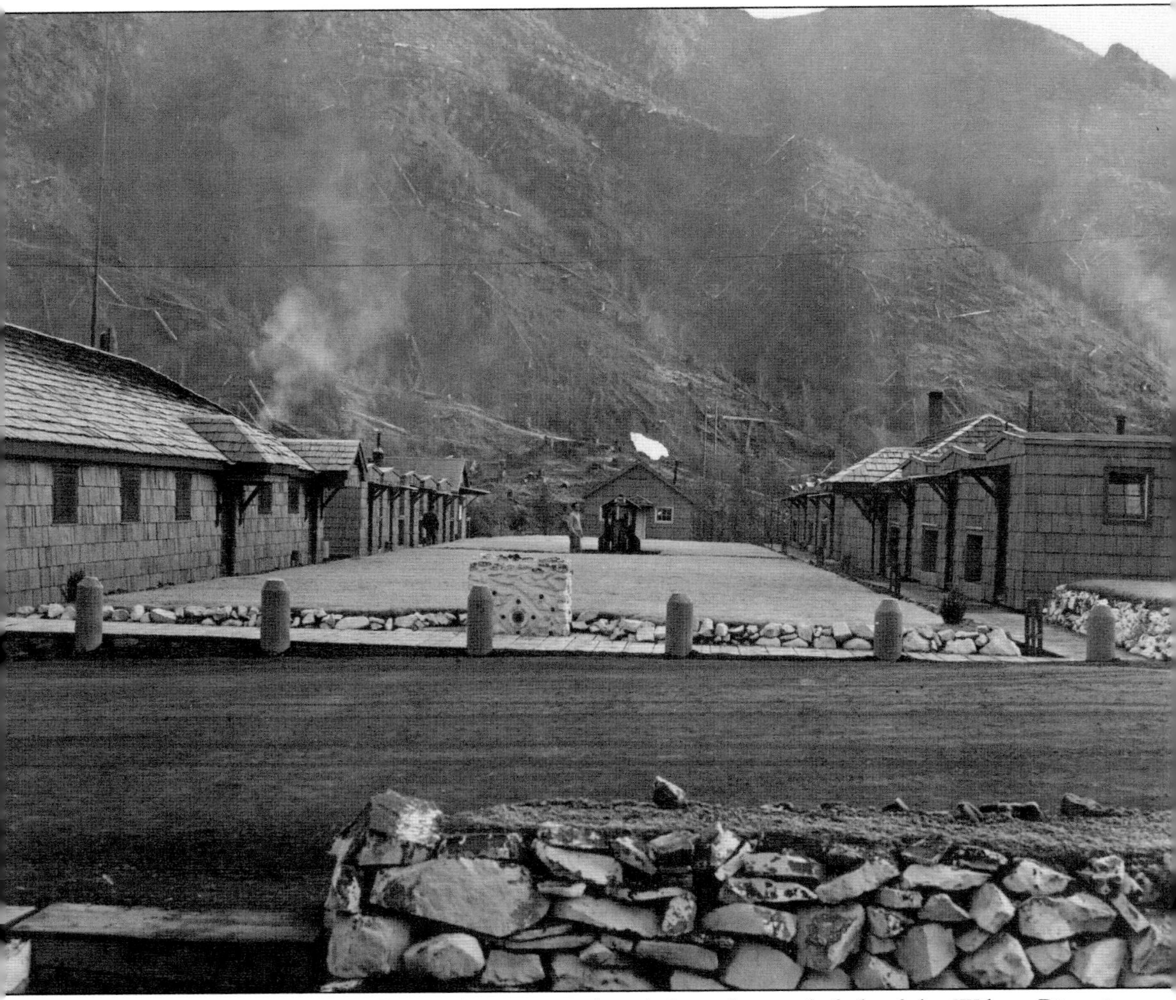

The first forest camp in Oregon history was founded on the south fork of the Wilson River in 1951 to plant trees, remove old stumps, and assist the State Forestry Department. The camp had 15 prefabricated buildings for about 50 inmates, who arrived on November 1. The buildings included housing for six men each, a mess hall and cookhouse, recreation rooms, washrooms and showers, and guards' quarters. This is the South Fork Camp, in the Tillamook Burn, not far from Forest Grove. Primarily established as part of the $10.5 million plan to rehabilitate the Tillamook Burn, the prisoners were also trained in firefighting techniques. The prisoners who worked here received $1 a day plus good-time days off their sentences. Between 1952 and 1958, they planted 36 million trees.

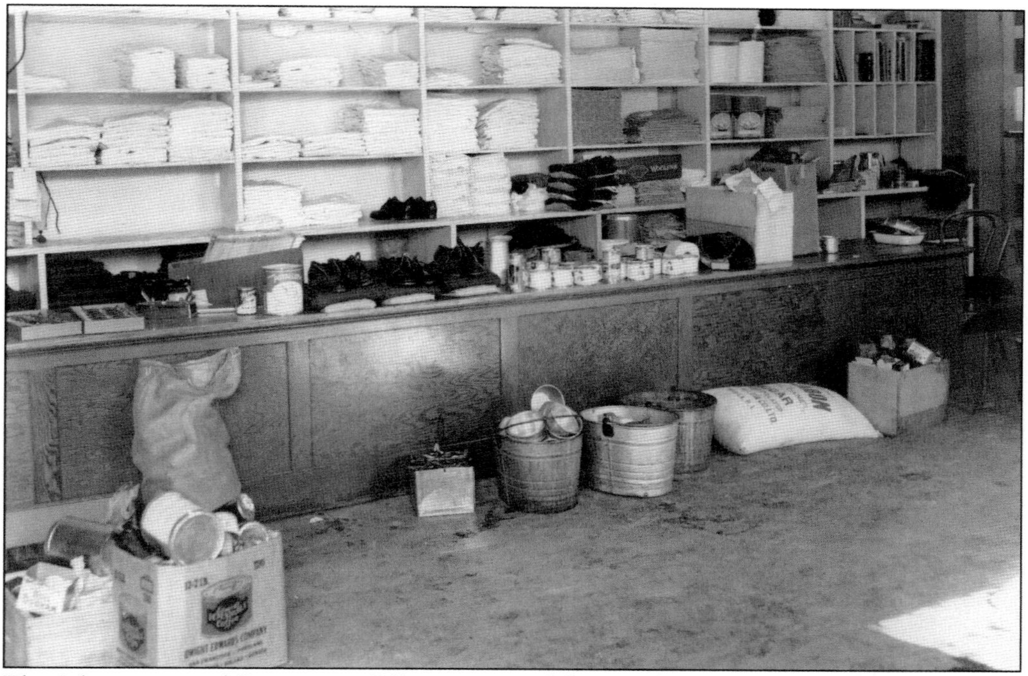

The Admittance and Orientation Office supervised the use of prison supplies and superintended the cooking and feeding of the prisoners. When new convicts arrived, they were given clothing and a tobacco ration. The prisoners were not allowed to play cards or swear. A hired civilian monitored the prison's supplies and helped prevent stealing.

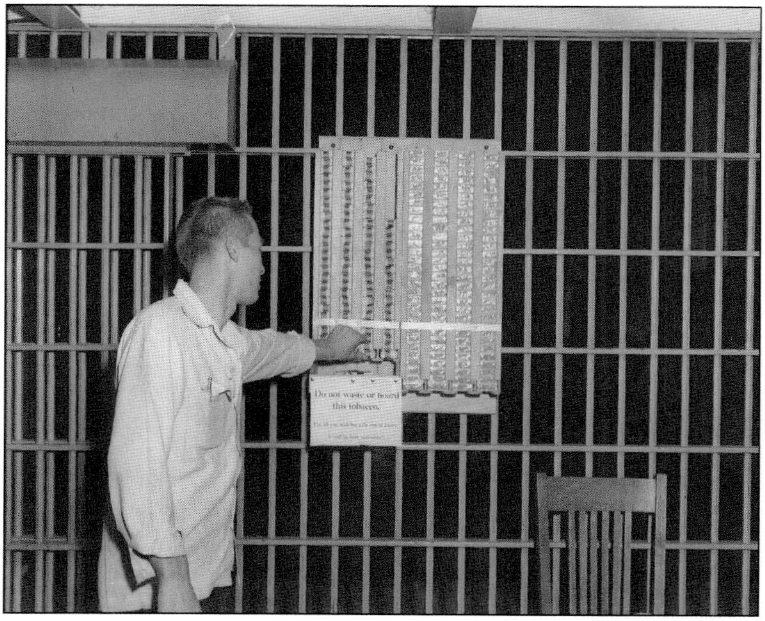

When Clarence Gladden was named warden in 1953, he discovered prisoners using tobacco as currency in a black-market scheme. To stop the problem, he installed these dispensaries in all the cellblocks. The sign read, "Do not waste or hoard this tobacco. Use all you wish but take one at a time. It will be here tomorrow." That solved the problem. (Courtesy of OSA.)

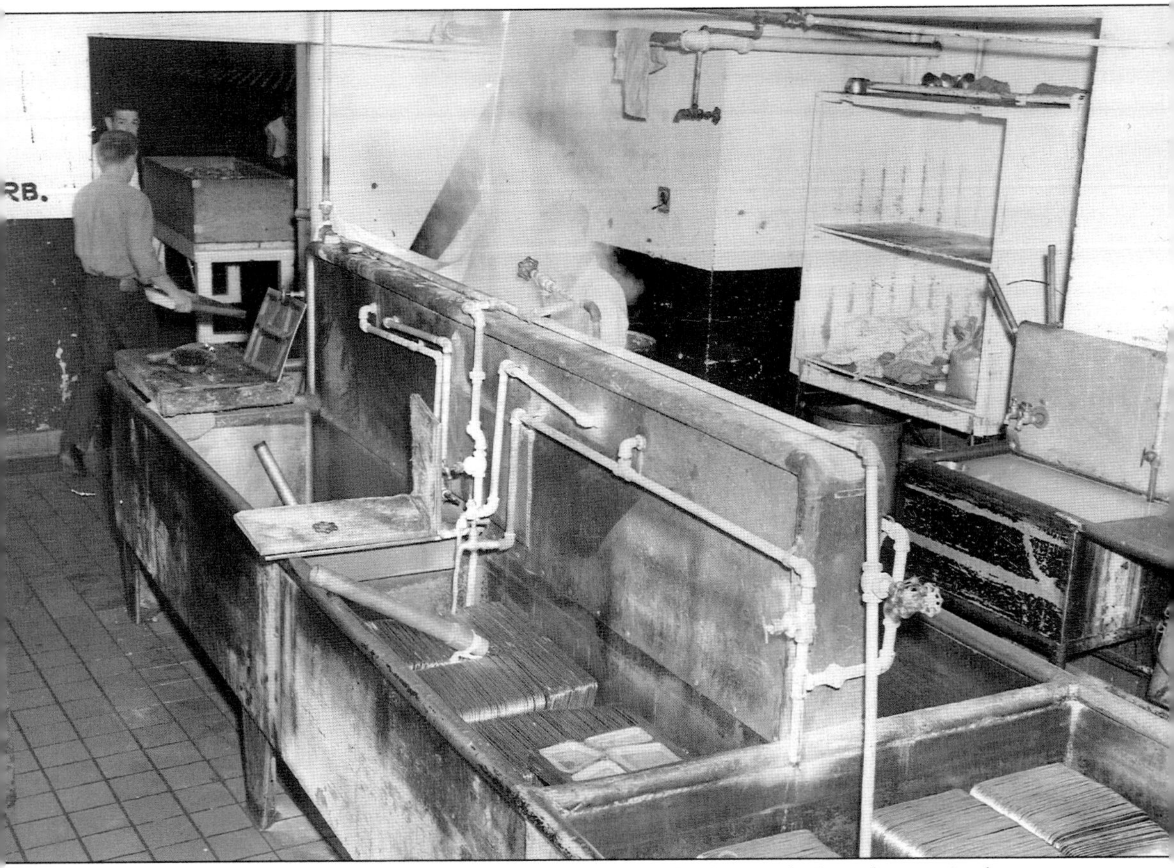

In 1918, it cost $10,747 for the guards' kitchen supplies, which served 45 employees. At the same time, it cost $25,654 for the prisoners' kitchen supplies, which served 566 convicts. This photograph of the dish-washing facility in the prison kitchen was taken in 1953. It shows dirt crusted on machines, dirty dishes floating in a back sink and a bucket under a counter to catch dripping utensils. By 1956, there were 1,638 prisoners and 292 employees. The 1957 biennium report stated, "While every care is taken to insure that only suitable food is obtained for preparation, great emphasis is placed on its careful preparation and serving." Between 1954 and 1956, the prison farm produced 1,381,643 pounds of root vegetables, which included 767,945 pounds of potatoes. Much of that produce went to the prison kitchen and had to be processed by inmates. (Courtesy of OSA.)

A national standard, the "Food Ration System" was adopted by the prison in 1954. This system mandated that each inmate received five pounds of foodstuffs per day based on the total weight of meats and vegetables. It was a formula the prison used to make sure each inmate received the right proportion of specific nutrients to maintain a good nutritional balance. (Courtesy of OSA.)

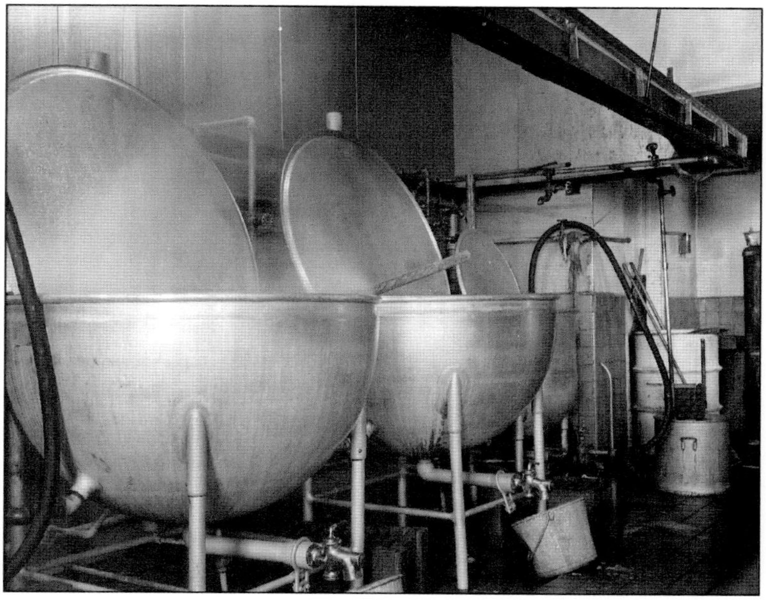

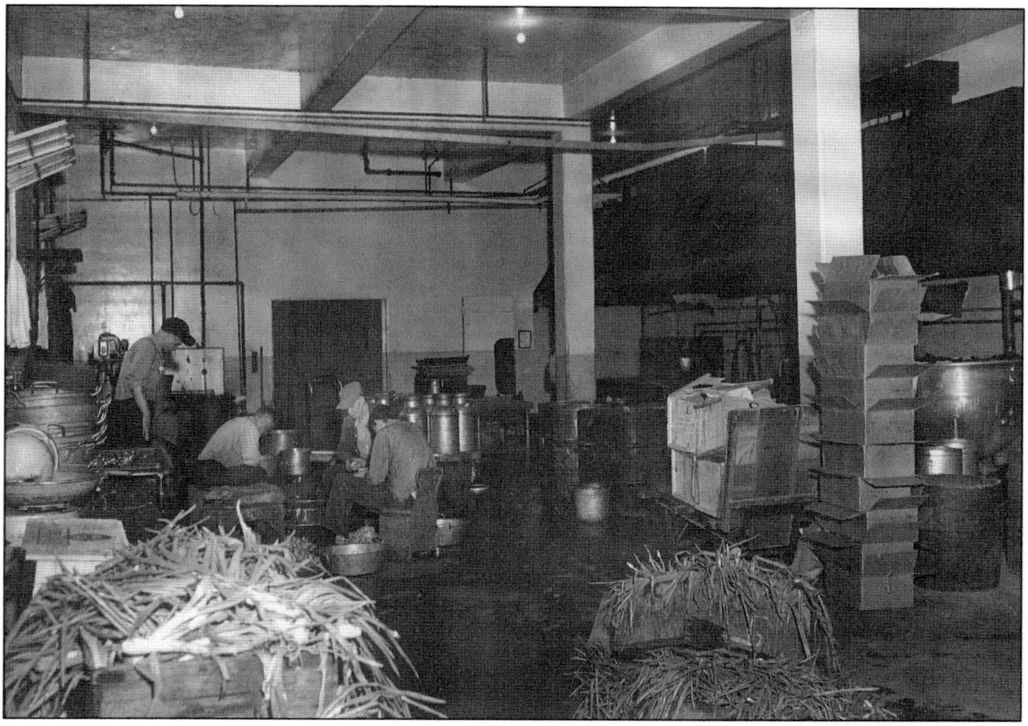

Inmates grew a wide variety of vegetables within the prison walls at the lifer's garden and even raised chickens for a time. Most of the vegetables for the cannery came from the prison farm, which operated from 1910 until 1968. They were transported from the farm to the cannery inside the walls. Inmates did all the produce handling and enjoyed working with the fresh food and helping preserve it. (Courtesy of OSA.)

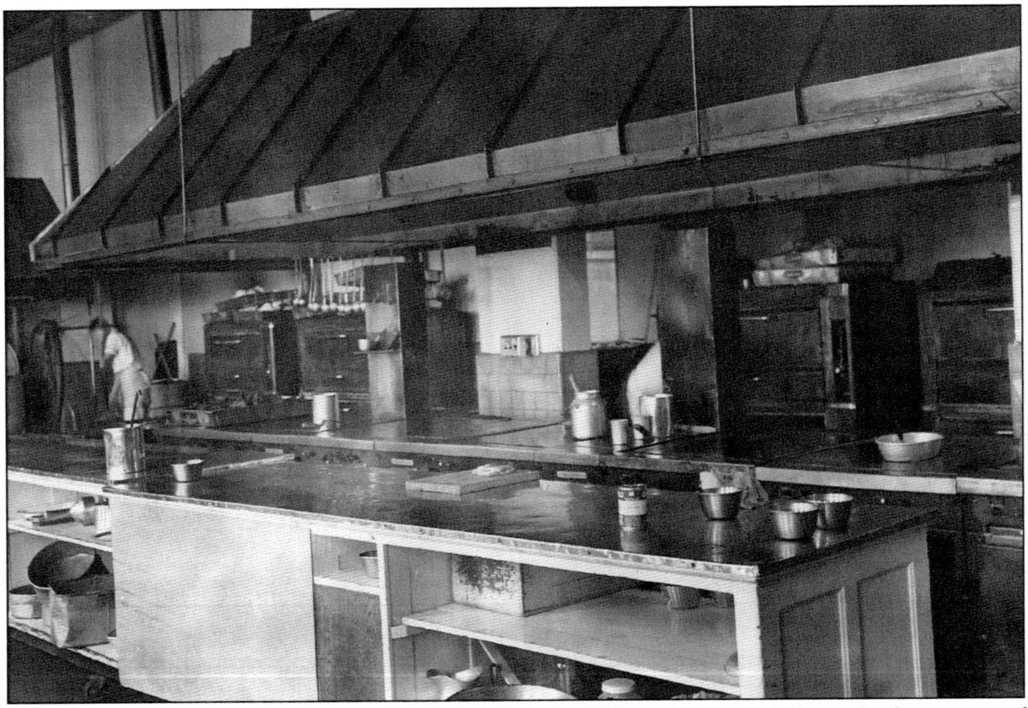

An original brick oven was built in 1901 when the kitchen was moved from the basement of the administration building to its own building. The kitchen was equipped with steam cookers and roasters direct from Philadelphia and St. Louis. In 1929, a double oven costing $2,500, a Middleby-Marshall No. 50 model B, was installed. This 1953 kitchen cooked and served three meals a day. (Courtesy of OSA.)

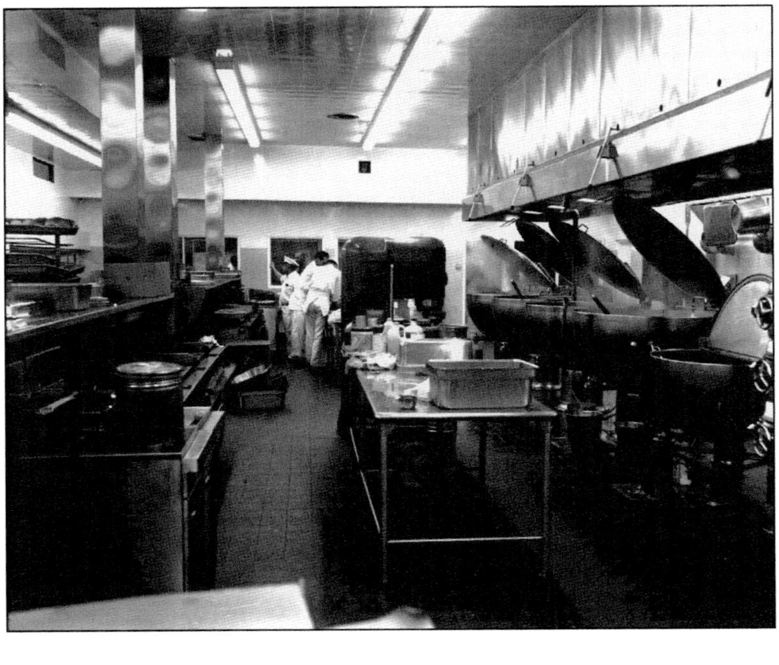

Inmate culinary staff prepared all the food for the prison. They often worked three shifts, cooking in large steam kettles for the prison. Average meals included two vegetables, one starch, a meat dish, a dessert, and all the fresh bread an inmate could eat. It cost an average of 57¢ a day to feed a prisoner in 1963. (Courtesy of OSA.)

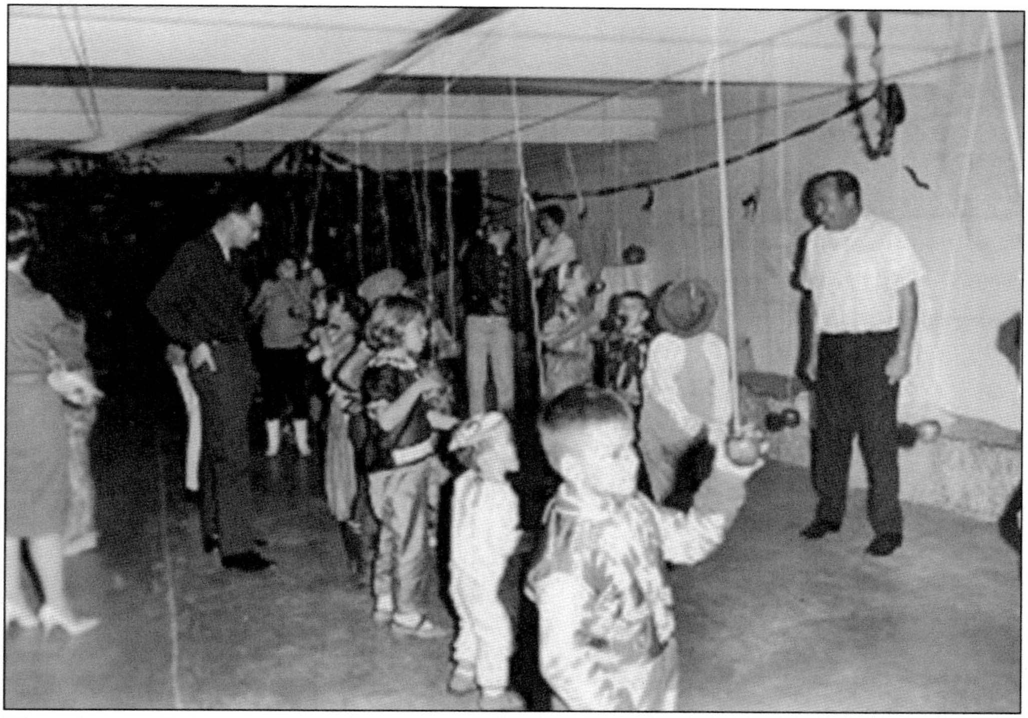

The prison staff always supported activities with the inmates and their families. Birthday parties and marriages and seasonal celebrations were often held at the prison for inmates' families and guests. This photograph is an example of prison personnel putting on a Halloween party for inmates' children. The prison Lifer's Club provided all the food and the prizes awarded to the children.

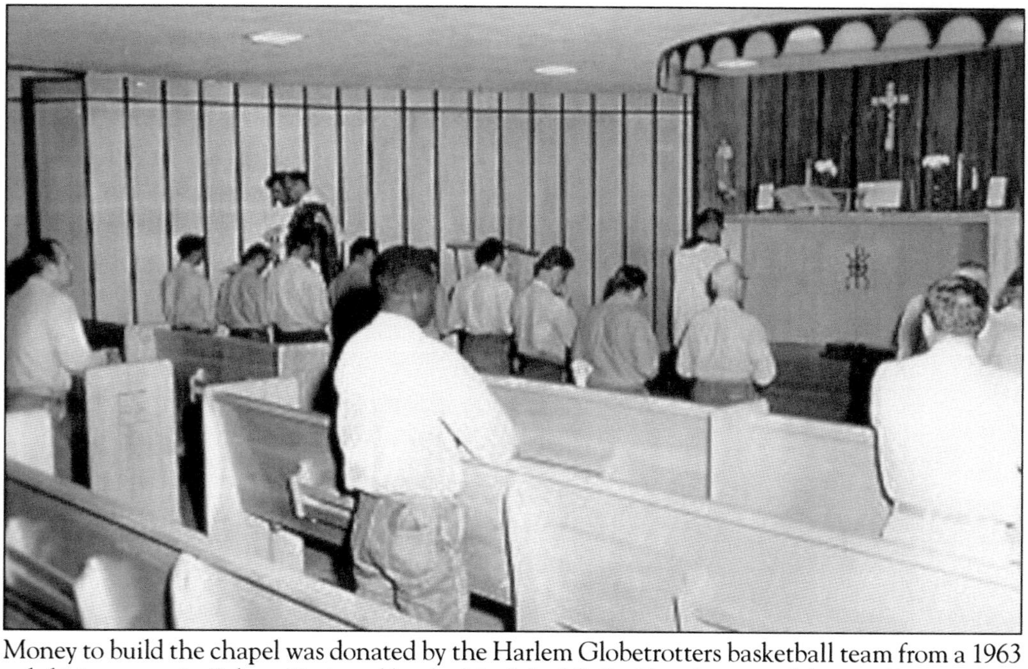

Money to build the chapel was donated by the Harlem Globetrotters basketball team from a 1963 exhibition game in Salem. Designed by the Mockford & Rudd architectural firm in Oregon City, the new chapel was completed in 1963. It was designed to serve as a worship space for all faiths.

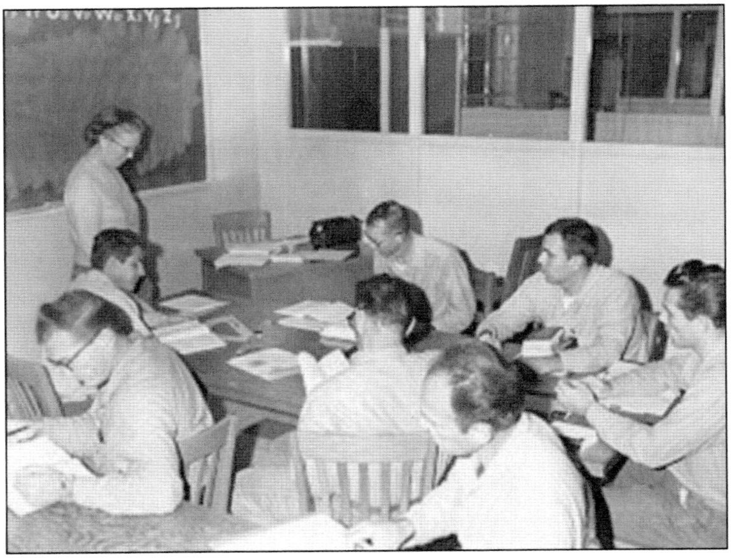

Jean Overholser was the first female educator to teach in the Oregon State Penitentiary. During the day, she taught at Oregon State University, but one night a week she volunteered to teach calculus with several others in the new college-level program started at the prison. During the 1965–1966 school year, 44 inmates earned their eighth-grade diplomas and 63 earned their GEDs.

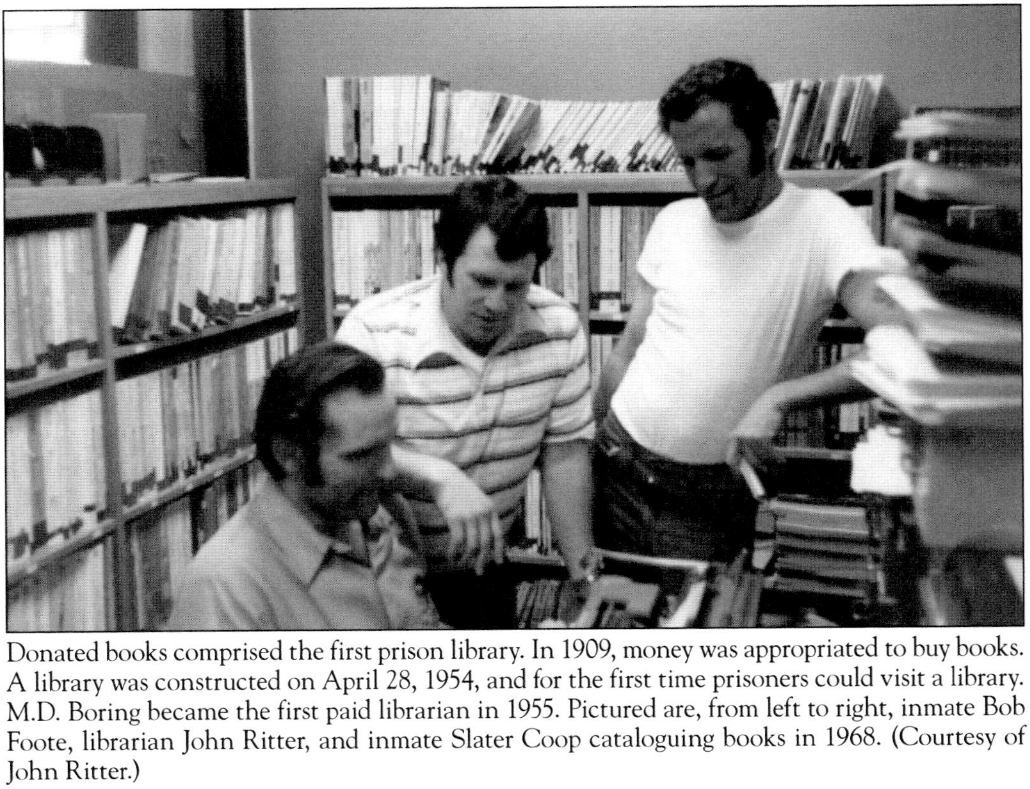

Donated books comprised the first prison library. In 1909, money was appropriated to buy books. A library was constructed on April 28, 1954, and for the first time prisoners could visit a library. M.D. Boring became the first paid librarian in 1955. Pictured are, from left to right, inmate Bob Foote, librarian John Ritter, and inmate Slater Coop cataloguing books in 1968. (Courtesy of John Ritter.)

Three

Riots, Escapes, Fires, and Floods

Prison officials had no idea how to control inmates in the early years of Oregon State Penitentiary history. They based their penal philosophy on the Calvinistic theory that convicts would do their time and come out reformed; instead, any chance they got, the inmates ran, crawled, climbed, or squeezed their way out. On August 31, 1866, the warden removed the prisoners' shackles, believing in the honor system. Immediately, nine prisoners attacked him, taking his gun, and ran into the nearby woods. Oregon became famous for the Oregon Boot, or Gardner shackle, which was invented in 1866 and used to prevent escapes. It was sold to prisons throughout the United States.

The first major fire occurred in 1875, and the first violent outbreak occurred on July 3, 1883, when a guard shot and killed four inmates. The most famous escape was that of Harry Tracy and David Merrill in 1902. In 1915, warden Harry Minto was killed by an escapee, and in 1918 Jefferson Baldwin, later known as Charley Panzram, escaped. He was later executed in Leavenworth after being identified as a serial killer. Major riots in 1926, 1936, and 1953 resulted in severe damage to the prison. Occasionally, floods and high water cut the prison off from the nearby roads. The 1964 flood and the Columbus Day storm of 1962 caused severe damage to the prison.

Oregon became known as a "hard prison," with floggings and "water cross" punishments, in which an inmate was stripped to the waist, handcuffed to a wall with arms outstretched, and sprayed with a powerful stream of water, nearly drowning him and causing severe bruising. Another punishment consisted of tying an inmate's wrists to the bars of his cell so he was left hanging there for up to eight hours. Of course, prisoners were also assigned to the segregation and isolation cells for varying amounts of time for breaking prison rules. Arson-caused fires regularly swept through the prison, usually in the industrial section. The last major fire before the 1968 riot was in 1964, causing about $70,000 in damage.

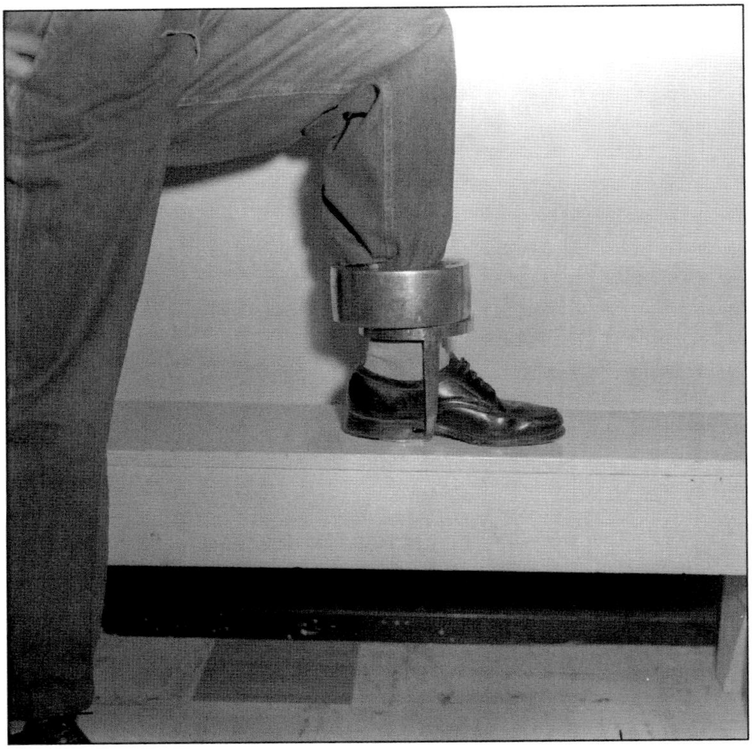

Warden J.C. Gardner became frustrated with all the prisoners escaping from the penitentiary in 1862, so he designed a means of keeping them from running away. It was called the Gardner shackle, or Oregon boot. It weighed 40 pounds and was made of heavy iron. He patented the invention, and Oregon paid him $5,000 to use it over the next 50 years before it was declared inhumane and discontinued.

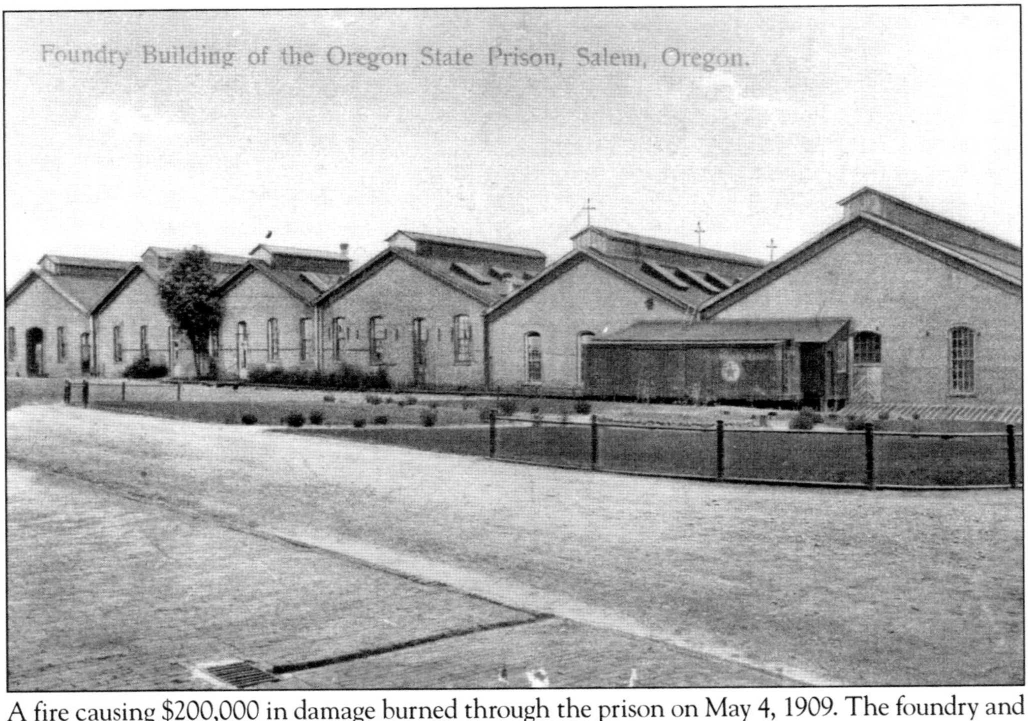

A fire causing $200,000 in damage burned through the prison on May 4, 1909. The foundry and stove manufacturing building had employed 225 convicts and 25 civilians. The fire started at 10:30 p.m. In addition to the prison fire crew, the asylum crew assisted hundreds of Salem citizens who rushed to help. Many of the prison records stored in the superintendent's office were destroyed.

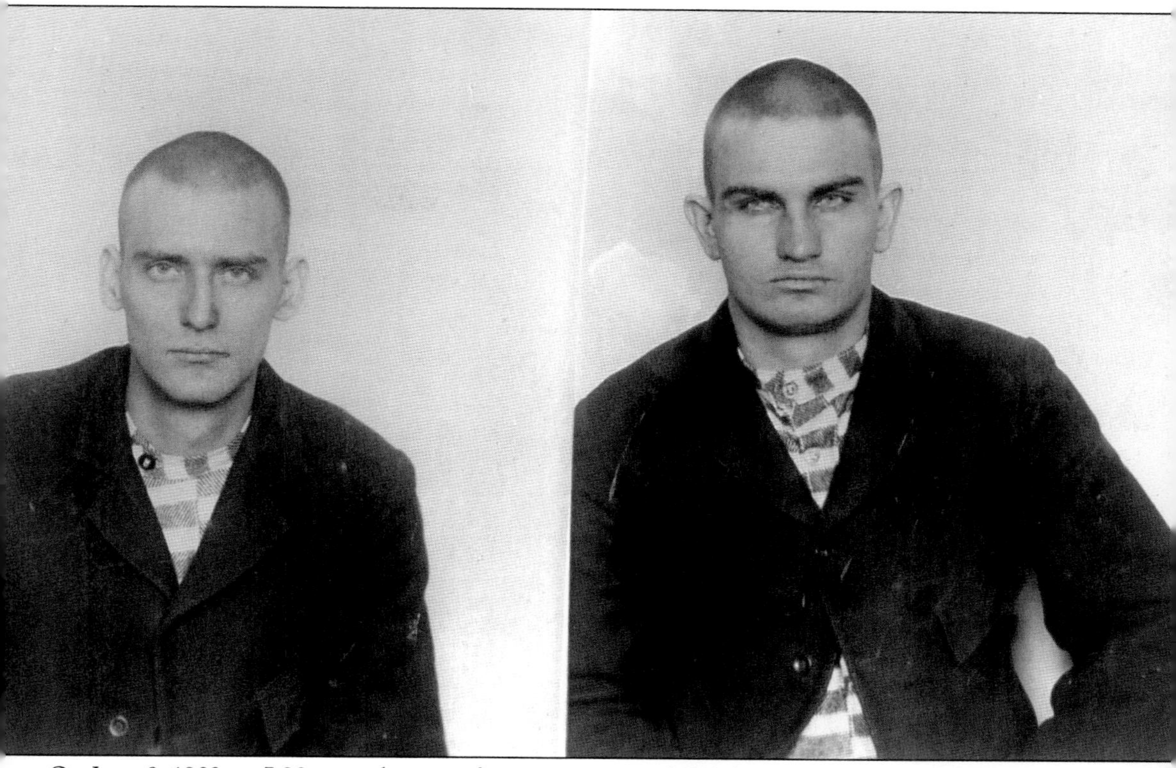

On June 9, 1902, at 7:00 a.m., the most famous escape in OSP's history took place. Harry Tracy (right), age 24, and David Merrill (left), age 28, had smuggled in guns and shot guard Frank Ferrell, age 32. Running through the prison and shooting at every guard they could see, they killed guard S.R.T. Jones, age 49, and shot inmate Frank Ingram. As the escape continued, another guard, B.F. Tiffany, age 35, was shot and killed. On June 28, Tracy shot his companion and brother-in-law in the back near Napavine, Washington, and hid his body. In a rampage across the state with a posse following him, he met deputy sheriff Charles Raymond on June 3 and killed him. Later the same day, he shot and killed policeman E.E. Breese and deputy game warden Neil Rawley. After a month of searching, he was spotted on August 5. Harry Tracy killed himself on August 6, 1902, after being trapped in a field outside Davenport, Washington, where a local posse wounded him. (Courtesy of OSA.)

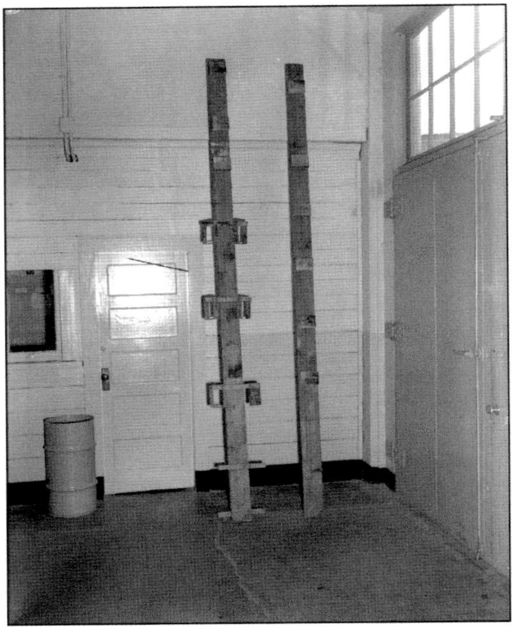

On December 11, 1911, Fred Weaver broke out of the bakery in the penitentiary by prying apart the bars on the window and crawling into the basement. From there, he escaped into the front yard by the same method. Many convicts tried to escape using homemade ladders meant to scale the stockade walls. Very few ever escaped for long.

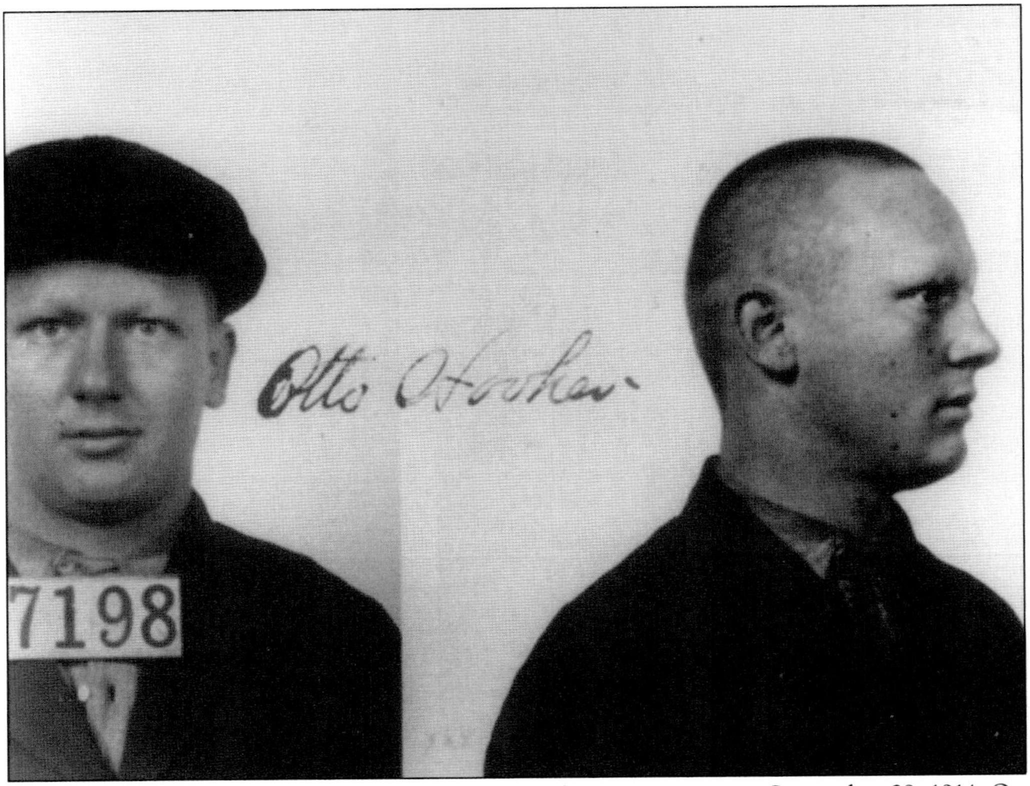

Otto Hooker, age 21, was convicted of burglary and sent to prison on September 29, 1914. On September 27, 1915, Hooker escaped from the prison, and during the ensuing manhunt he killed warden Harry Minto, age 51, and Jefferson City marshal J.J. Benson. A posse of 200 men with bloodhounds trailed the convict across the Oregon countryside, and he was shot and killed the next day in Albany, Oregon. (Courtesy of OSA.)

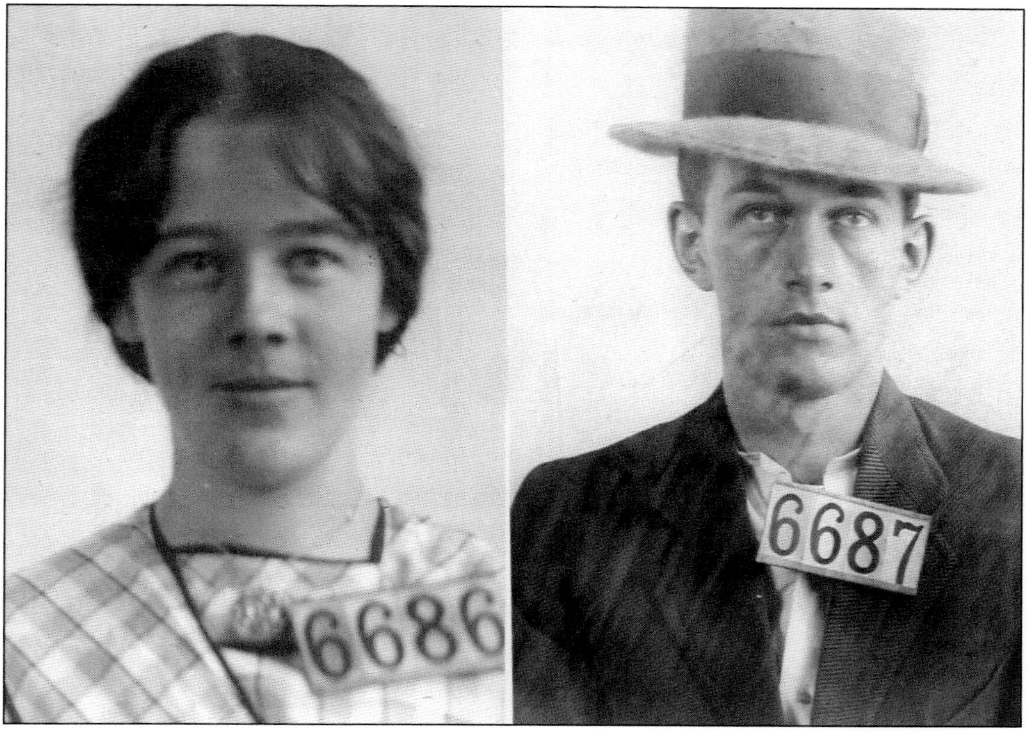

The most unusual escape attempt in the prison's history occurred on September 29, 1916, when William Tanner disappeared. Ten days later, he and his girlfriend, Hazel Erwin, attacked Carrie Kersch in the women's quarters, where he had been hiding, but she managed to scream for help. When the guards and matron arrived, they found Tanner hiding on top of a large bookcase. (Courtesy of OSA.)

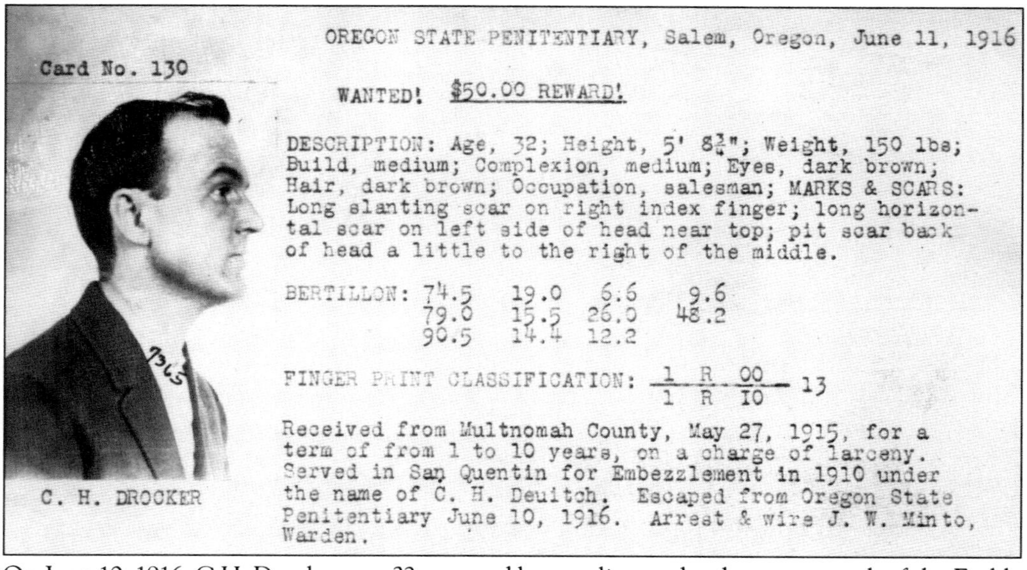

OREGON STATE PENITENTIARY, Salem, Oregon, June 11, 1916

Card No. 130

WANTED! $50.00 REWARD!

DESCRIPTION: Age, 32; Height, 5' 8¾"; Weight, 150 lbs; Build, medium; Complexion, medium; Eyes, dark brown; Hair, dark brown; Occupation, salesman; MARKS & SCARS: Long slanting scar on right index finger; long horizontal scar on left side of head near top; pit scar back of head a little to the right of the middle.

BERTILLON: 74.5 19.0 6.6 9.6
79.0 15.5 26.0 48.2
90.5 14.4 12.2

FINGER PRINT CLASSIFICATION: $\frac{1 \quad R \quad 00}{1 \quad R \quad 10}$ 13

Received from Multnomah County, May 27, 1915, for a term of from 1 to 10 years, on a charge of larceny. Served in San Quentin for Embezzlement in 1910 under the name of C. H. Deuitch. Escaped from Oregon State Penitentiary June 10, 1916. Arrest & wire J. W. Minto, Warden.

C. H. DROCKER

On June 10, 1916, C.H. Drocker, age 32, escaped by crawling under the motor truck of the Feeble Minded Institution and riding out the main gate. A standard $50 reward was offered for his return, but he was never captured. He had attempted to escape by cutting through his cell bars on November 4, 1915, and was put in the dungeon for 10 days. (Courtesy of OSA.)

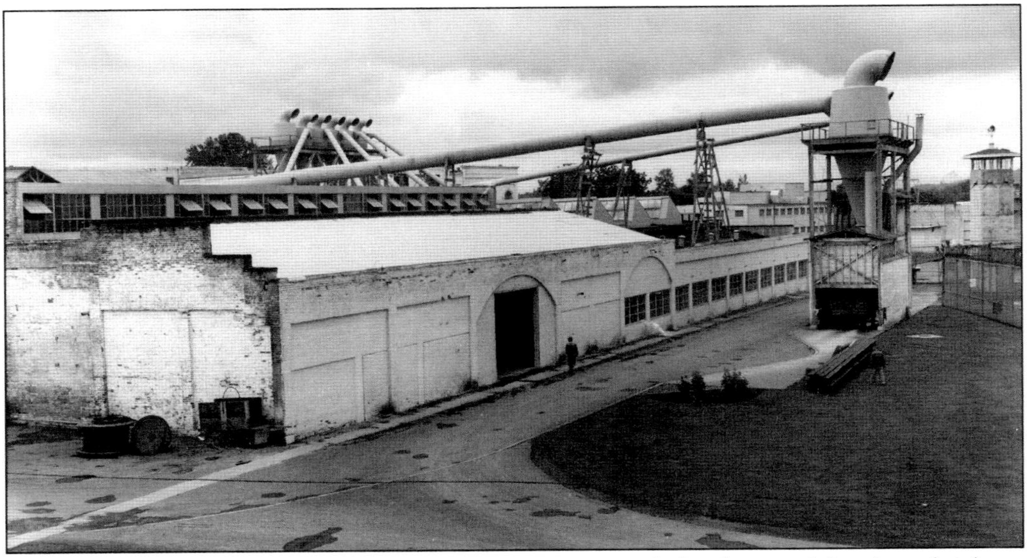

A fire destroyed four large brick buildings housing this flax plant at the prison on May 18, 1916. Flames were seen shooting from the building around 4:45 p.m. and were fanned by high winds. Nearly $25,000 worth of equipment and 20 tons of retted flax valued at $25 a ton were burned along with the steam plant and the shoe shop.

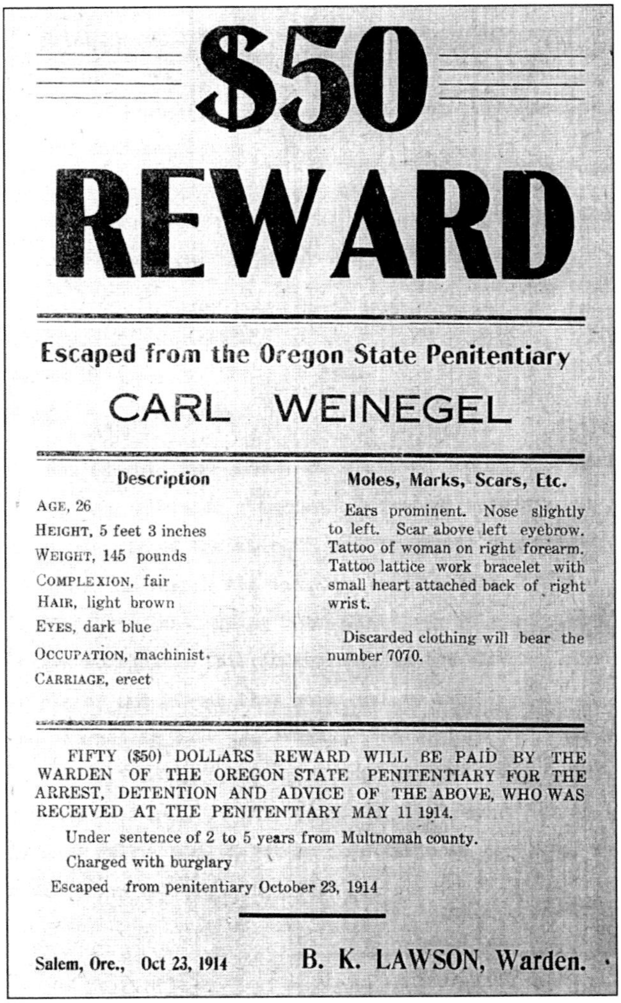

$50

REWARD

Escaped from the Oregon State Penitentiary

CARL WEINEGEL

Description	Moles, Marks, Scars, Etc.
AGE, 26 HEIGHT, 5 feet 3 inches WEIGHT, 145 pounds COMPLEXION, fair HAIR, light brown EYES, dark blue OCCUPATION, machinist. CARRIAGE, erect	Ears prominent. Nose slightly to left. Scar above left eyebrow. Tattoo of woman on right forearm. Tattoo lattice work bracelet with small heart attached back of right wrist. Discarded clothing will bear the number 7070.

FIFTY ($50) DOLLARS REWARD WILL BE PAID BY THE WARDEN OF THE OREGON STATE PENITENTIARY FOR THE ARREST, DETENTION AND ADVICE OF THE ABOVE, WHO WAS RECEIVED AT THE PENITENTIARY MAY 11 1914.

Under sentence of 2 to 5 years from Multnomah county.

Charged with burglary

Escaped from penitentiary October 23, 1914

Salem, Ore., Oct 23, 1914 B. K. LAWSON, Warden.

Two convicted safe crackers, Carl Weinegel and Frank Wagner, dug through brick walls and a concrete floor to escape from the penitentiary on October 23, 1914. The cell mates used an improvised drill made of a heavy steel spike, which fit into the heel of a shoe. They avoided the new electric lights installed on the cellblock walls, but guard J.H. Evans caught sight of them, fired a warning shot, and stopped them. (Courtesy of OSA.)

On February 3, 1917, three convicts tried to escape and were recaptured by the trusties working with them. Carl Weinegel, recaptured from his escape in 1914, was one of the people who tried to escape. Lothar F. Von Falkenthale, age 28, who was convicted of burglary, and Julius Keil, age 27, were also recaptured. (Courtesy of OSA.)

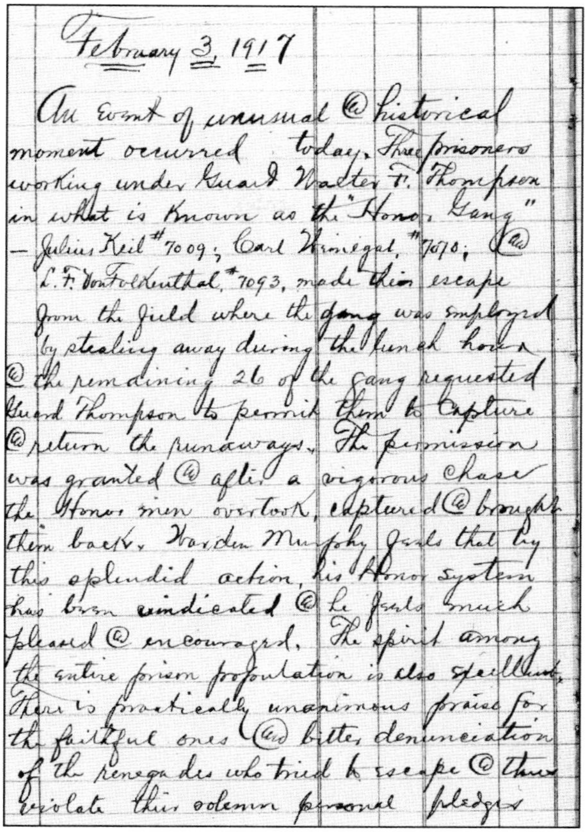

February 3, 1917

An Event of unusual & historical moment occurred today. Three prisoners working under Guard Walter F. Thompson in what is known as the "Honor Gang" — Julius Keil #7009; Carl Weinegal, #7070; & L. F. Von Falkenthal, #7093, made their escape from the field where the gang was employed by stealing away during the lunch hour & the remaining 26 of the gang requested Guard Thompson to permit them to capture & return the runaways. The permission was granted & after a vigorous chase the Honor men overtook, captured & brought them back. Warden Murphy feels that by this splendid action, his Honor system has been vindicated & he feels much pleased & encouraged. The spirit among the entire prison population is also excellent. There is practically unanimous praise for the faithful ones & bitter denunciation of the renegades who tried to escape & thus violate their solemn personal pledges

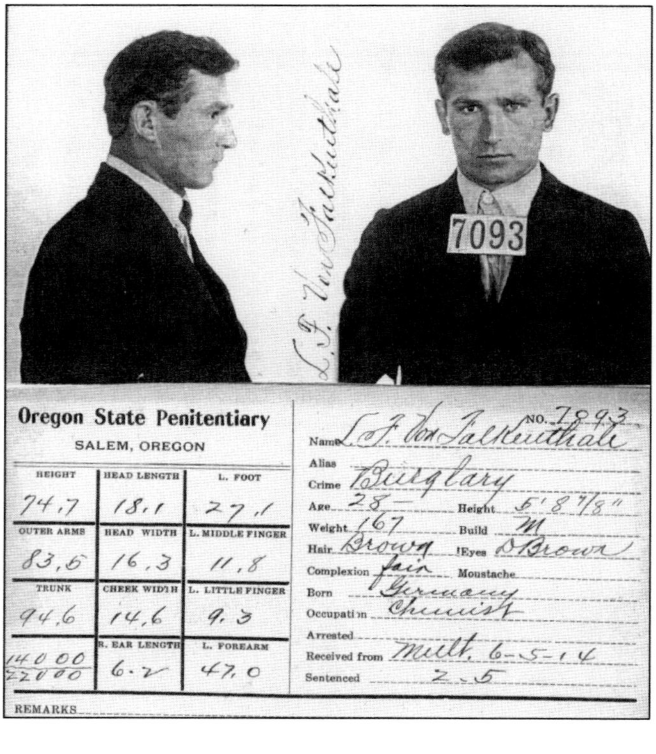

Lothar Von Falkenthale was one of the convicts involved in the attempted escape. There were 58 escapes during the two years Charles Murphy was superintendent (1917–1918). His reform policy abolished corporal punishment and instituted peeling potatoes for rule infractions. The board of control in charge of the prison was so dissatisfied that they fired him. (Courtesy of OSA.)

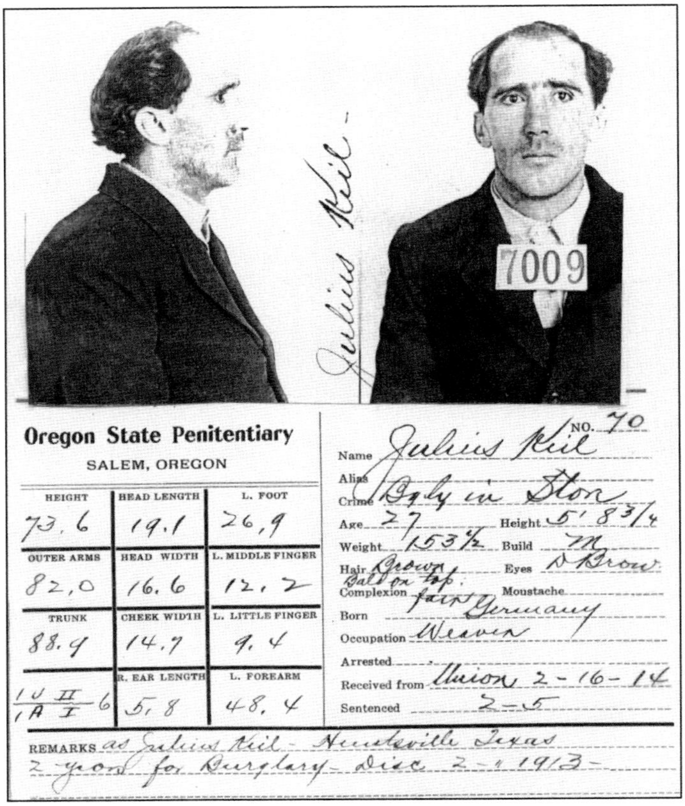

Julius Keil was the third member of the group of attempted escapees and had an extensive criminal history. The prison began taking photographs of the prisoners about 1894 using outside photographers. OSP purchased its first camera in 1904 to take convict pictures. Superintendent Joseph D. Lee introduced the Bertillon system of measurements and identification to the prison in 1901. Prisoners began being fingerprinted in 1908. (Courtesy of OSA.)

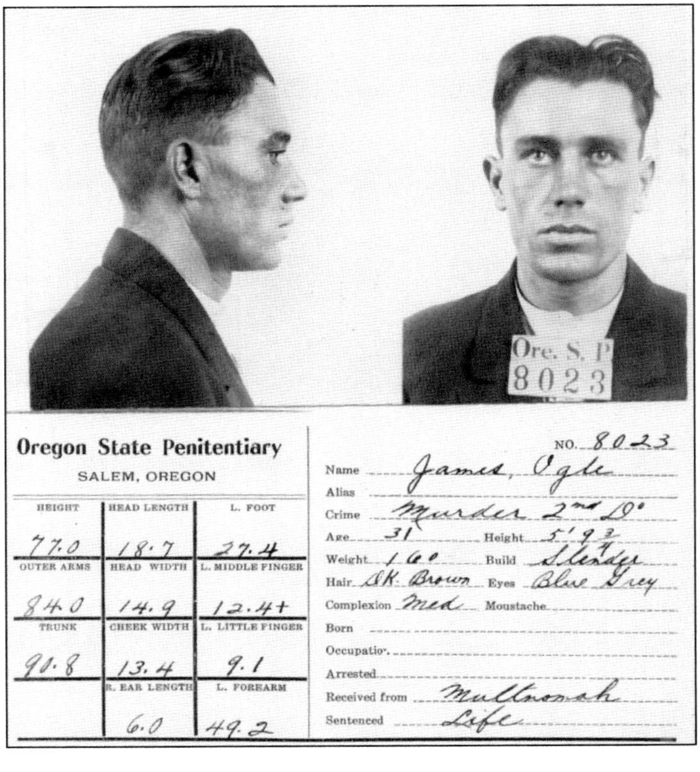

Inside the prison, it was a capital crime to defy a guard. Guard John Davidson was warned that James Ogle, convicted of second-degree murder, was going to make an escape. On the morning of March 21, 1922, Ogle and Davidson entered the bullpen for exercise. Ogle threw a rock, just missing the guard's head. Immediately, Davidson fired his gun, killing Ogle. A grand jury exonerated him. (Courtesy of OSA.)

Jeff Baldwin, also known as Charley Panzram, was an inmate at OSP from June 24, 1915, to September 18, 1917, when he escaped. He had previously been confined to solitary confinement for 61 days. Recaptured seven days later after a wild gun battle in Shedd, Oregon, he escaped again on May 12, 1918. During his stay in OSP, he took a sledgehammer and tried to break all the locks on any cell he could reach. In 1916, he set fire to the flax shed and caused $25,000 worth of damage. He spent four days hanging from his cell door by his wrists after one escape attempt. He became the most notorious criminal in the United States by the time he was hanged at age 39 in Leavenworth, Kansas, on September 5, 1930. Before his death, he confessed to 22 murders. (Both courtesy of OSA.)

$50 REWARD

Escaped from the Oregon State Penitentiary

JEFF BALDWIN

Description

AGE when received, 27
HEIGHT, 5 feet 9 1-2 inches
WEIGHT, 168 pounds
COMPLEXION, medium
HAIR, med. brown
EYES, grey blue
BUILD, heavy
NATIVITY, Alabama
OCCUPATION, thief

FINGER PRINT $\frac{32 \quad M \quad O}{32 \quad I \quad I}$

Moles, Marks, Scars, Etc.

Slanting scar on left side of head; horizontal scar under right side of mouth; pit scar under right cheek; scar on second joint of middle finger right hand.

Discarded clothing will bear the number 7390

Formerly in Montana penitentiary

FIFTY ($50) DOLLARS REWARD WILL BE PAID BY THE WARDEN OF THE OREGON STATE PENITENTIARY FOR THE ARREST, DETENTION AND ADVICE OF THE ABOVE, WHO WAS RECEIVED AT THE PENITENTIARY June 24, 1915

Under sentence of 7 years from Clatsop county.
Charged with larceny in a dwelling
Escaped from Prison September 18, 1917

Anyone seeing above please phone or telegraph to the Warden, State Penitentiary, and charge to penitentiary. Phone 12.

Salem, Ore., Sept 18, 1917 **CHAS. A. MURPHY, Warden**

OREGON STATE PENITENTIARY,
SALEM

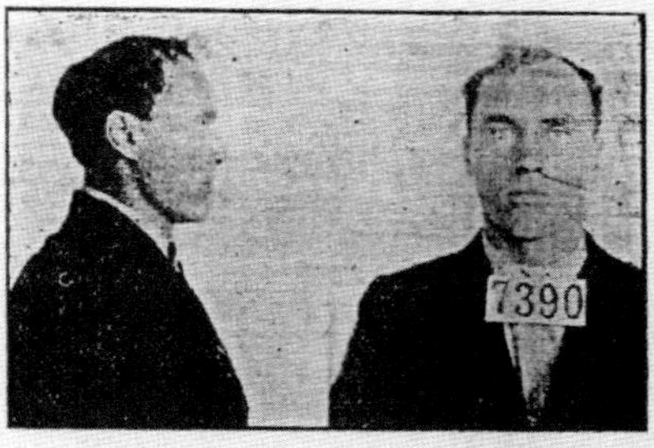

JEFF BALDWIN, No. 7390
Escaped May 12, 1918

Received June 24, 1915, from Clatsop county for a term of seven years, on a charge of larceny in a dwelling.

Age when received 27; height 5 feet 9½ inches; weight 168 pounds; complexion med; hair med brown; eyes grey blue; build medium heavy; nativity Alabama; occupation thief.

Finger Print $\frac{32 \quad M \quad O}{32 \quad I \quad I}$

Bertillon: 76.2 | 82.0 | 92.5 | 19.3 | 15.9 | 15.0 | 6.6 | 27.1 | 11.6 | 9.2 | 47.4

MARKS: Slanting scar on left side of head; horizontal scar on left side of mouth; pit scar under right cheek; scar on second joint right middle finger; large tattoo covering both breasts. Two terms in Montana prison under names of Jeff Davis and Jeff Rhodes.

$50 Reward for Arrest and Detention

Captured Nos. 6862, 7397, 6347, 6472, 6338, 7255, 7507, 7365, 7168, 7141, 6634, 6546, 6106, 5751

NOTICE—Place in book previously sent you.

86

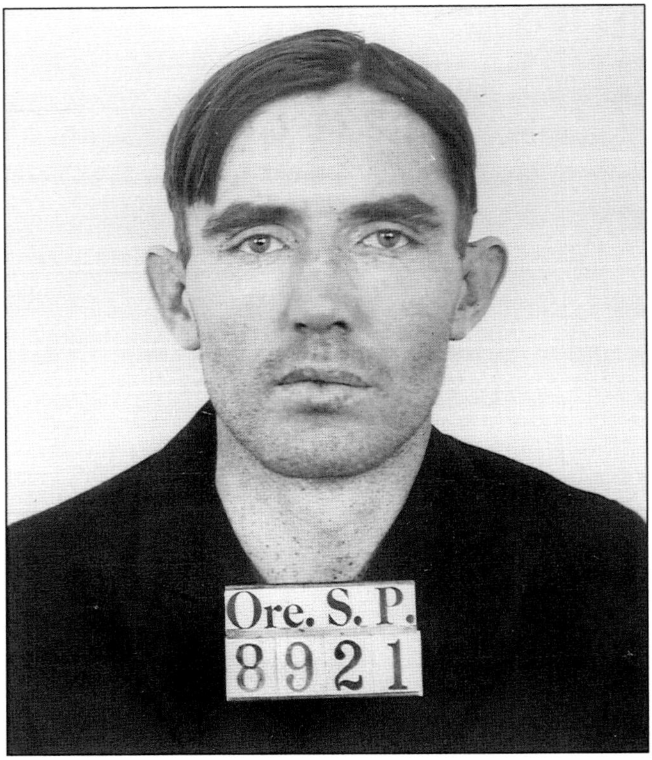

Frank Fallon was caught when a man tried to smuggle a gun in to him. The authorities put him in the bullpen and then in the dungeon on bread and water. A noisy riot in support of him ensued on November 21, 1925, with convicts yelling, banging on their cells, and throwing materials out through the bars. Eight more convicts joined the seven already in the bullpen. (Courtesy of OSA.)

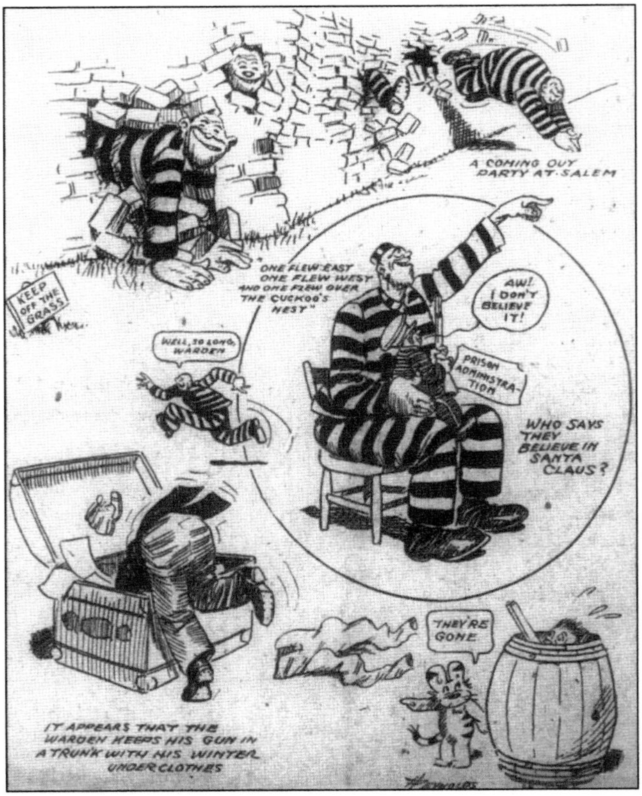

This cartoon from the August 15, 1925, *Oregonian* illustrates how escapes from the prison had become a well-known joke. During the term of warden Johnson Smith, from January 15, 1923 to October 8, 1923, a total of 41 convicts escaped. Amos Dalrymple was subsequently chosen as warden. His brother-in-law was killed during a prison escape on August 12, 1925. (Courtesy of the *Oregonian*.)

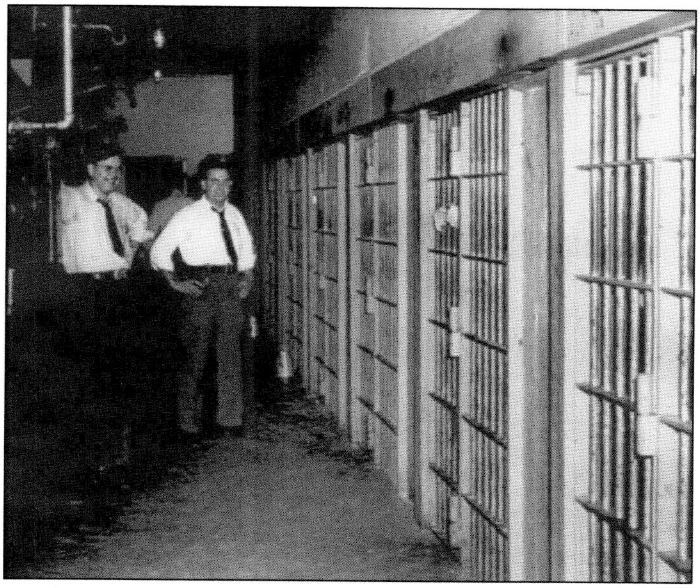

Corrections officers William H. Hill, Orland J. Cox, and George P. Karl gaze into the isolation cells used for violent and dangerous inmates. These segregation and isolation cells were located in the basement of cellblock C until 1953, when a new building was erected. Many of the most dangerous men in Oregon history were incarcerated here. (Courtesy of SJ.)

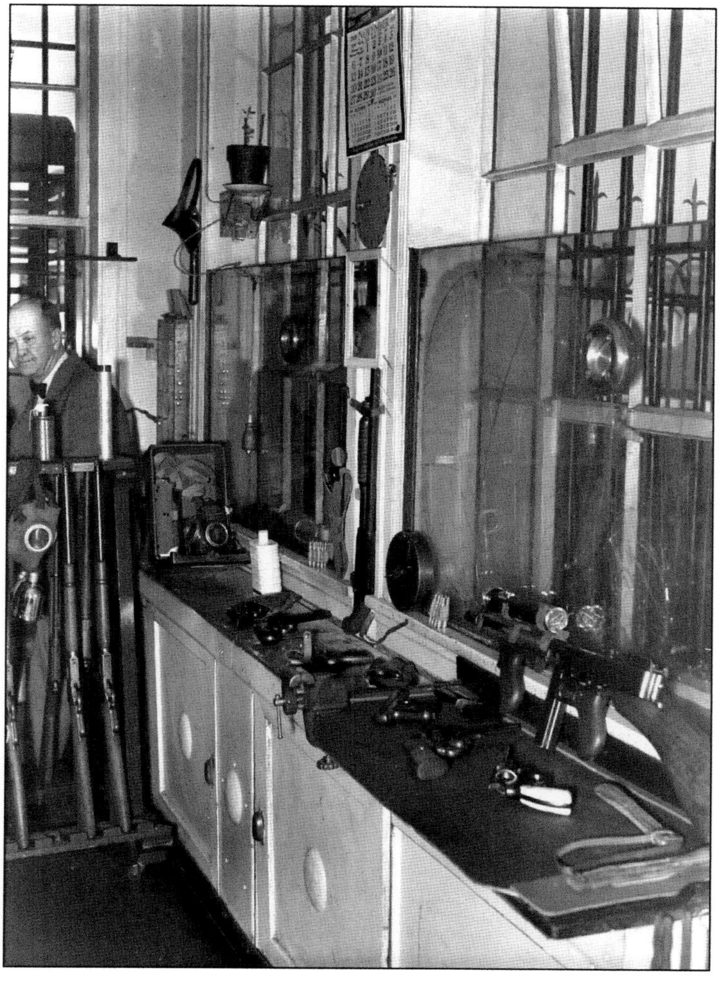

Between 1866 and 1870, the prison acquired 13 Henry rifles, one Spencer rifle, two Sharps rifles, and 12 Army Colt pistols. In 1900, the prison added seven 30-30 Winchester rifles, two double-barreled shotguns, and a revolver. The threat of riots and violent escapes prompted officials at OSP to create the arsenal seen here by 1950. Guards on the wall carried rifles, while guards working inside the prison did not carry guns. (Courtesy of SPL.)

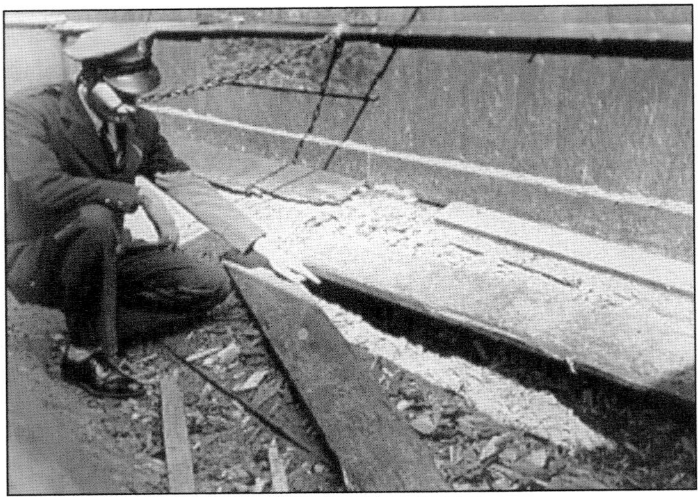

A guard examines the boards covering the hiding place of two convicts who escaped on September 13, 1952. Gerald Macomber, age 29, and Charles Crozier, age 28, hid under some loose boards in an empty sawdust truck as it left the prison during a small fire. A third man attempted to copy the two successful escapees the next day but was caught by an alert guard. Macomber and Crozier were later captured.

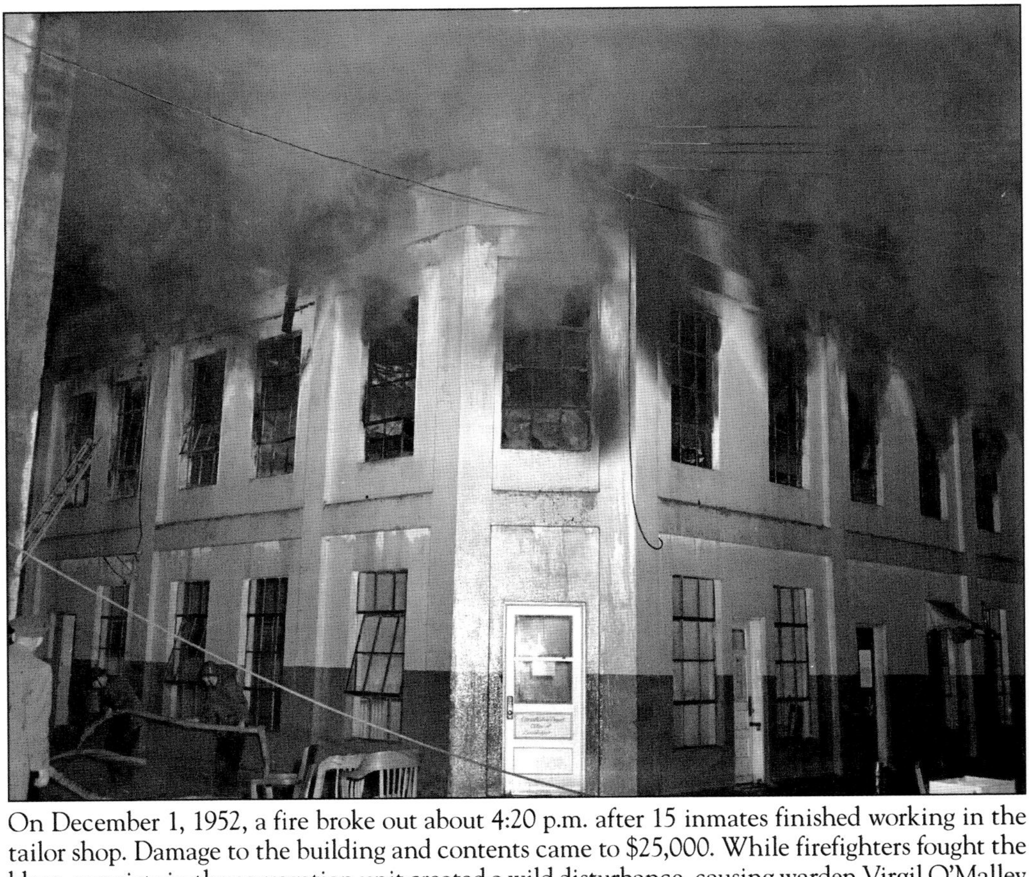

On December 1, 1952, a fire broke out about 4:20 p.m. after 15 inmates finished working in the tailor shop. Damage to the building and contents came to $25,000. While firefighters fought the blaze, convicts in the segregation unit created a wild disturbance, causing warden Virgil O'Malley to authorize the use of tear gas. Prisoners in cellblock C, above the unit, were allowed outside for fresh air.

Two convicts attempted to escape via the prison sewer pipes on July 15, 1952. Harold Hayes, age 21, crawled 350 feet before dying from exposure to sewer gas. His partner, Franklin Clingenpeel, age 19, managed to call for help and was rescued.

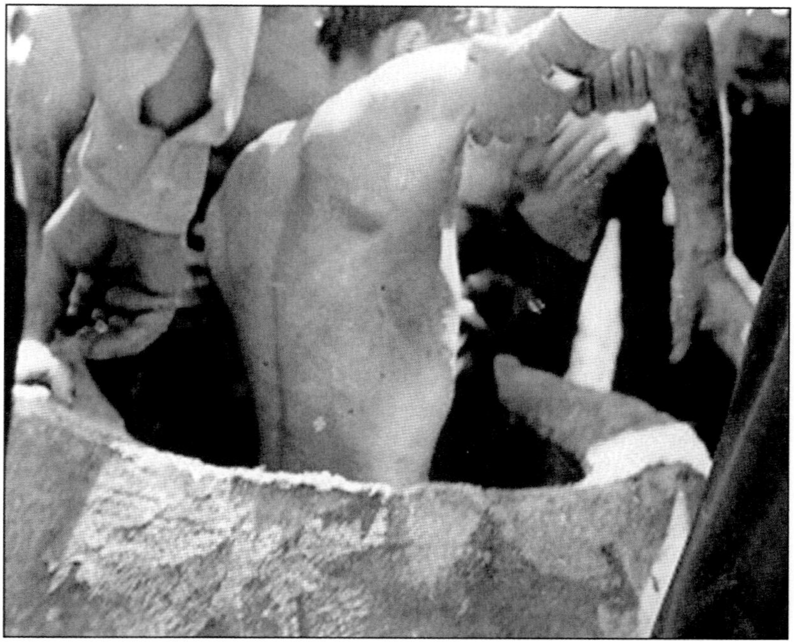

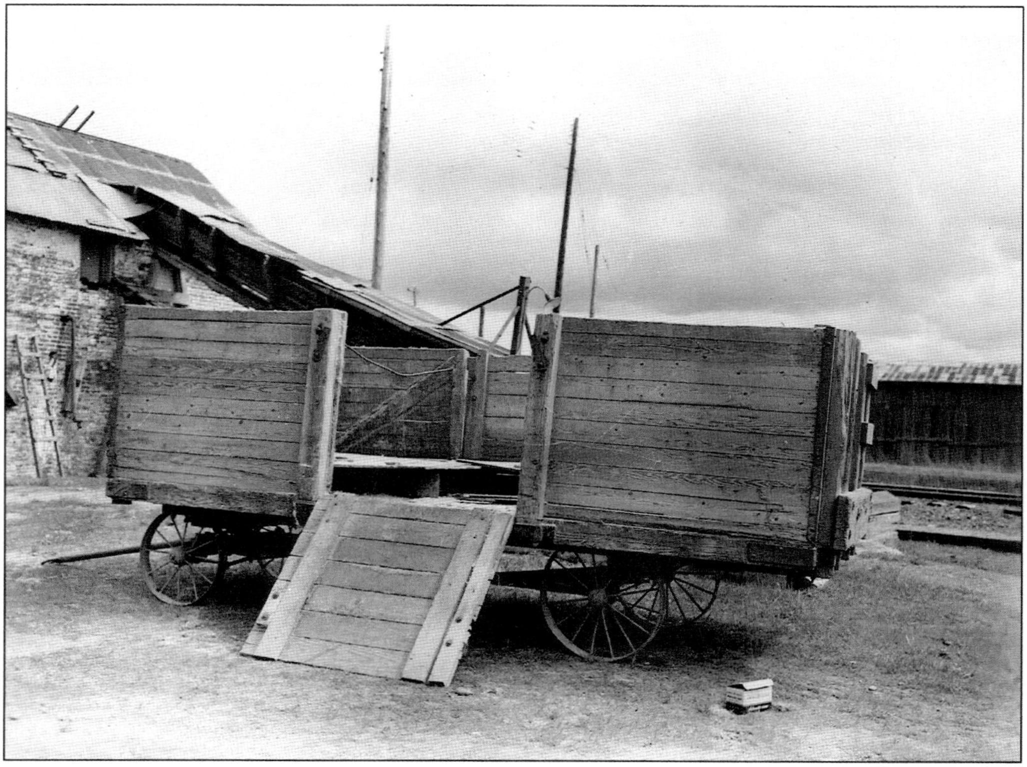

In April 1953, five convicts attempted to escape the prison by hiding in the false bottom of this flax wagon. A prison report dated April 2, 1953, warned that OSP was on the verge of exploding: "Inmates seemed to roam at will throughout the cell blocks. There seemed to be no uniformity in the clothing of the inmates." (Courtesy of OSA.)

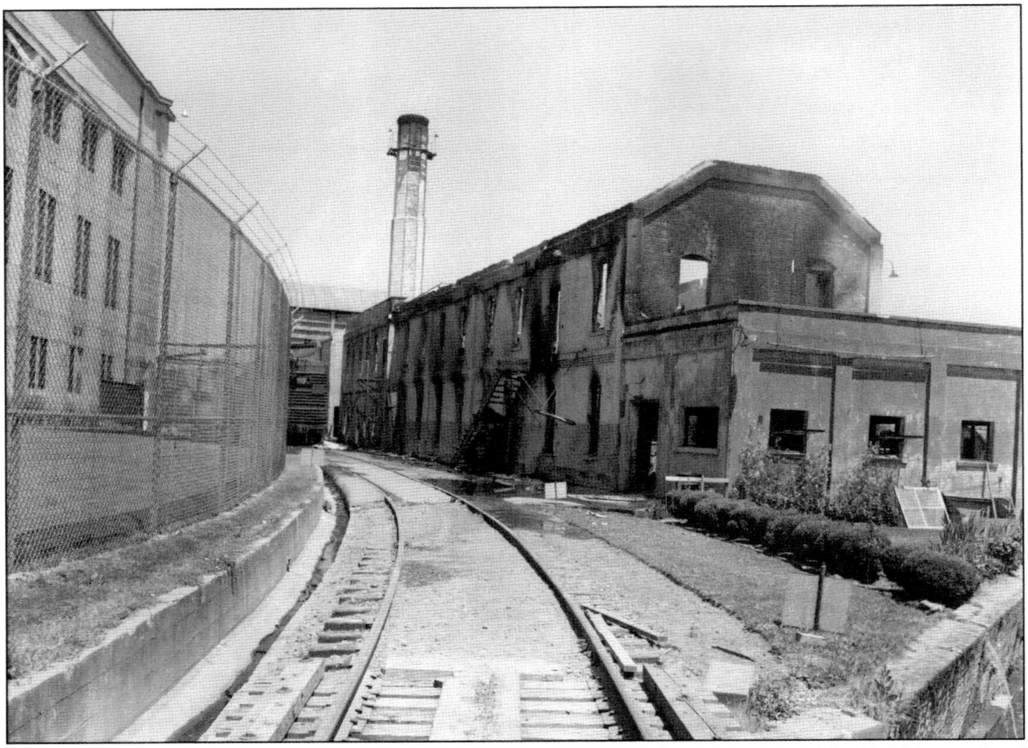

This photograph shows some of the damage from a riot and fire that caused $150,000 worth of damage on Friday, July 11, 1953. After prisoners refused to work at 7:00 a.m., they were confined to the baseball yard. Guards had to fire twice into the unruly crowd, wounding a convict. To the left are the laundry, the flax shop, and the hydro plant. (Courtesy of OSA.)

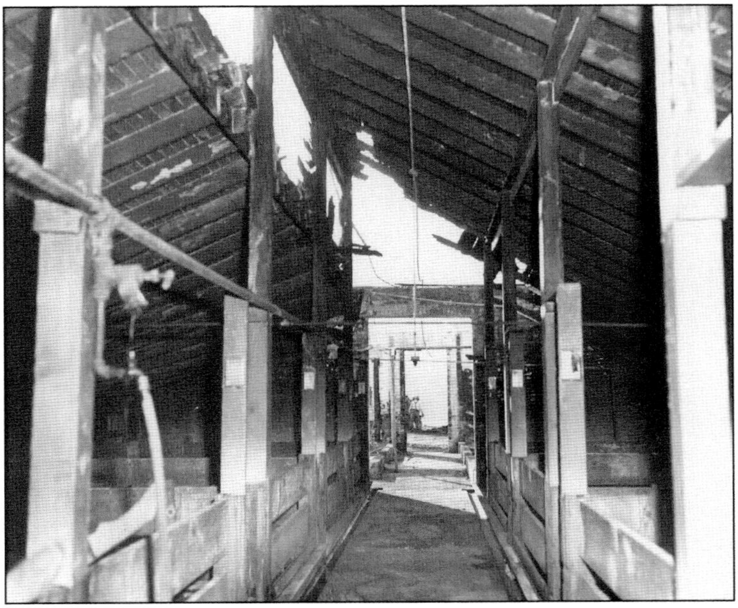

On Saturday, guards had to fire tear gas into the crowd after they broke into the dining area and plundered kitchen supplies. In retaliation, the convicts started a fire in the laundry and tailor shop, the machine shop, and the flax plant. After four days, the men finally returned to their cells. Two convicts escaped, stole a truck, and careened through Salem's streets before they were caught. (Courtesy of OSA.)

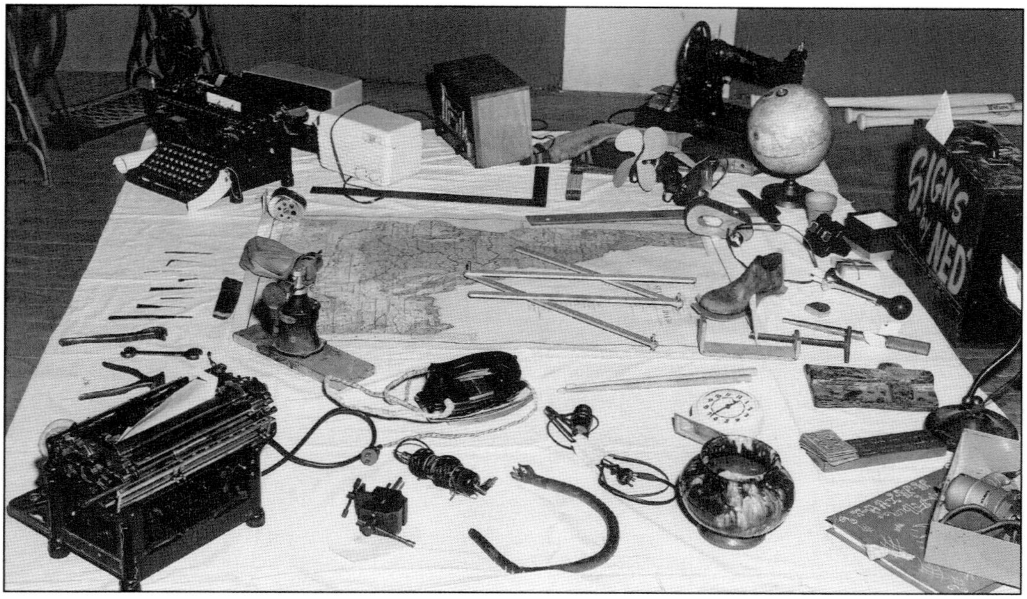

After a sit-down strike and fire on July 11, 1953, warden Clarence Gladden ordered an inch-by-inch search of the penitentiary. Several days later, 30 truckloads of contraband were confiscated. Besides the baseball bats, two tridents, and other weapons seen above, there were guitars, sewing machines, model airplanes, irons, typewriters, lamps, fans, radios, maps, cans of rubber cement, and electrical parts of all kinds. (Both courtesy of OSA.)

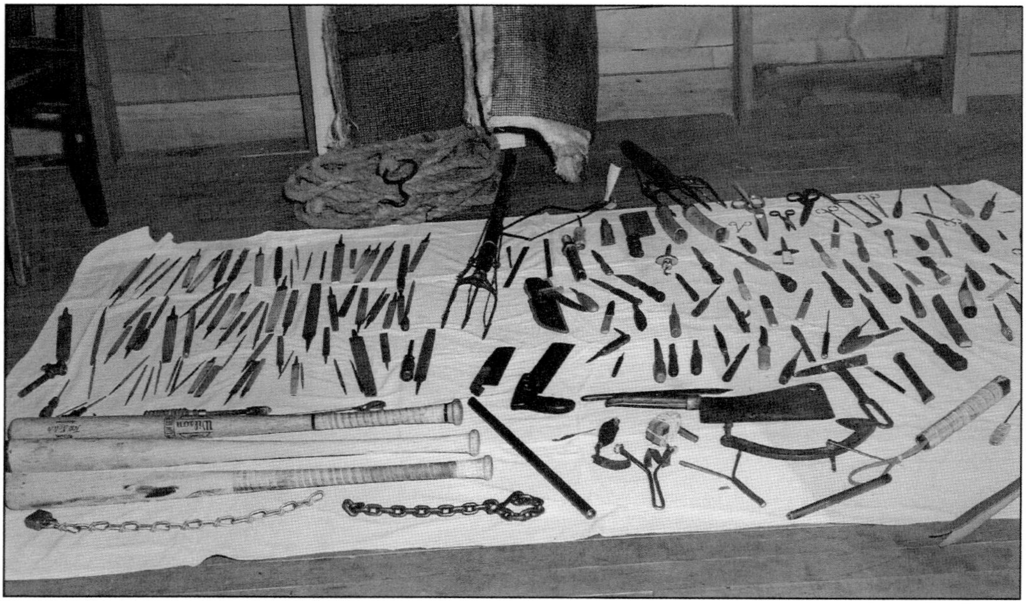

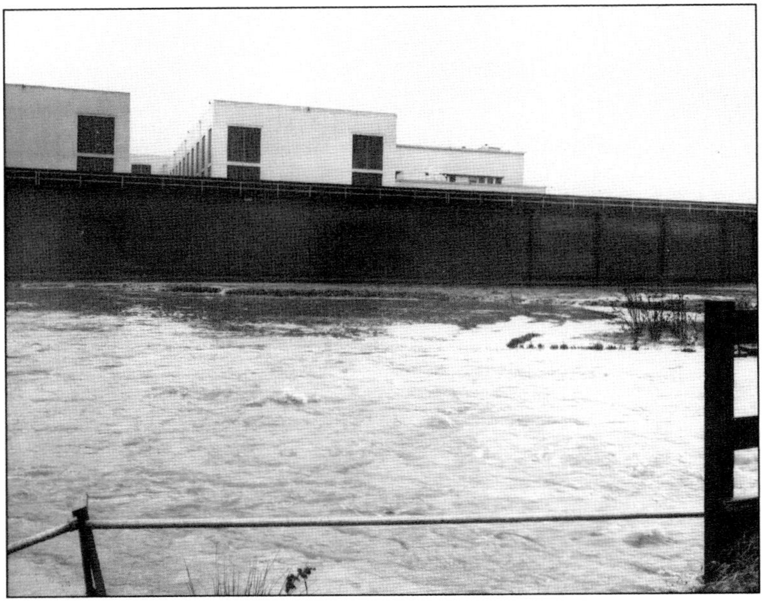

The 1964 Christmas flood severely impacted Salem and the prison. On Christmas Eve, the nearby Willamette River crested at 29.5 feet. The water surrounded the prison walls, making it nearly impossible for employees to get in or out. Clean drinking water was scarce. For nearly a week, Salem residents struggled to save their homes and businesses. (Courtesy of OSA.)

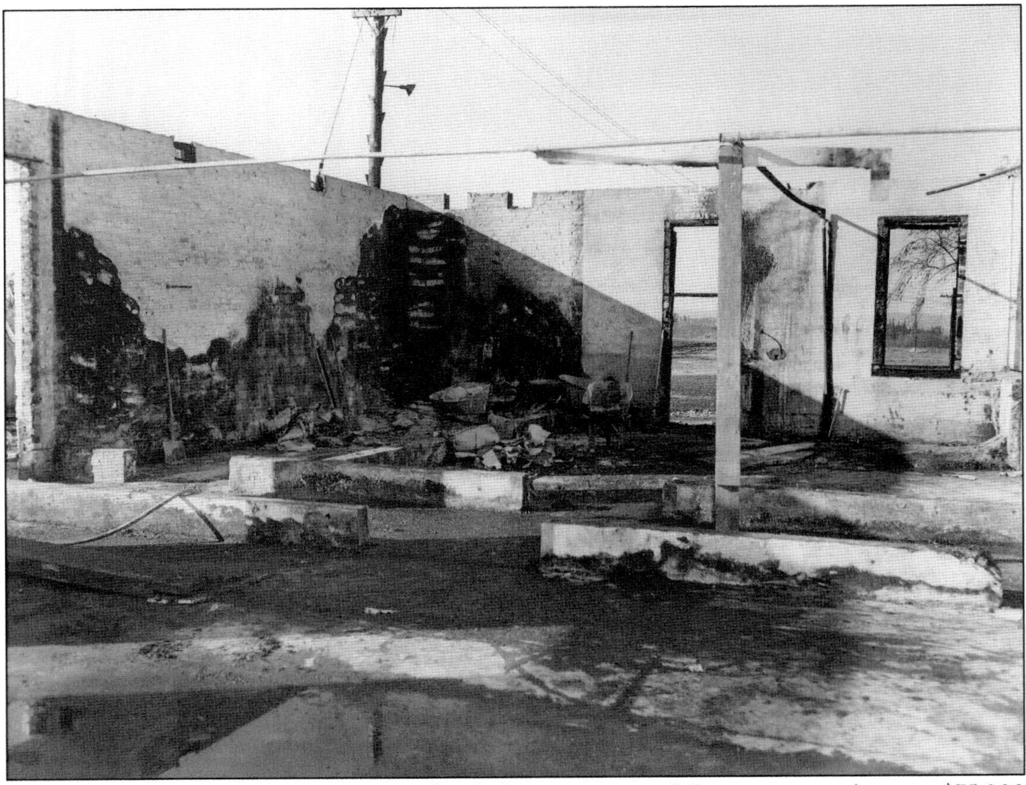

Arson caused a fire in the mattress and upholstery section of the prison, resulting in $75,000 worth of damage on January 29, 1964. Earlier in the day, another fire had broken out in the same place but had been immediately extinguished. The second blaze, at 11:30 a.m., brought out the Salem Fire Department. The 200-foot-by-60-foot mattress factory was housed in the old cannery building, erected in 1950. (Courtesy of OSA.)

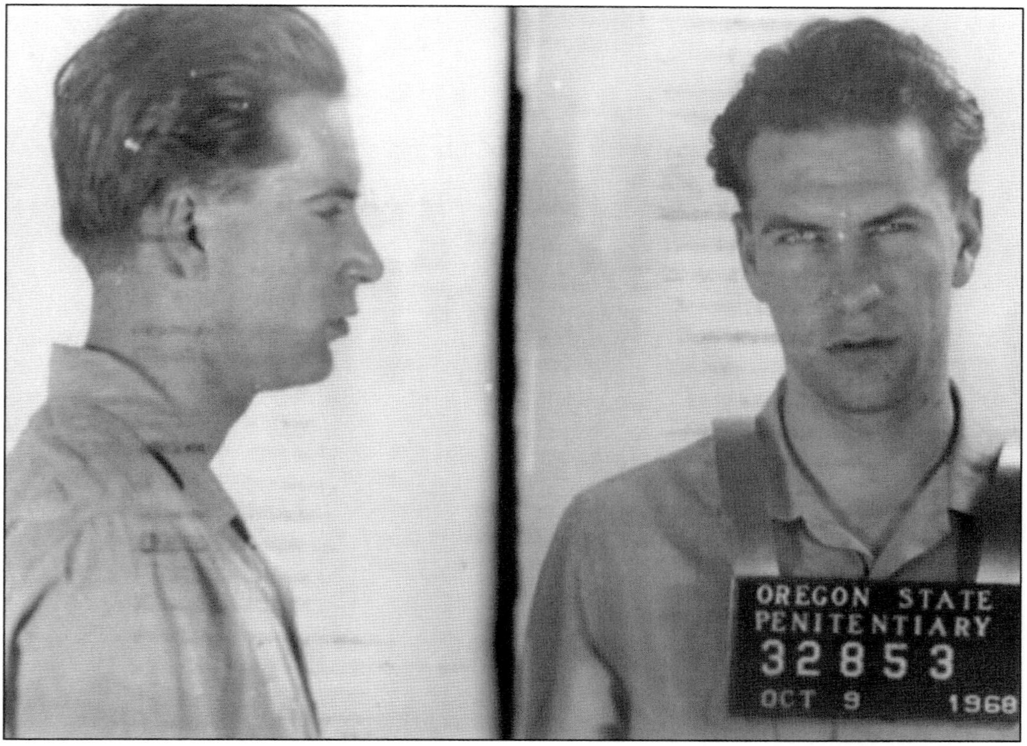

Thomas Grenfell, age 24, and Marvin Andres, age 31, attacked inmate Raymond Chinn on April 12, 1969. Guard Alvin Schmitt was attempting to break up the fight when Grenfell stabbed him. Two days later, Schmitt died in a Salem hospital. At Grenfell's trial, he was declared innocent by reason of insanity and sent to the Oregon State Hospital. (Courtesy of OSA.)

Warden Hoyt Cupp reported that a small uprising occurred on February 4, 1971, in which some damage and two small fires occurred. The strike started in the dining hall on Thursday evening. On Saturday, 126 inmates rebelled and were herded into the segregation and isolation building, where they tore up parts of the building. A large amount of contraband was discovered.

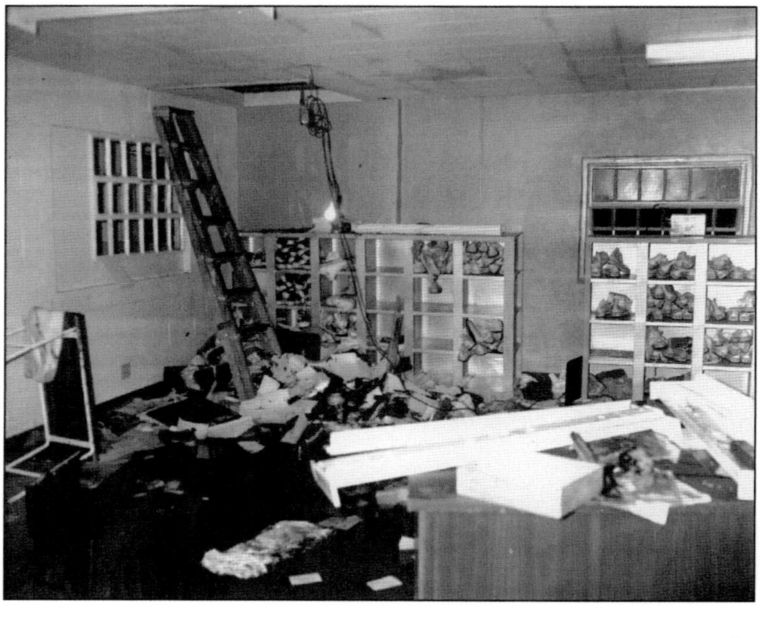

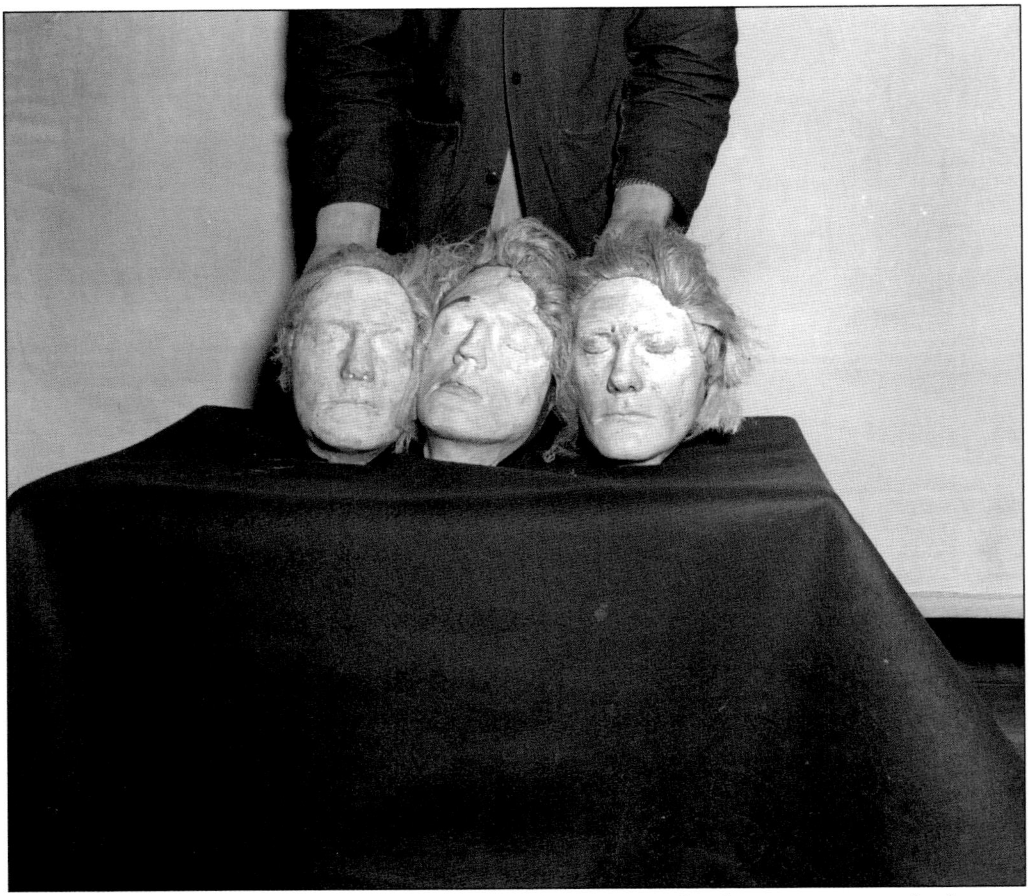

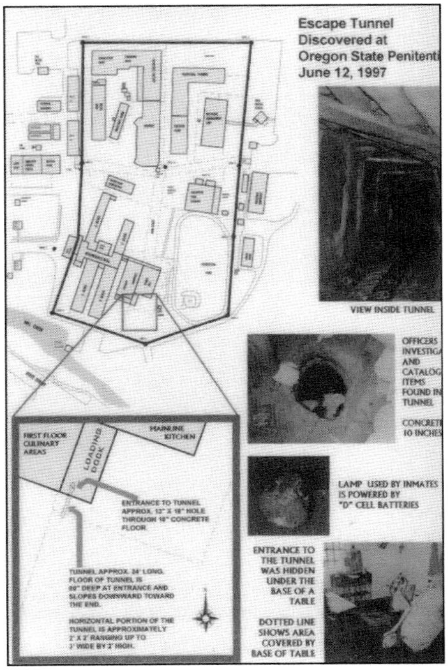

On February 14, 1952, three convicts made these masks in an aborted escape attempt. Warden Virgil O'Malley and his guards caught the men before they were able to get out of the cellblock. One of the men changed his mind in the end and did not use his mask. The men had made perfect replicas of their faces out of latex composition and placed the masks on their pillows.

A mysterious 24-foot-long tunnel was discovered at the prison on June 12, 1997. Hidden under a table in the loading dock, the 13-foot-by-18-foot entrance was found by a suspicious kitchen supervisor. The escapees carved through 10 inches of concrete and were 120 feet short of the south prison wall. Seven prisoners were later identified as participating in the escape plan.

Four

The 1968 Riot

On March 9, 1968, the most devastating riot in Oregon State Penitentiary history took place. The riot began at 4:10 p.m. on a Saturday as the prisoners were returning from the recreation yard to their cells. When it was over, at 10:30 a.m. Sunday, the 700 convicts involved had committed an estimated $5 million in damages. During the riot, 22 guards had been held hostage, six guards were injured, one convict was dead, and numerous convicts had injuries. Also, 13 civilians who were caught inside the walls were rescued and released.

The fires destroyed all the prison's rehabilitation facilities, the industrial plant that provided vocational training, more than half of the cells, and the kitchen and dining room. The offices of the chaplains, sociologists, and counselors were destroyed. The prison hospital was severely damaged. Fires burned over the 22 acres inside the prison walls on Saturday night and early Sunday morning before firemen were able to enter the prison. The four guards held hostage for 16 hours included Lt. Ralph Pribble, age 42, Charles Laudette, age 27, William Lowery, age 27, and Sgt. Lowell Hamby, age 56.

Warden Clarence Gladden was too ill to take control, so George Randall, the director of state corrections, assumed the role. A Marion County grand jury investigation determined that Randall's failure to allow the prison riot squad to use force against the rioters was the critical failure in controlling the convicts. The grand jury also stated that a breakdown of custody, together with general unrest, was the greatest contributing factor to the riot.

It was determined that four inmates and 25 conspirators planned and started the riot. Estimates of damages ranged from $1,630,696 to $5 million. The total cost of the riot will never be truly known. George Randall was fired in disgrace, and eventually the board of control was dissolved and control of the penitentiary was transferred to the governor. Hoyt Cupp was appointed the new warden shortly afterward.

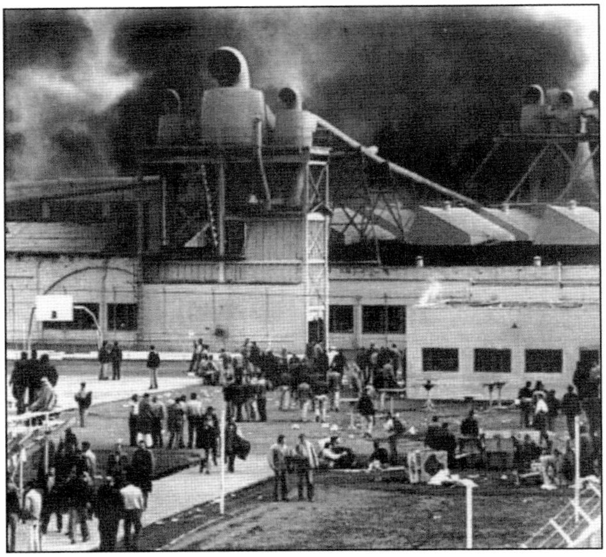

The riot broke loose at 4:15 p.m. on Saturday, March 10, 1968, as the prisoners were coming in from the recreation yard. After aimless rioting, the inmates in the segregation and isolation block issued an ultimatum at 7:30 p.m., warning that "a guard will come out with his head off, and this will continue every 30 minutes" if their demands were not met. (Courtesy of SJ.)

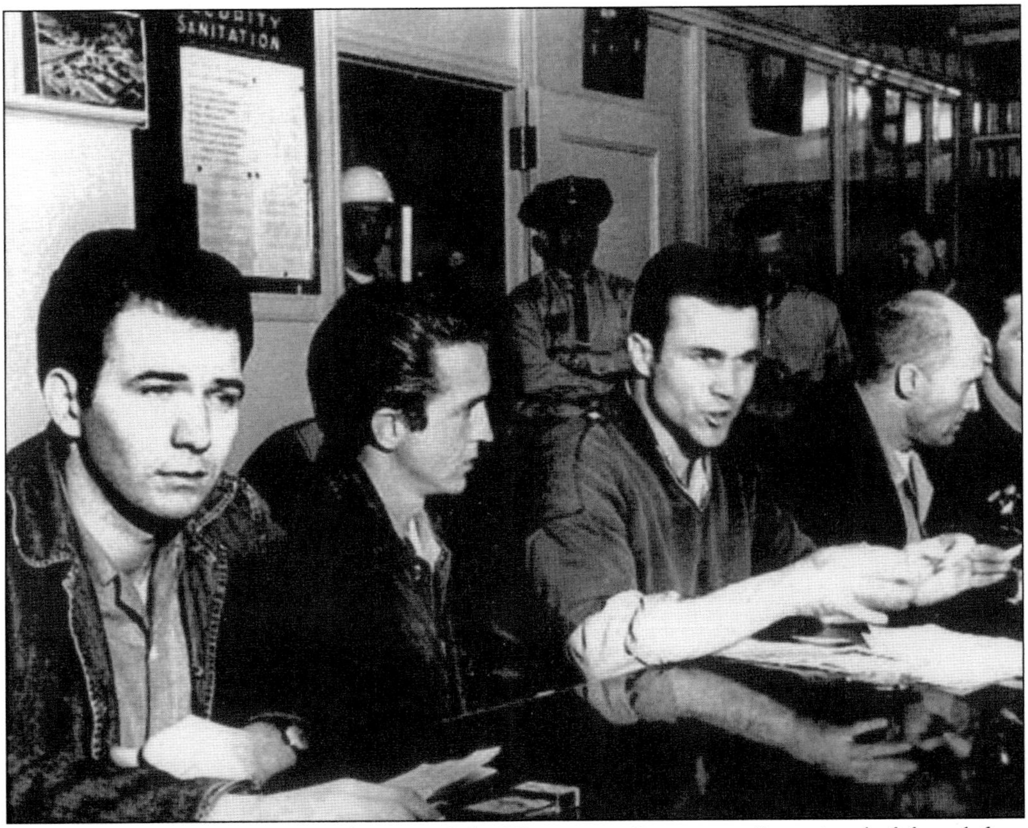

The prisoner negotiating team, designated the "Grievance Committee," consisted of, from left to right, Ronnie W. Hancock, age 24, serving life; Richard Dornack, age 28, serving 15 years; Lendel Buttram, age 30, serving six years; and Billy Ray Bowling, age 37, serving life. Others not in the photograph include Calvin Dow, age 20, serving two years, and Jimmy Ennis, age 22, serving 30 months. Hancock and Bowling had been released from the segregation unit after being assigned there because of an escape attempt on September 21, 1967. (Courtesy of SJ.)

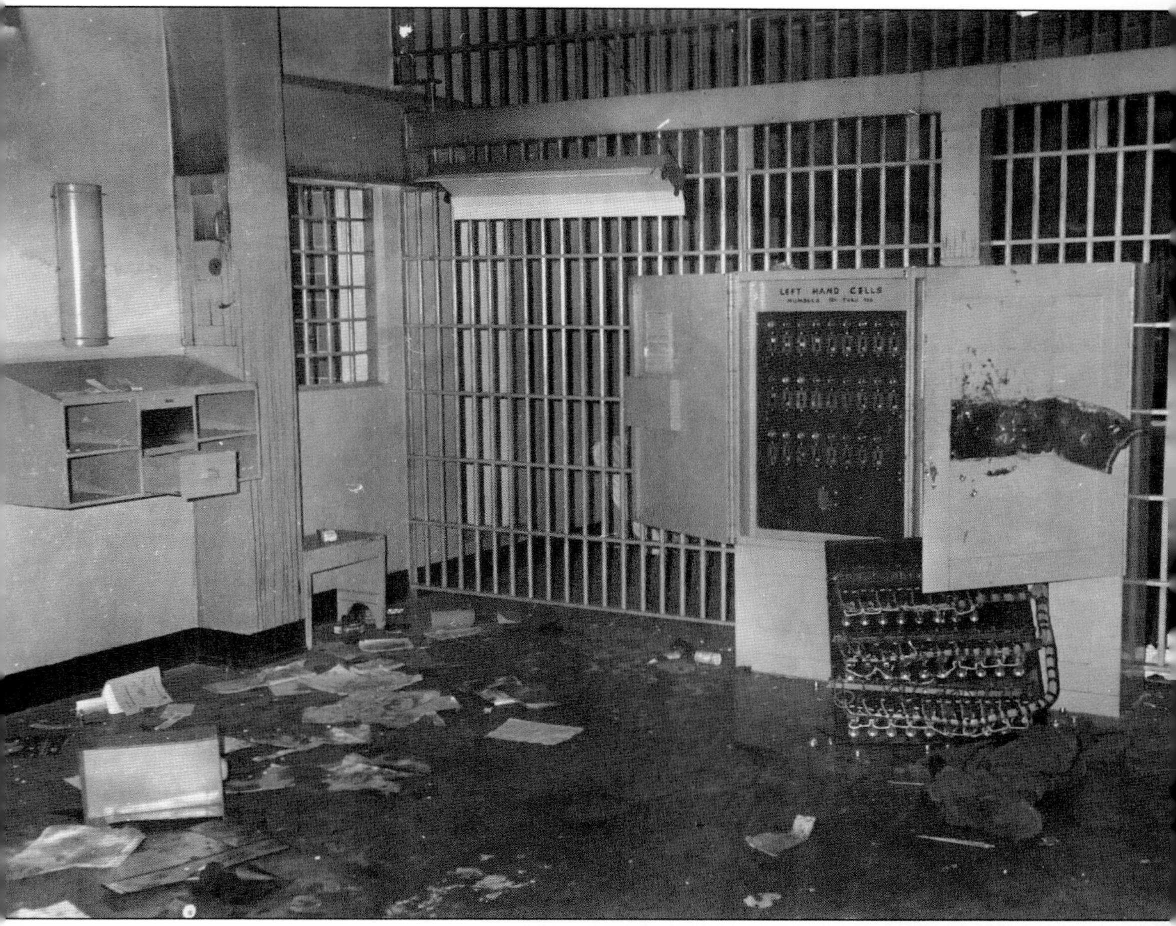

Very soon after the rioting began, the convicts took over the prison control center, which gave them access to all radio and telephone communications. Nearly 40 employees were inside the walls. By 9:00 p.m., most had escaped or been released by prisoners. After the negotiations were finished, the last prisoner, Francis Petrie, was released. Corrections officer Petrie used prison clothing as a disguise to get away from the rioting prisoners. Convicts stayed in the yard until Monday at 5:00 p.m. By 7:30 p.m., about 250 had returned to their cells. The rest huddled under tarps in the rain. (Courtesy of OSA.)

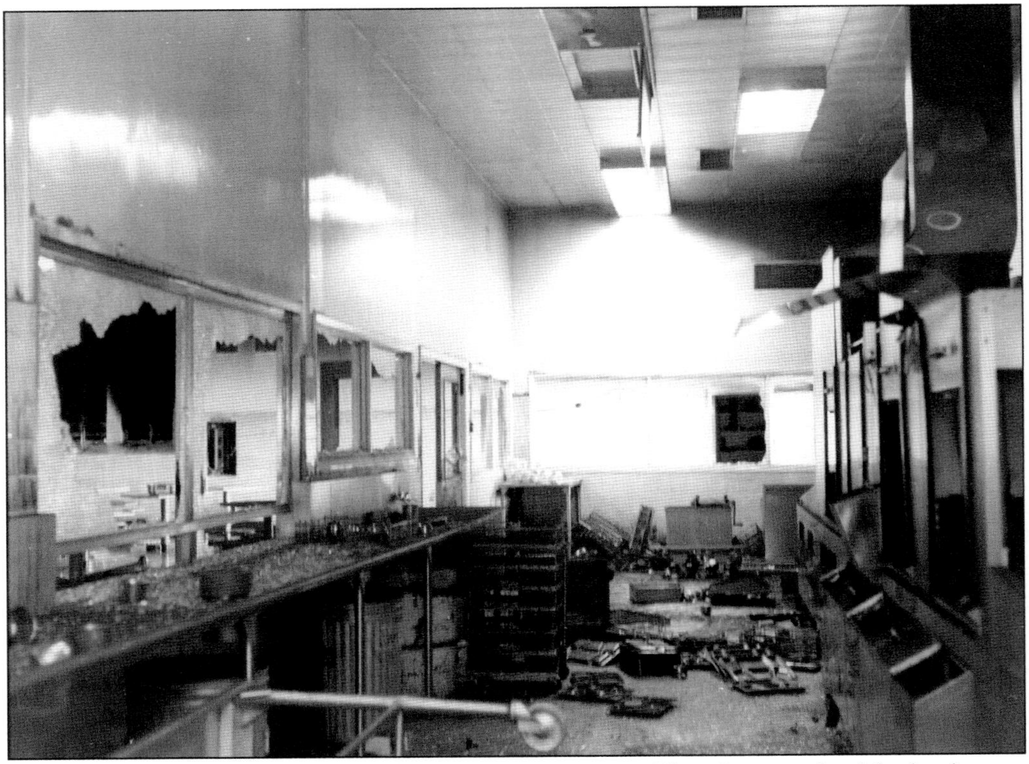

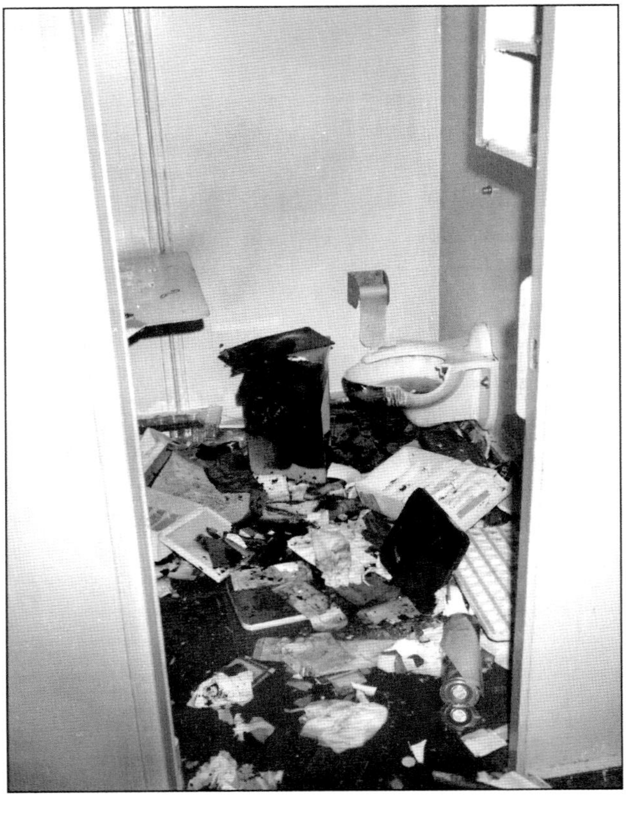

This photograph of the kitchen shows the destruction. Corrections officer Robert Geer was released early in the riot with a bleeding head wound. Because he resisted the convicts, they marched him into a cell and beat him. Lt. Hal Masterson suffered three broken ribs when a convict struck him with a pipe. Three other guards received injuries. Geer was later killed by an inmate in 1972.

Dwight Reinwald finally reached tower no. 9 on the telephone and reported that 30 people were trapped. For three hours, the group hid in the smoke. Finally, a 70-foot-high ladder was hooked to the window, and Salem fireman Don Hill started climbing toward them. Using an acetylene torch, he cut through the bars, freeing the group. Francoise Goeury, a French teacher, was the first to climb down, and Reinwald was the last.

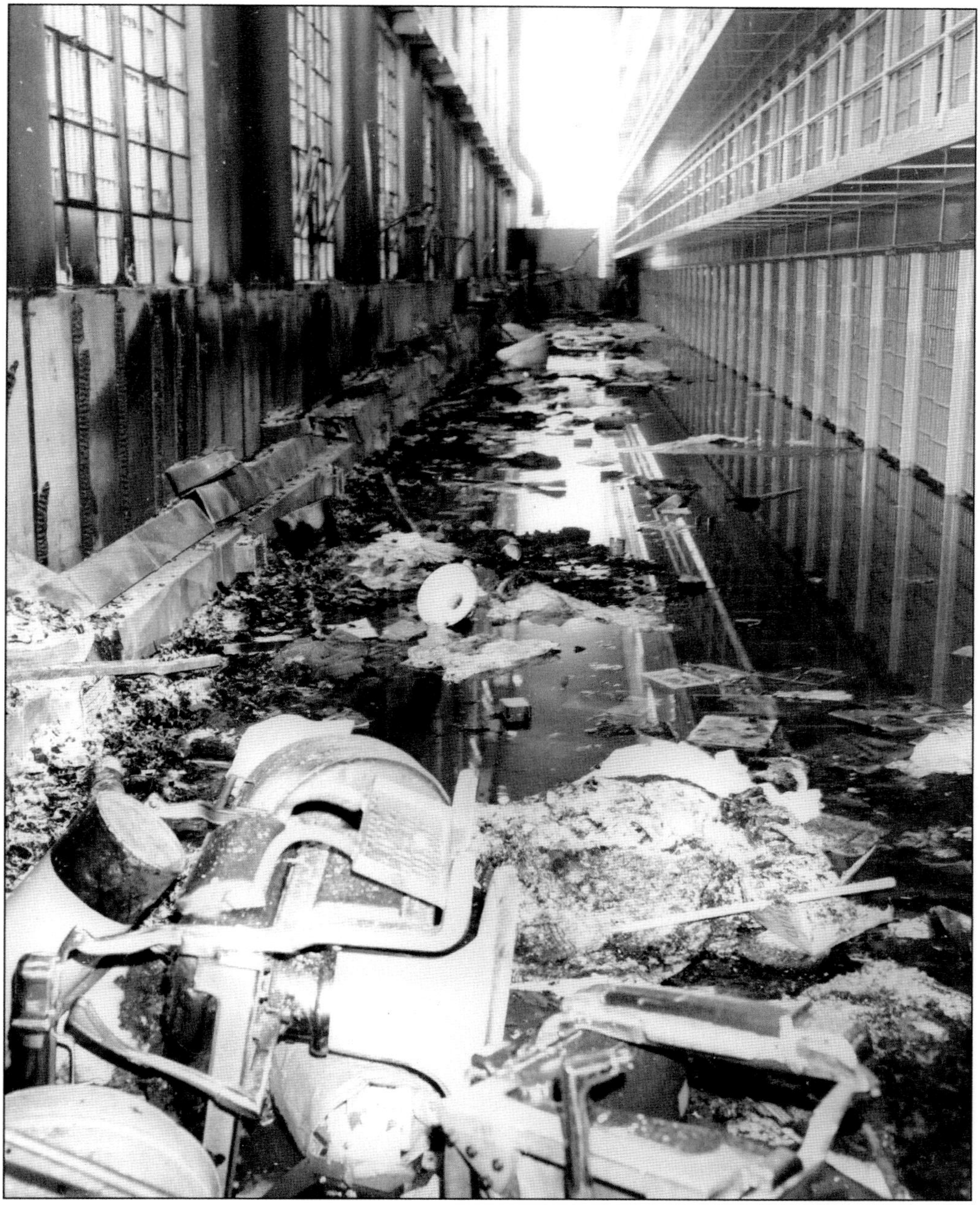

After wrecking the control center, convicts proceeded to trash deputy warden Lloyd Francis's office, immediately south of the central control station, which sits between cellblocks D and E, housing 400 prisoners each. Nearly 40 employees were inside the main area when the riot began. Four hostages, Lt. Ralph E. Pribble, Sgt. R.D. Meyers, Lt. Hal Masterson, and corrections officer C.R. Mahan, were held hostage. Riot damage totaled between $1,630,696 and $5 million. Because of an efficient sprinkler system, the furniture factory suffered less damage than anticipated. The treatment and education building was badly damaged by fire. The main control room and deputy warden's office were demolished, and many records were destroyed. The new dining room and kitchen were lightly damaged. Ironically, the prisoners were generally happy with the vocational department, yet those were the buildings hit hardest by the fires.

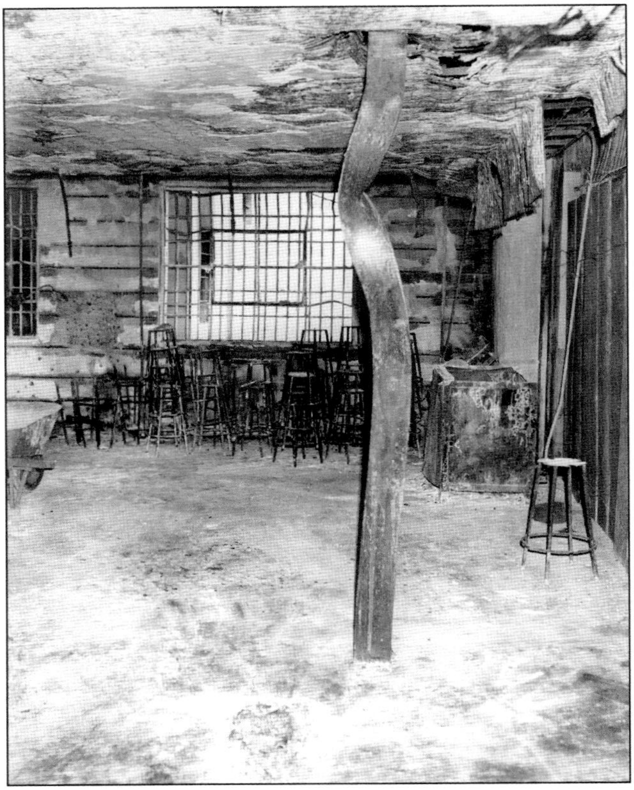

All of the 25,000 volumes in the library were destroyed. When it was over, the library was gone. All that remained was ankle-deep water and black debris strewn around. Convict negotiations procured a change of wardens and promises of improvement or change in medical services, recreation, the prison canteen, letter writing, visiting privileges, the work release program, and other items.

This metal shop was part of the vocational department. Convicts also did considerable damage to the prison hospital, smashing cabinets, burning mattresses, upsetting a dental chair, and strewing debris over the floors.

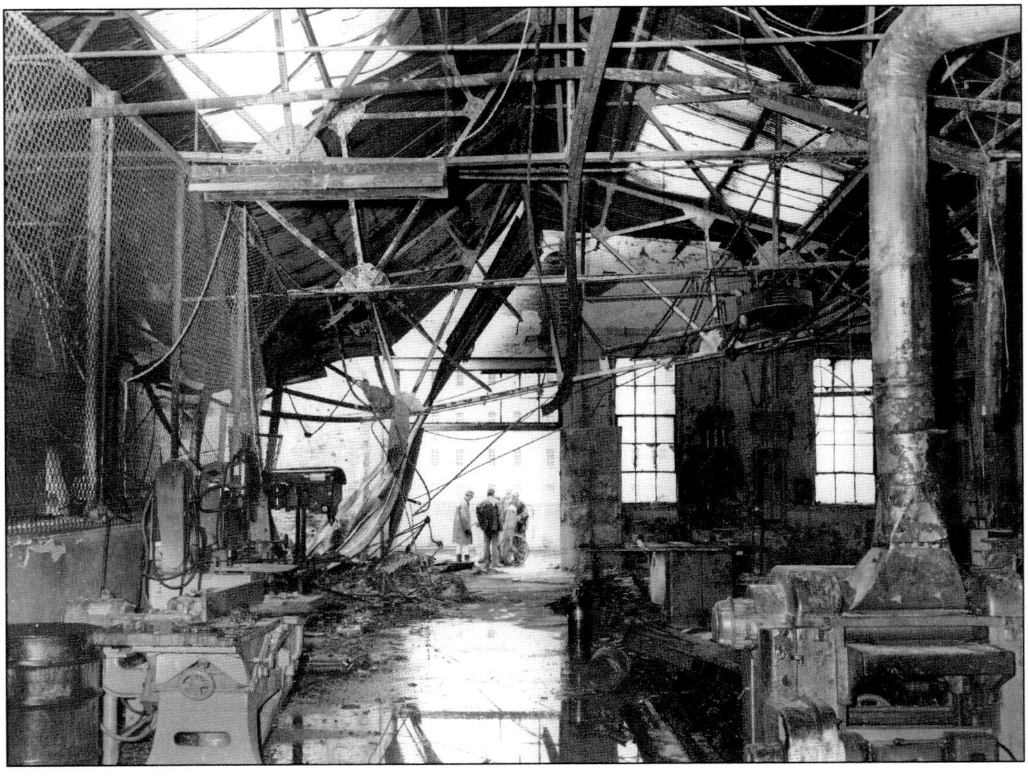

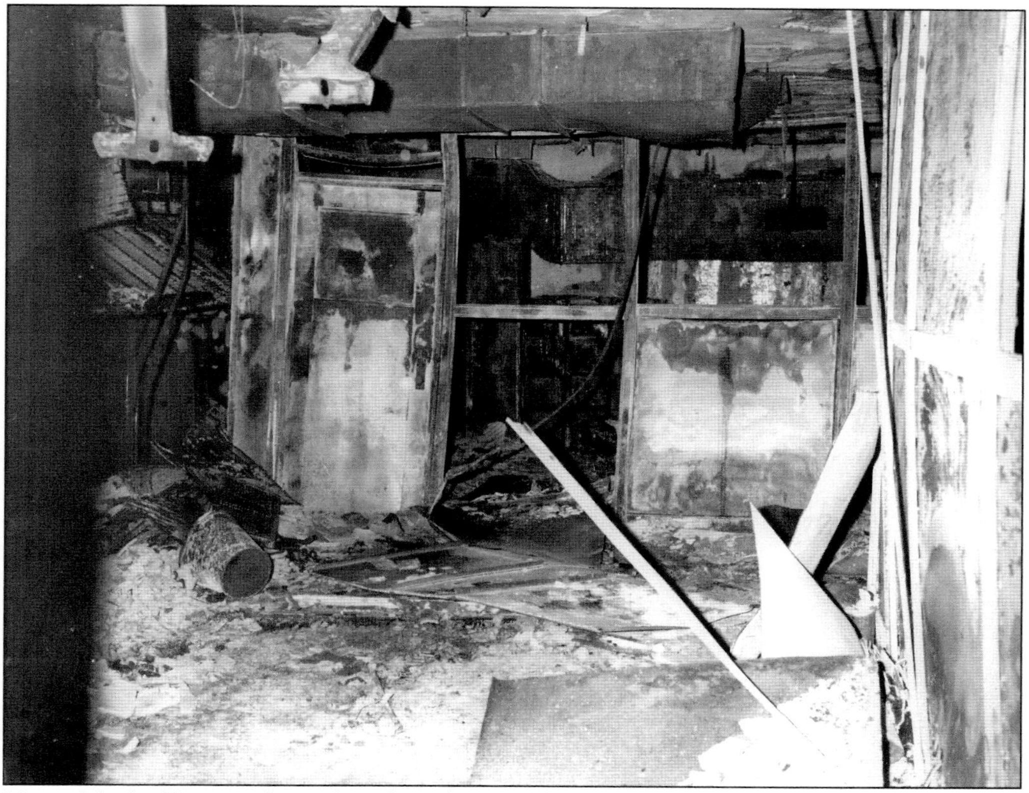

Most of the bedding was burned, and windows and heating ducts were smashed in the cellblocks. In this photograph, damage included receptacles for dirty sheets. Anything that could be broken was piled together and set on fire. The vocational carpentry shop was destroyed. Several thousand dollars in wood lathes, saws, drill presses, and wood-carving tools were burned.

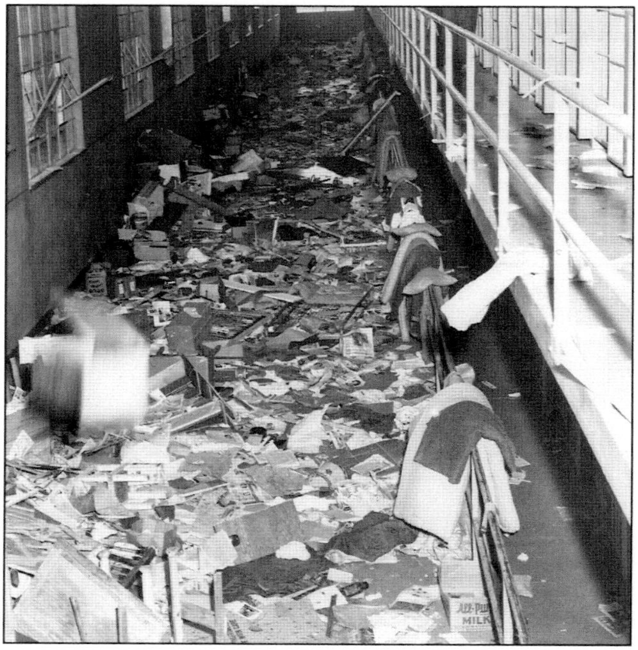

Most of the contraband discovered after the riot came from inside the prisoners' cells. This was just a small sample of the thousands of articles found strewn around after the riot and during the cleanup. Besides hypodermic needles, there were hammers, knives, and other debris. The rioters seized the weapons from the prison shops, kitchen, and hospital. (Courtesy of OSA.)

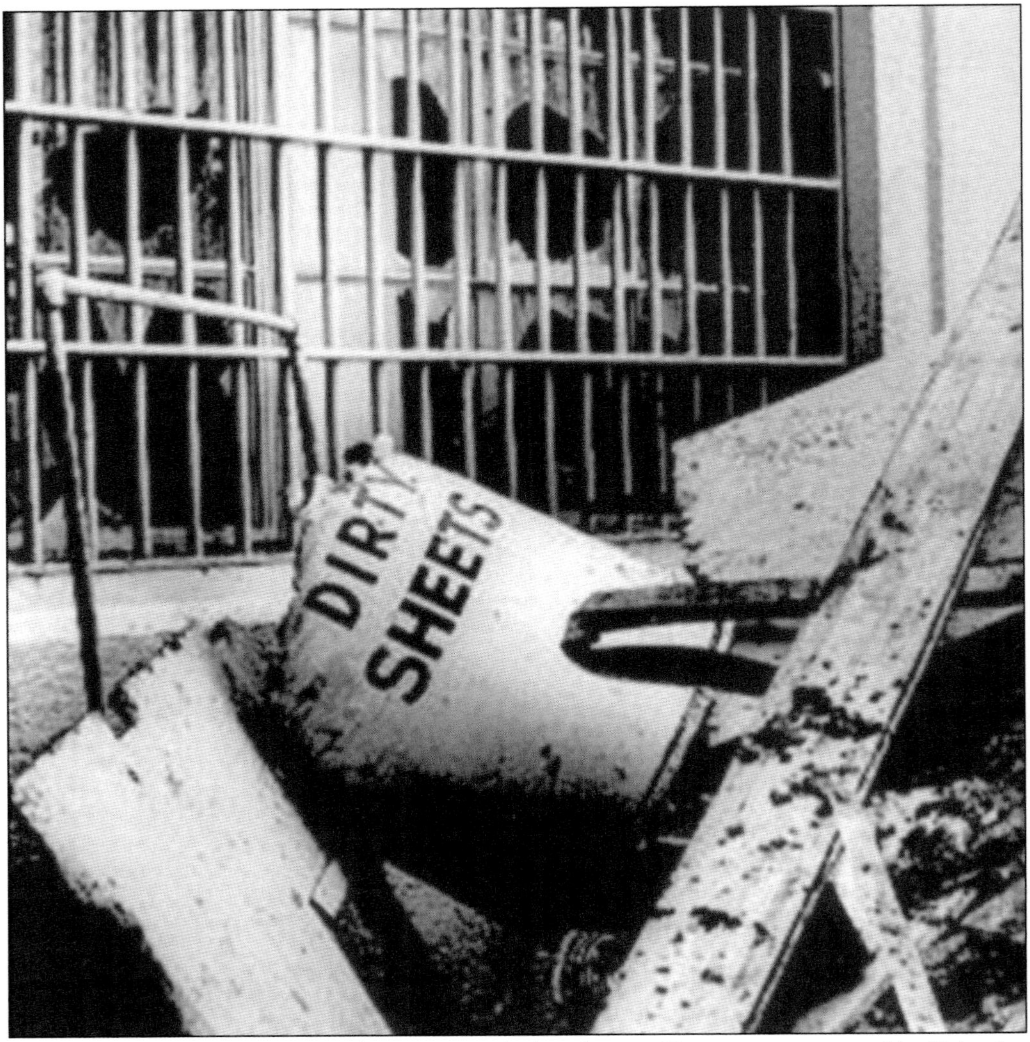

Four guards were held hostage and one inmate died in the riot. Two inmates were stabbed Monday night, one during the move back into the cellblocks and the other about 9:30 p.m. The wounded convicts were Delmar W. Dubray, age 30, and Melvin Newell, age 36. Both were taken to Salem Memorial Hospital. Three other inmates had only superficial knife wounds. Thomas J. Baughn, age 50, was shot through the lung and died an hour after the riot started. John Clemens, age 24, was shot in the right hand by guard H.H. Corey. Another inmate, Myron C. Ballain, age 46, was still in the hospital three days later. While roaming free in the yard, inmates ate fresh bread by the loaf and sheet cakes by the dozen, drank milk by the gallon, and cooked meat over bonfires.

Five

Industrial Programs

Like all state prisons in the 19th century, the Oregon State Penitentiary (OSP) began leasing prisoners to private contractors when it was first established. This was a very lucrative way to help pay for the prisoners' maintenance and keep them busy at the same time. All prison officials emphasized the need for productive work. The first work-related industry at OSP began in 1878 when superintendent W. Watkins instituted a tanning facility and a shoe factory. Prison-manufactured bricks were also used in the construction of many buildings and state institutions in Salem. Between 1866, when the first prisoners were moved to Salem, and 1924, millions of bricks were manufactured in the prison brickyard.

Private contractors paid the prison for inmate labor as well as prison-made products. A foundry was built inside the prison yard in 1883. Stoves made in the foundry were sold all over the world under the Monarch label. Aschael Bush, an early OSP warden, designed the first stoves. Other industries followed, including an enormous flax industry. Beginning in 1925, flax operations provided work for hundreds of inmates for about 25 years until advances in textile production reduced the need for flax products.

A farm operation begun in 1954 produced dairy products, eggs, and meat for the penitentiary and other Oregon institutions. The farm also provided fruit and vegetables for a large cannery operated by inmates between 1948 and 1960. The canned food was served in various state institutions and donated to food kitchens around the state.

The prison began making furniture as early as 1920, and it continues to be a major industry today. Vocational training included classes in small engine repair, automotive repair, cosmetology, woodworking, welding, and building maintenance. The vocational classes were affiliated with two unions, and an apprenticeship program was developed where inmates could apply to join the union and seek outside employment once they were discharged.

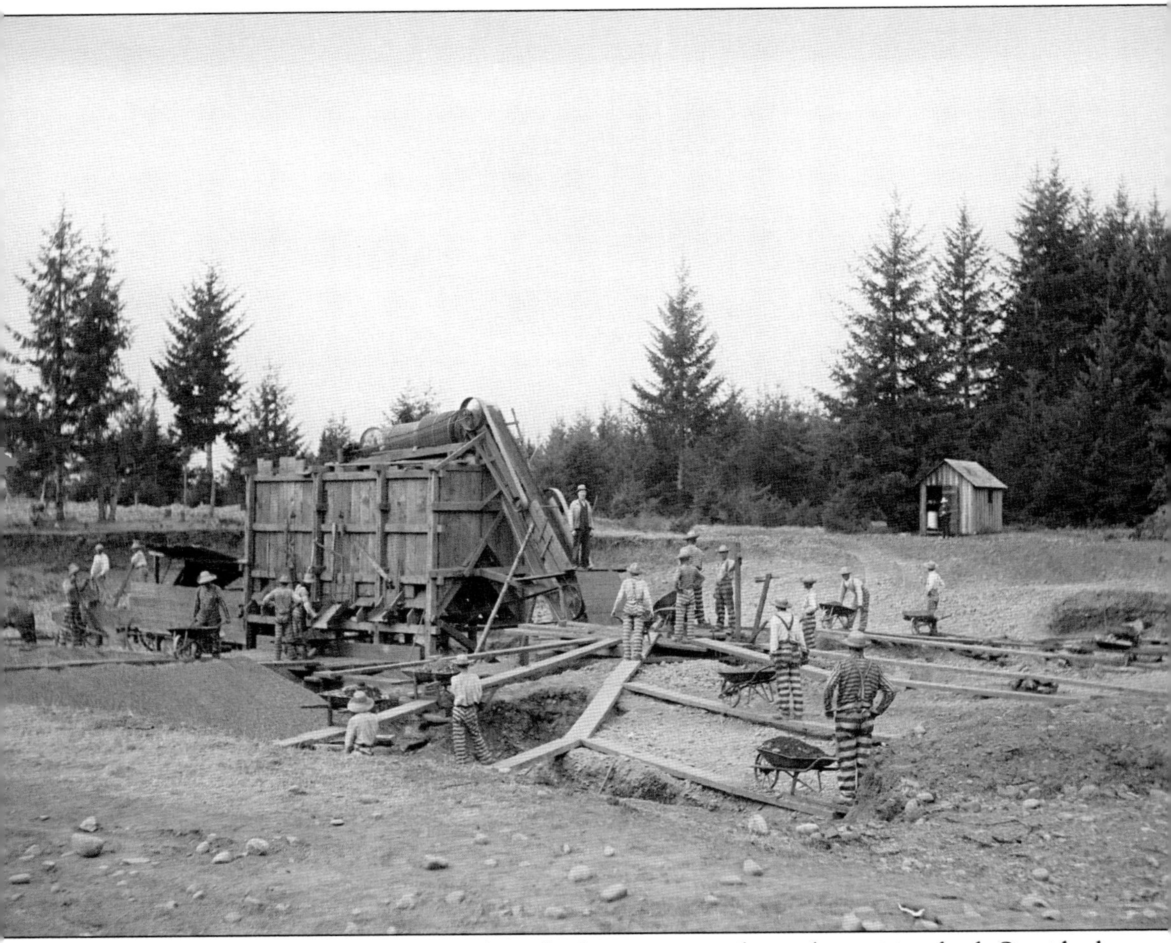

By 1880, nearly all the open ground inside the prison was devoted to raising food. Outside the walls, prisoners were leased to various county and state improvement projects. Between 1887 and 1888, the prison earned $34,379 from convict labor, which went straight into the state treasury. The men in this photograph are working at a rock crusher at the Aumsville quarry. (Courtesy of SPL.)

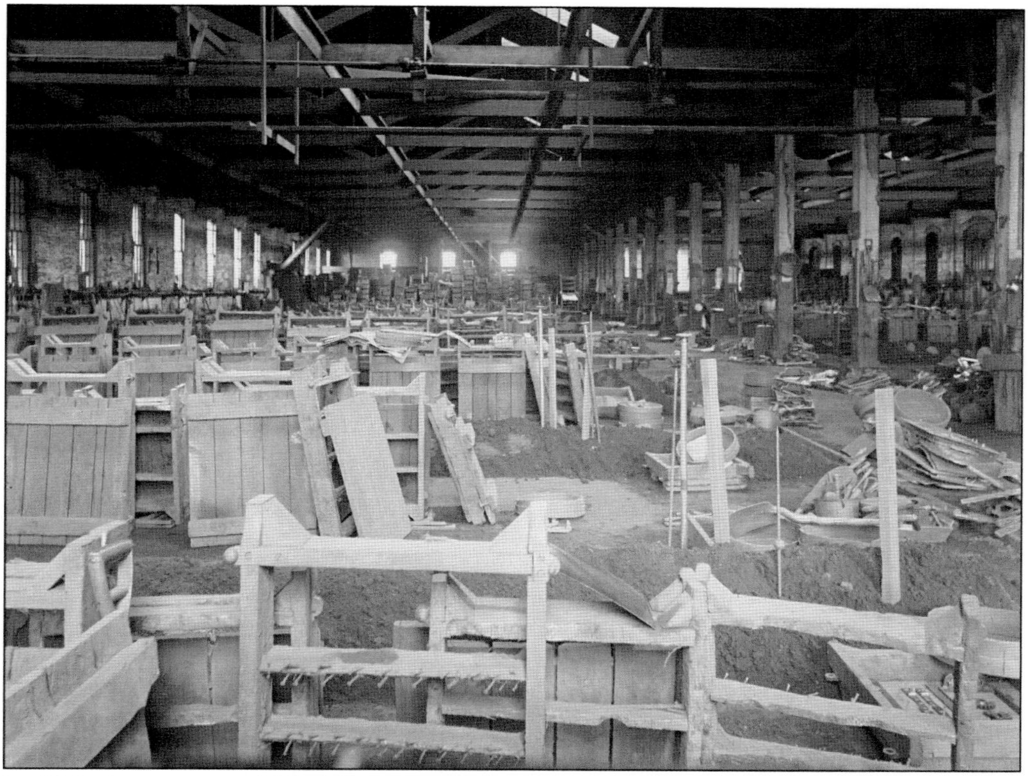

In 1921, the prison used $30,000 to install new machinery for an up-to-date furniture factory. Convicts were taught how to make kitchen cabinets, chairs, rockers, tables, and other pieces of furniture. After a fire, a new building was constructed in 1952, costing $45,000.

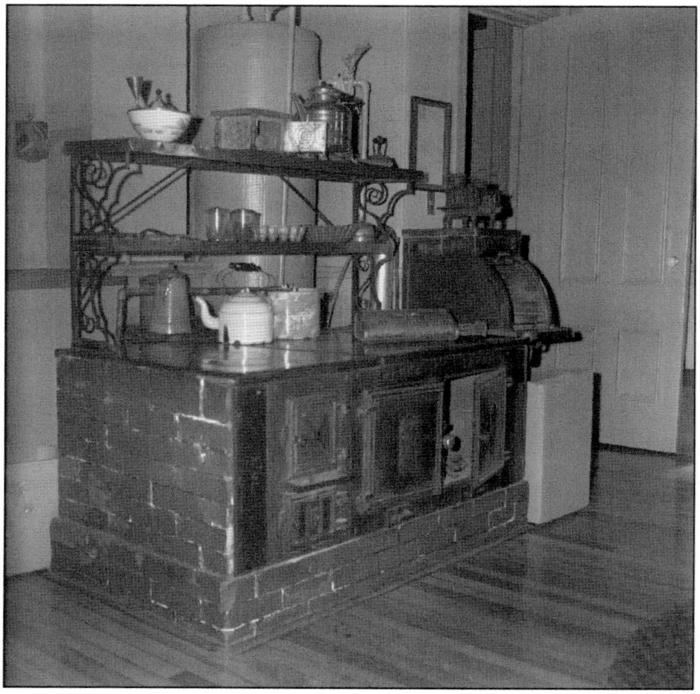

The stove foundry was established by the Northwestern Foundry Company in 1883. It paid 125 inmates 40¢ a day for their labor. Eight guards supervised. Over the next 10 years, the company paid the state $166,366 before its contract expired. The stove foundry was taken over by the Loewenberg-Going Company and paid the state $44,546 between 1899 and 1900. The contract expired in 1912.

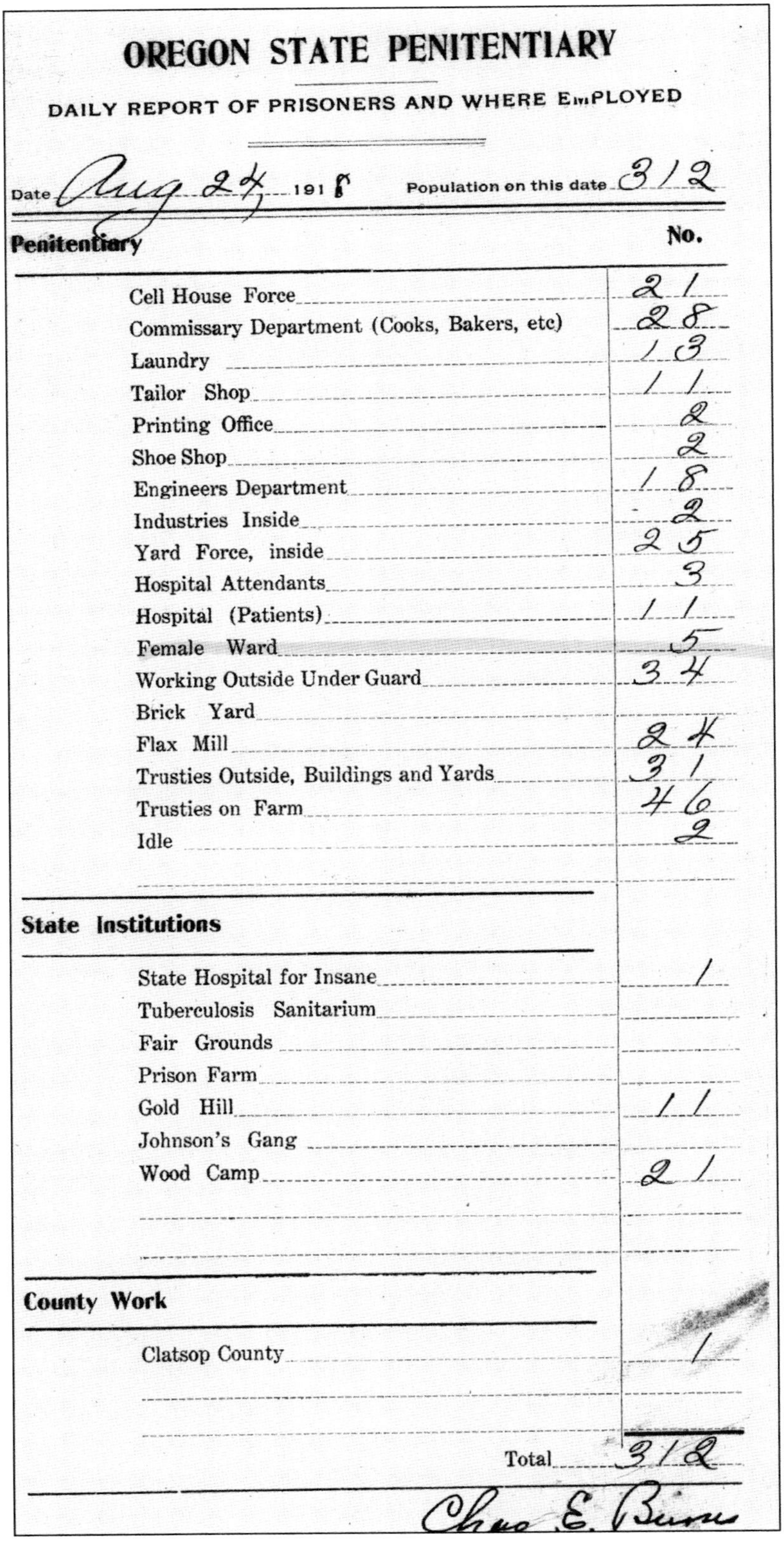

OREGON STATE PENITENTIARY

DAILY REPORT OF PRISONERS AND WHERE EMPLOYED

Date Aug 24, 1918 Population on this date 312

Penitentiary	No.
Cell House Force	21
Commissary Department (Cooks, Bakers, etc)	28
Laundry	13
Tailor Shop	11
Printing Office	2
Shoe Shop	2
Engineers Department	18
Industries Inside	2
Yard Force, inside	25
Hospital Attendants	3
Hospital (Patients)	11
Female Ward	5
Working Outside Under Guard	34
Brick Yard	
Flax Mill	24
Trusties Outside, Buildings and Yards	31
Trusties on Farm	46
Idle	2
State Institutions	
State Hospital for Insane	1
Tuberculosis Sanitarium	
Fair Grounds	
Prison Farm	
Gold Hill	11
Johnson's Gang	
Wood Camp	21
County Work	
Clatsop County	1
Total	312

Chas. E. B[illegible]

On August 24, 1918, there were 312 convicts in the prison. This report shows where each one was working that day. The majority were working on the farm, cleaning up the inside of the prison, or working in the commissary. Eleven were sick in the hospital, and one was confined to the Oregon State Hospital. Another large group was cutting wood needed to heat the buildings. (Courtesy of OSA.)

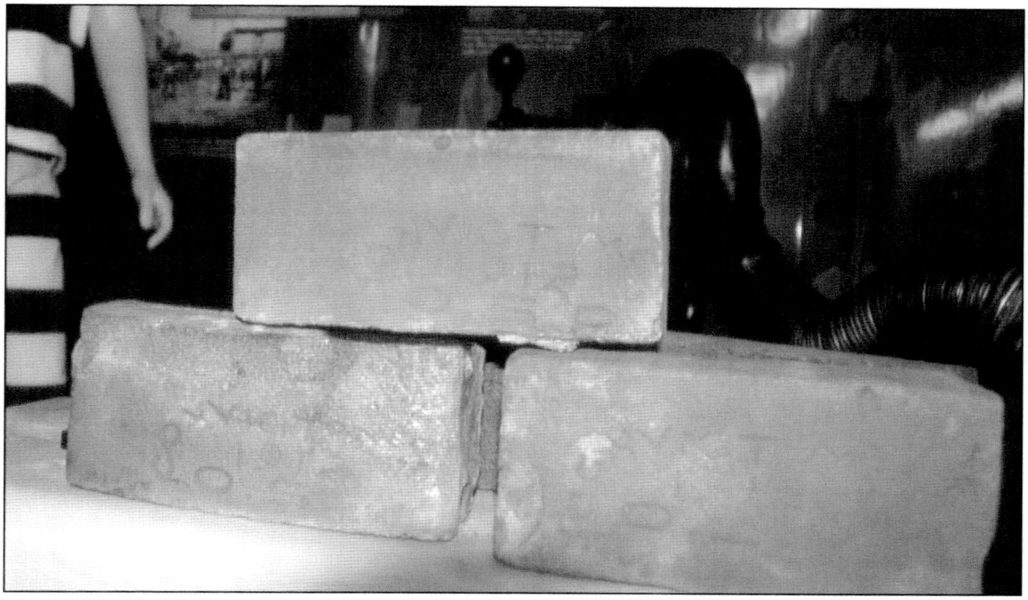

Bricks made in the prison were used to build most of the state institutions around Salem. Every prison building, including the stockade wall, was constructed of brick. Two and a half million bricks were used to build the original prison. In 1890, over one million bricks were used at the boys' reform school. In 1899 alone, over two million bricks were manufactured. (Courtesy of Diane L. Goeres-Gardner.)

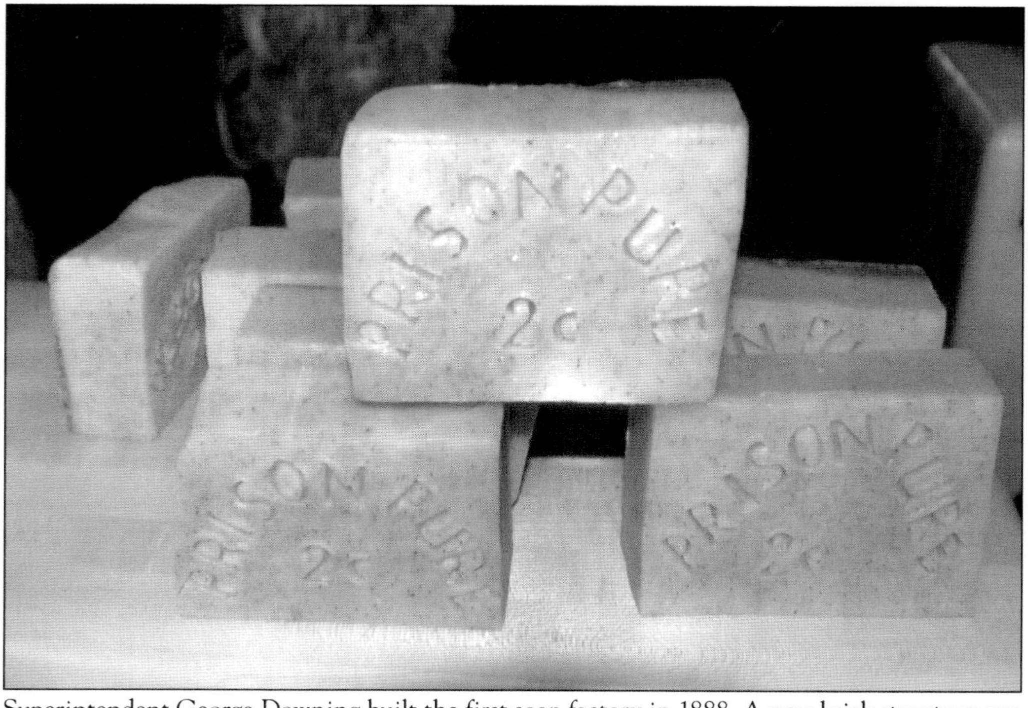

Superintendent George Downing built the first soap factory in 1888. A new brick structure was erected in 1904. Prison pure soap was manufactured from pig fat, lye, and pumice. It was then poured into a form and stamped. The form was lifted, punched out, and sold for 2¢ a block. The money went into the convicts' goodie fund. (Courtesy of Diane L. Goeres-Gardner.)

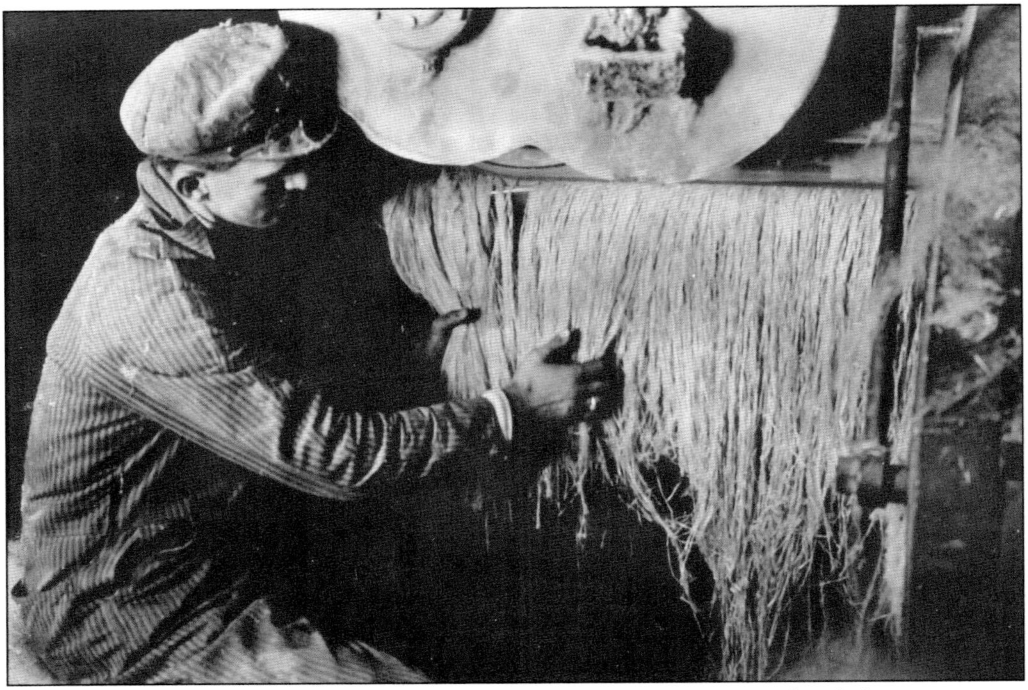

The flax industry was established about 1925, when the prison contracted with farmers to grow flax on 2,100 acres. A new warehouse constructed in 1924 allowed for threshing flax straw, making and baling tow, cleaning and grinding seed, and storing flax products. In addition, the old foundry building was reconstructed as a scotching mill and warehouse.

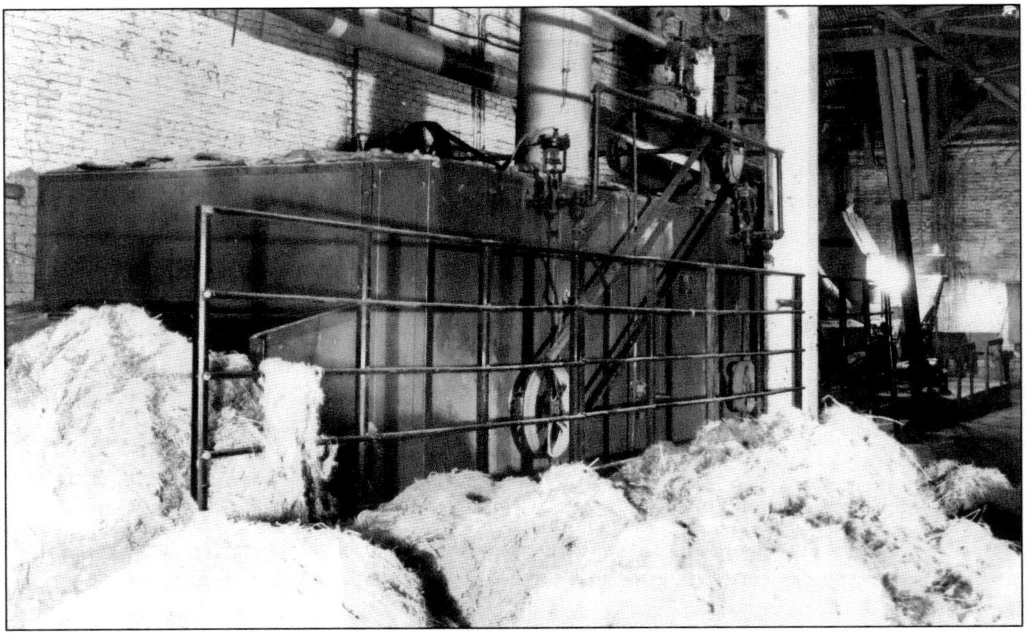

The first flax-pulling machine in Oregon began operating in 1923. The flax straw was pulled, bound into bundles, and soaked in ponds adjacent to the prison. After 48 hours, the bundled flax moved into the prison, where the husks were removed, or retted. The fiber was used to make linen, bootlaces, and hay-bailing twine.

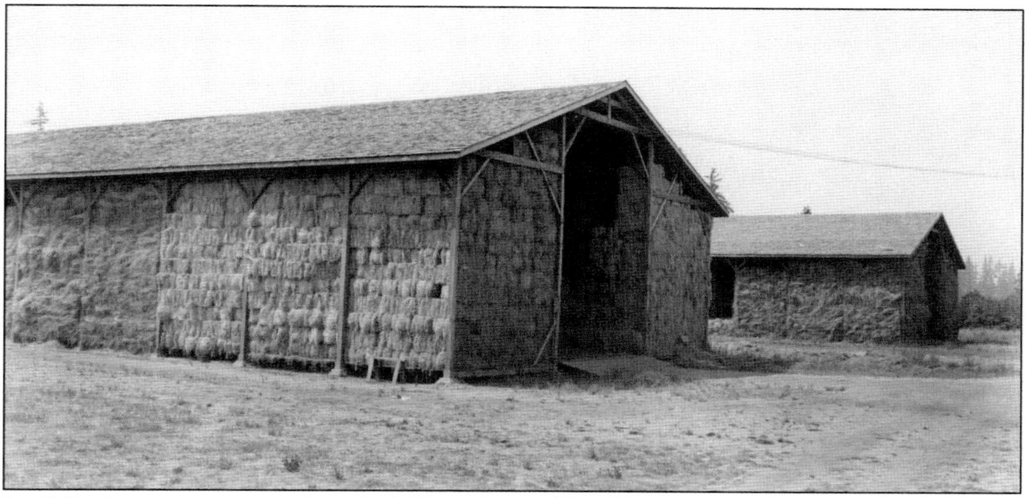

In 1940, the prison retting plant had 25 tanks capable of retting 300 tons of flax. Retted straw was arranged in wigwams for drying and bleaching in 80-acre fields. Straw also went through a deseeding mill, where the seed was whipped or thrashed from the straw.

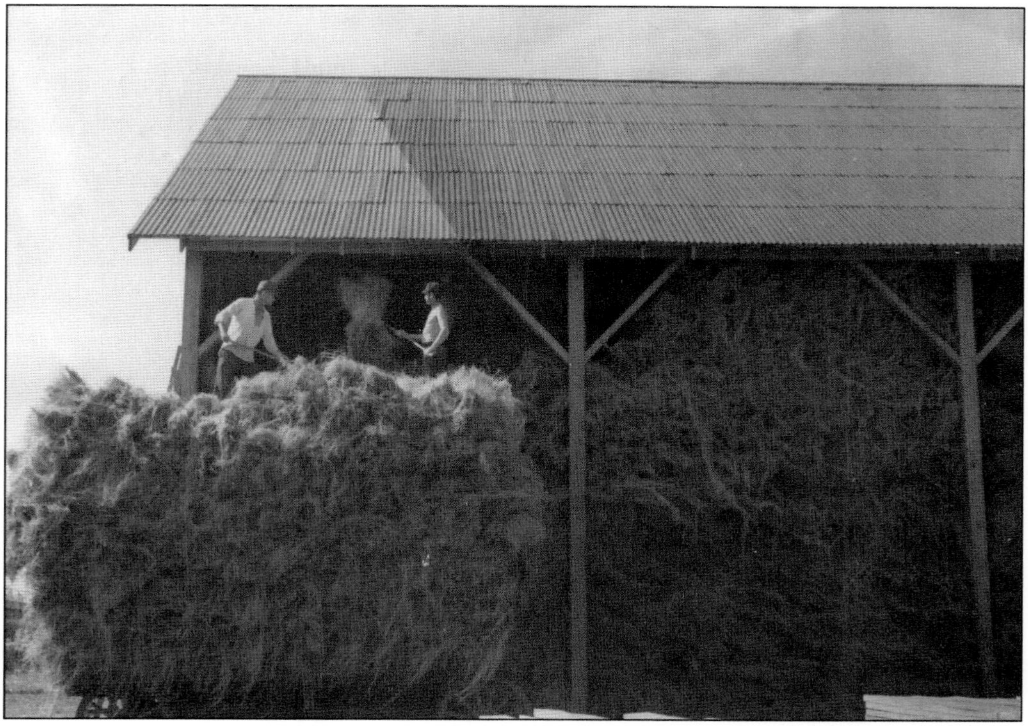

The baled flax was stored in two open-air warehouses situated near Hawthorne Street in Salem. The warehouses' foundations could still be seen in the 1960s, when they were finally broken up to make way for a soccer field. The flax industry was discontinued on July 1, 1957. The market had turned down because of the manufacture of nylon, acetate, and other synthetics.

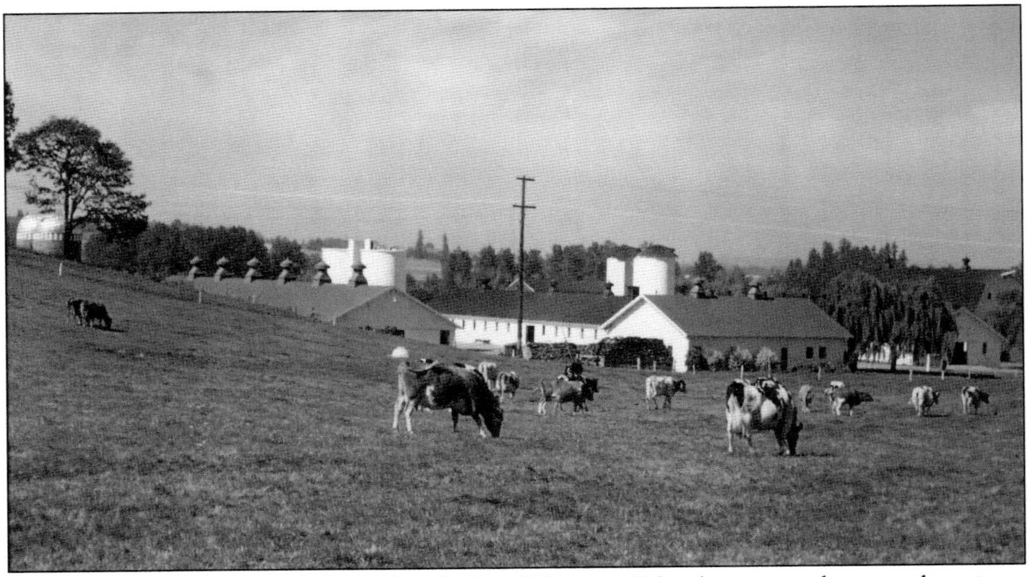

In 1929, property that once belonged to the Boys' Training School was turned over to the prison. Included were modern dairy and horse barns, poultry, a dairy herd, horses, and swine pens. It also included a dormitory capable of housing 75 prison trusties. The prison now owned 956.35 acres of land, of which 700 acres were cultivated. By 1932, there were 49 good Holstein milk cows and one purebred bull.

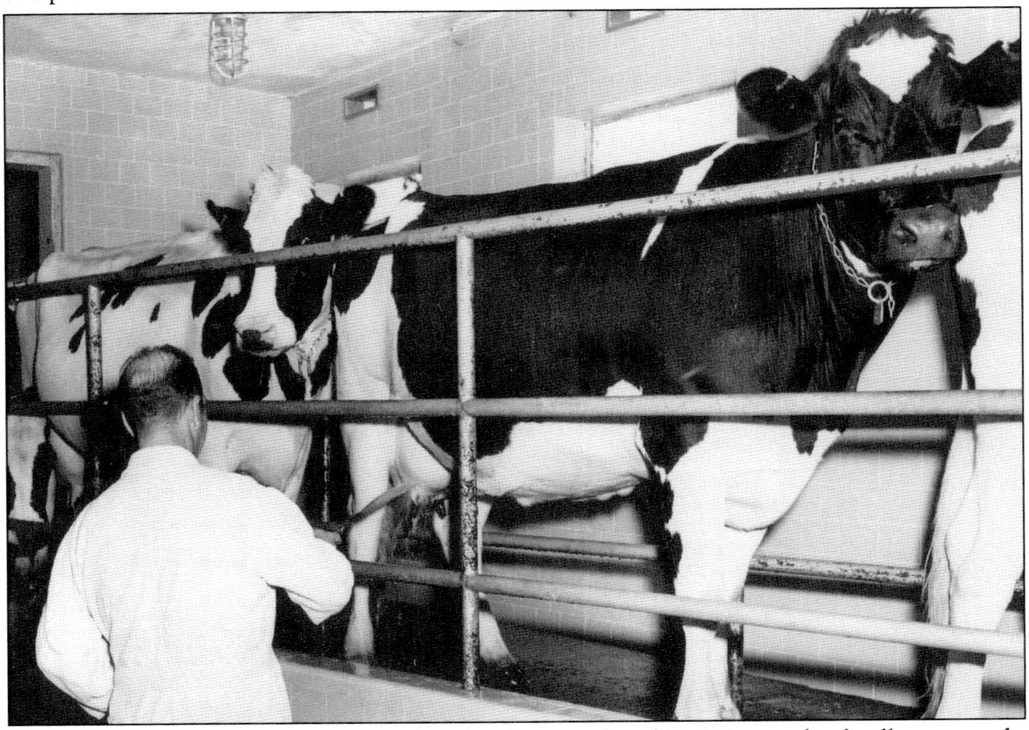

In 1940, the superintendent reported that the dairy produced 79,000 pounds of milk per month. This milking parlor was constructed in 1955. The modern dairy was almost completely mechanized and able to milk 200 cows in two hours. An inmate tended each individual cow and made sure it received the best possible care.

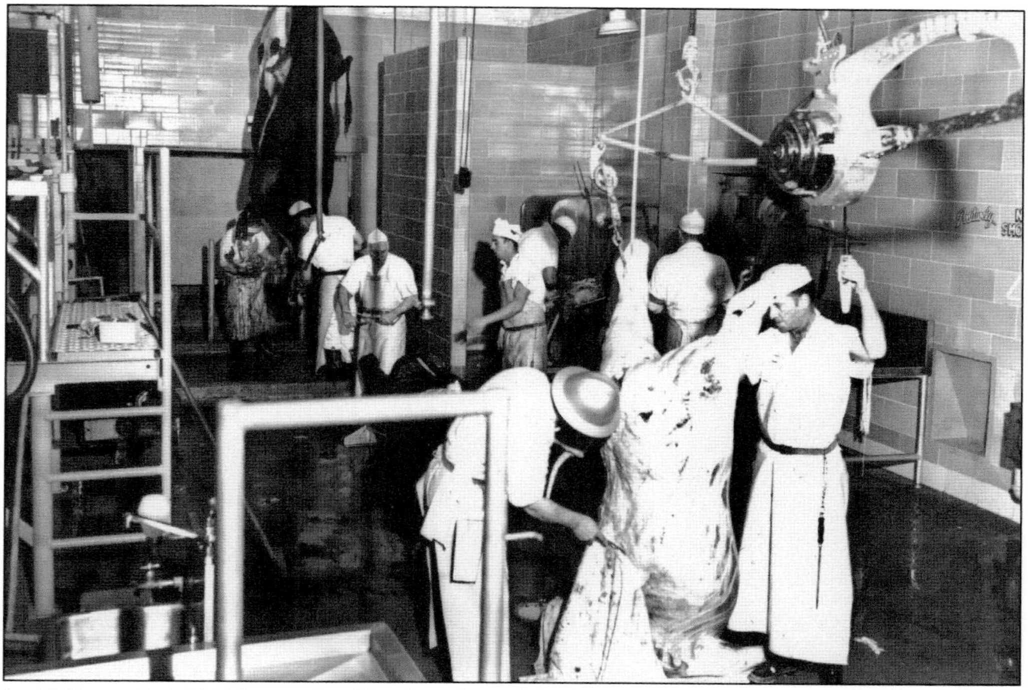

In 1955, nearly 564,113 pounds of beef, pork, and fowl were produced on the prison farm. It was manned by 200 minimum-security prisoners who worked eight hours a day, seven days a week, in an environment designed to promote good work habits. Instead of money, they had three days a month removed from their sentences in addition to good behavior time.

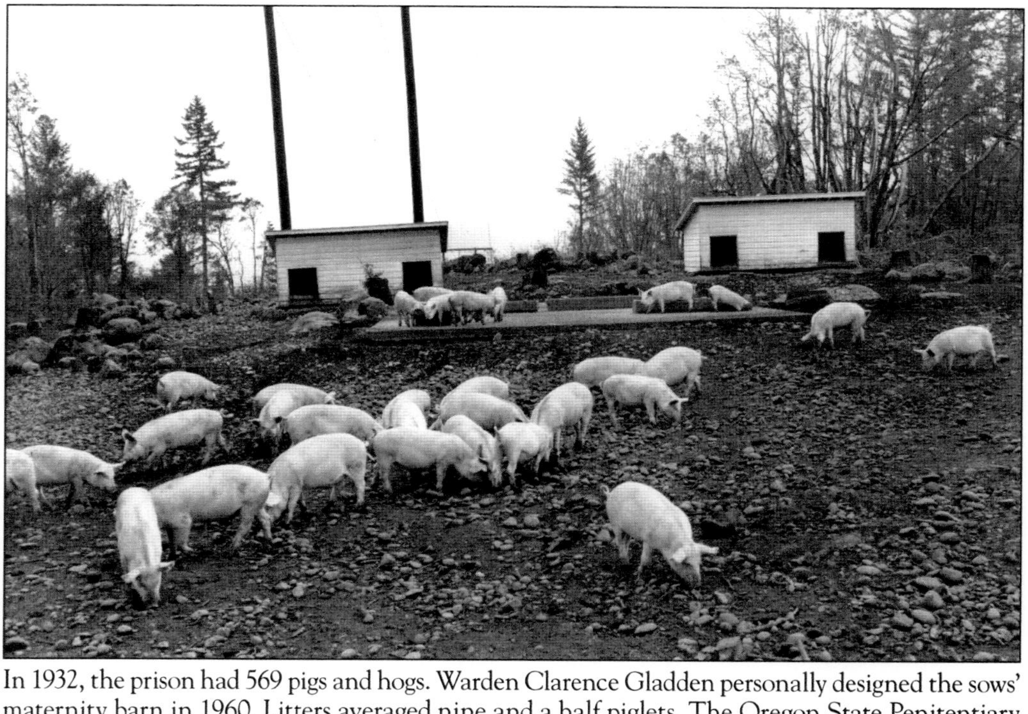

In 1932, the prison had 569 pigs and hogs. Warden Clarence Gladden personally designed the sows' maternity barn in 1960. Litters averaged nine and a half piglets. The Oregon State Penitentiary farm was named one of the 10 best penal farms in the nation.

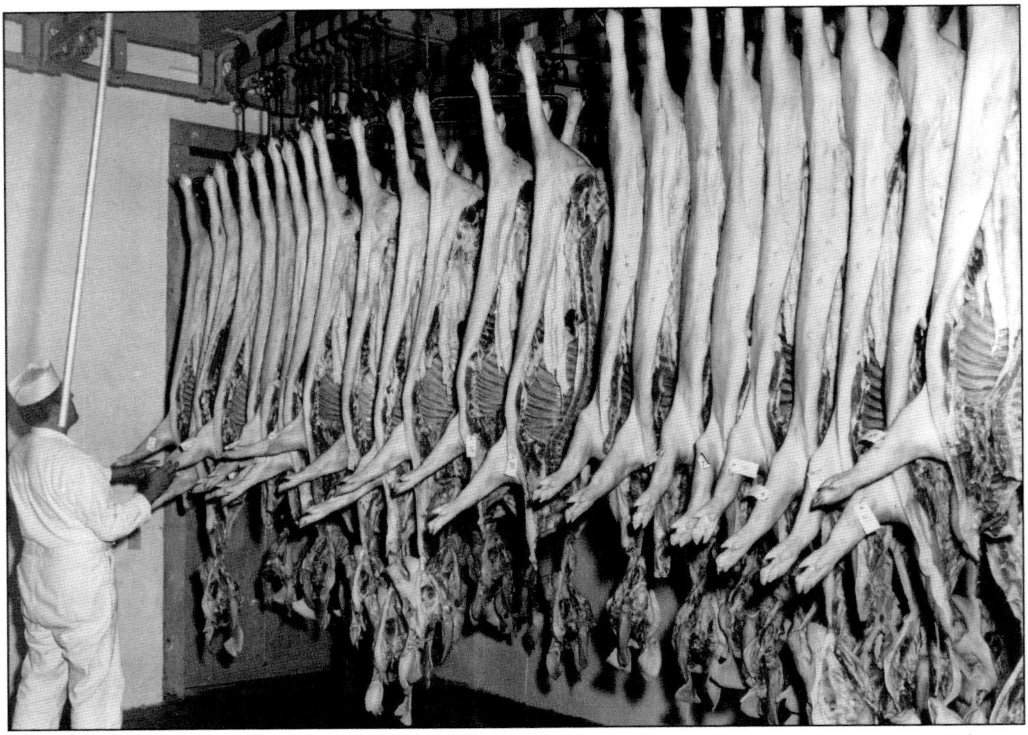

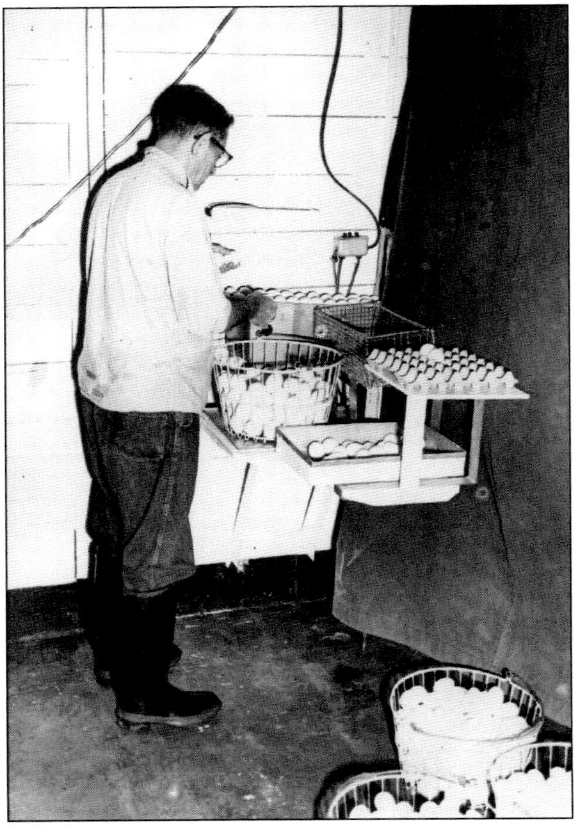

The convicts were fed pork several times a week after 1932. A butcher shop for pigs was built in 1952, costing $8,500. By 1961, the "pig factory" at the farm annex had the capacity to care for 2,000 hogs. About 24 were butchered every week. In 1964, an average crew of 12 men slaughtered 4,000 hogs and 600 beef cattle, creating 1.5 million pounds of meat a year.

In 1932, the poultry department consisted of 1,446 hens and 449 turkeys. By 1955, the hens laid 85,635 dozen eggs a year. In 1961, the chicken farm provided 520 dozen eggs a day at a cost of less than 16¢ a dozen, which were distributed to the prison and other state institutions. The prison farm increased its egg production capabilities until there were 10,000 layers in a modern poultry shed by 1964.

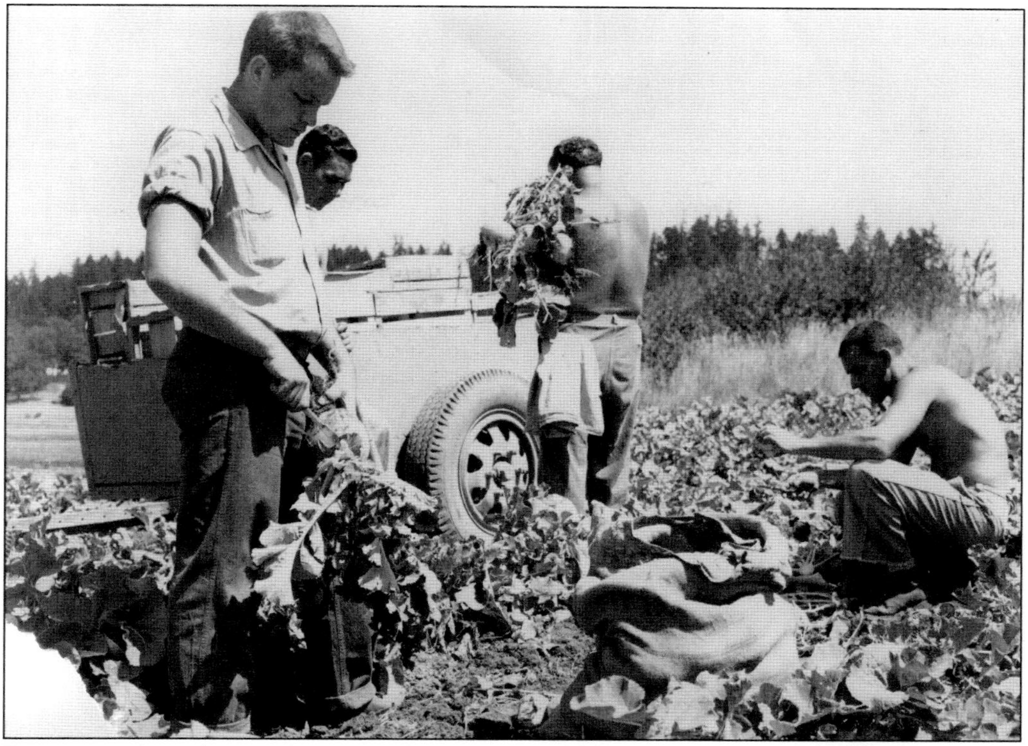

Between 1954 and 1956, the prison farm grew 1,381,643 pounds of root vegetables, including 767,945 pounds of potatoes. The cannery packed 78,136 cases, which provided a profit of $17,352 in 1953. About 200 convicts worked during the peak season and 20 during the winter season, and 78 percent of the fruits and vegetables were grown on prison land. The prison farms produced $1 million of food a year on 2,000 acres by 1964. (Both courtesy of OSA.)

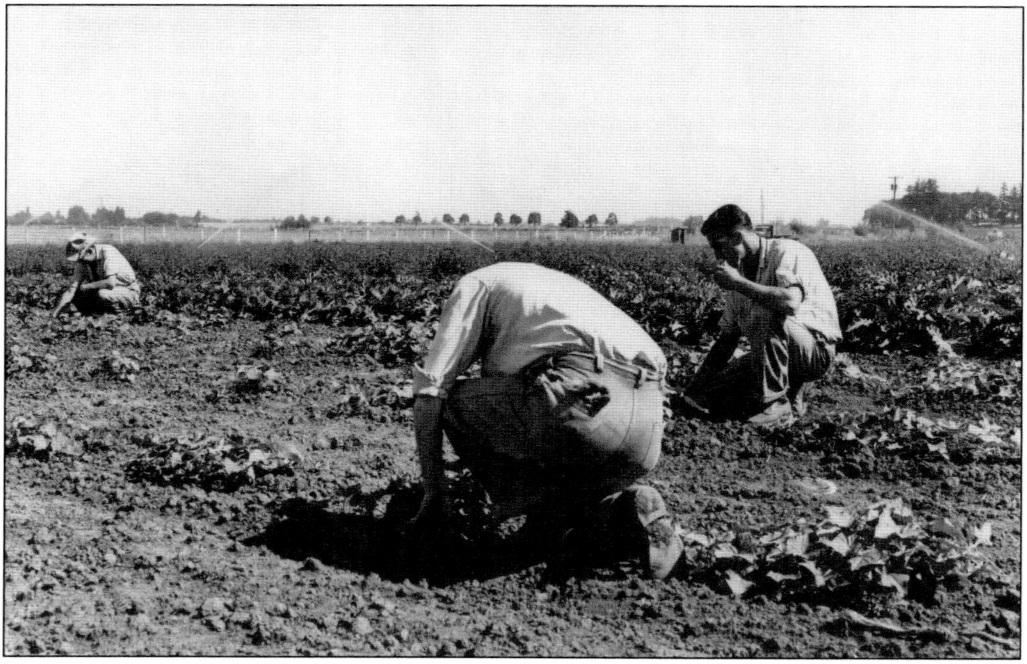

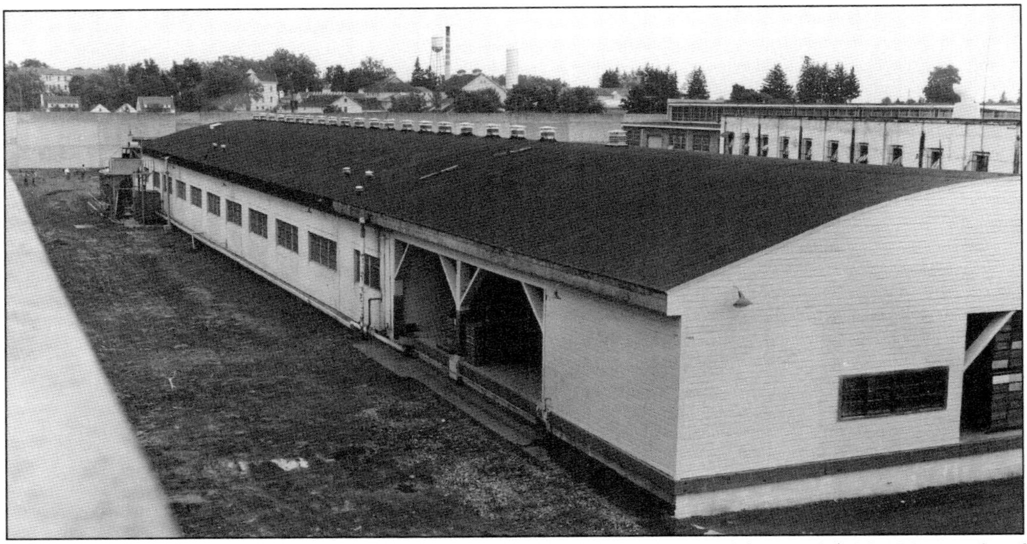

This cannery was constructed in 1947 of reinforced concrete and housed $66,000 worth of equipment. It cost $58,000 and was 60 feet long, 240 feet wide, and 12 feet high.

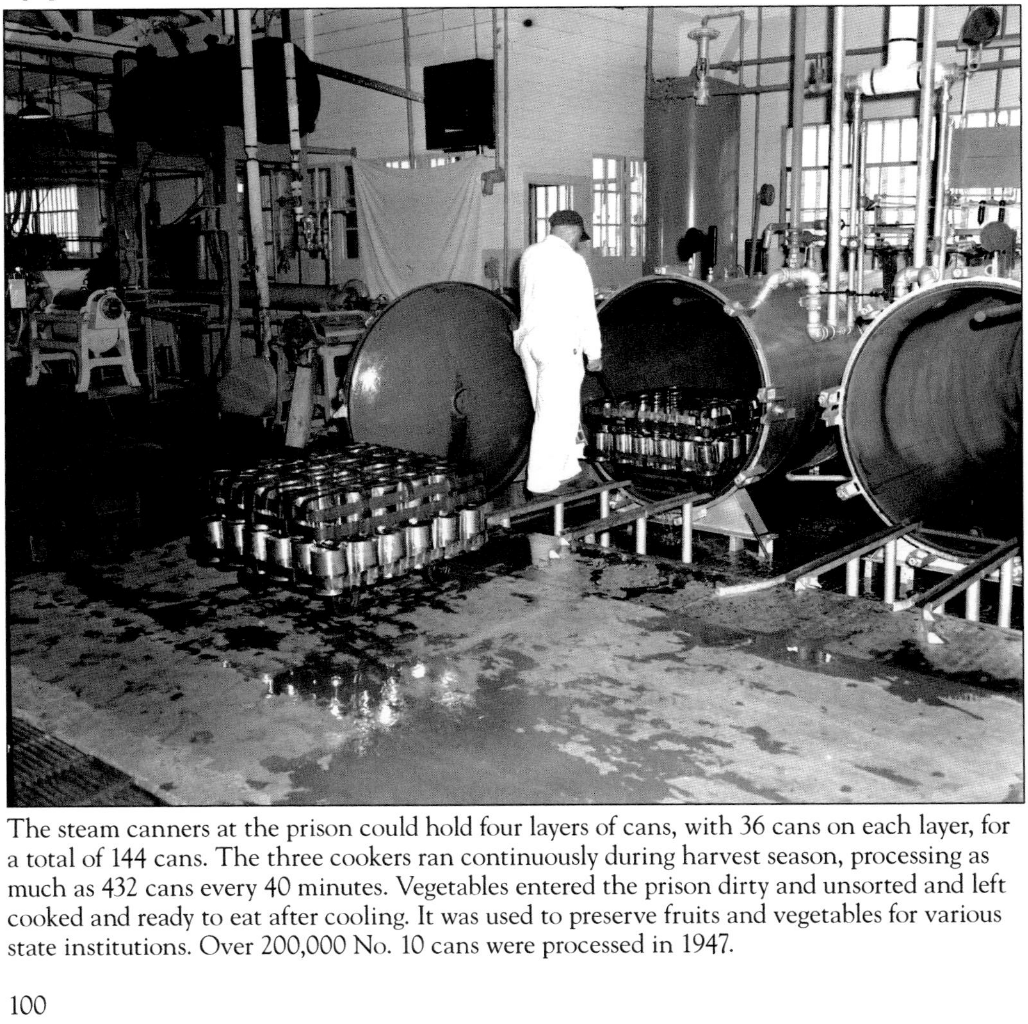

The steam canners at the prison could hold four layers of cans, with 36 cans on each layer, for a total of 144 cans. The three cookers ran continuously during harvest season, processing as much as 432 cans every 40 minutes. Vegetables entered the prison dirty and unsorted and left cooked and ready to eat after cooling. It was used to preserve fruits and vegetables for various state institutions. Over 200,000 No. 10 cans were processed in 1947.

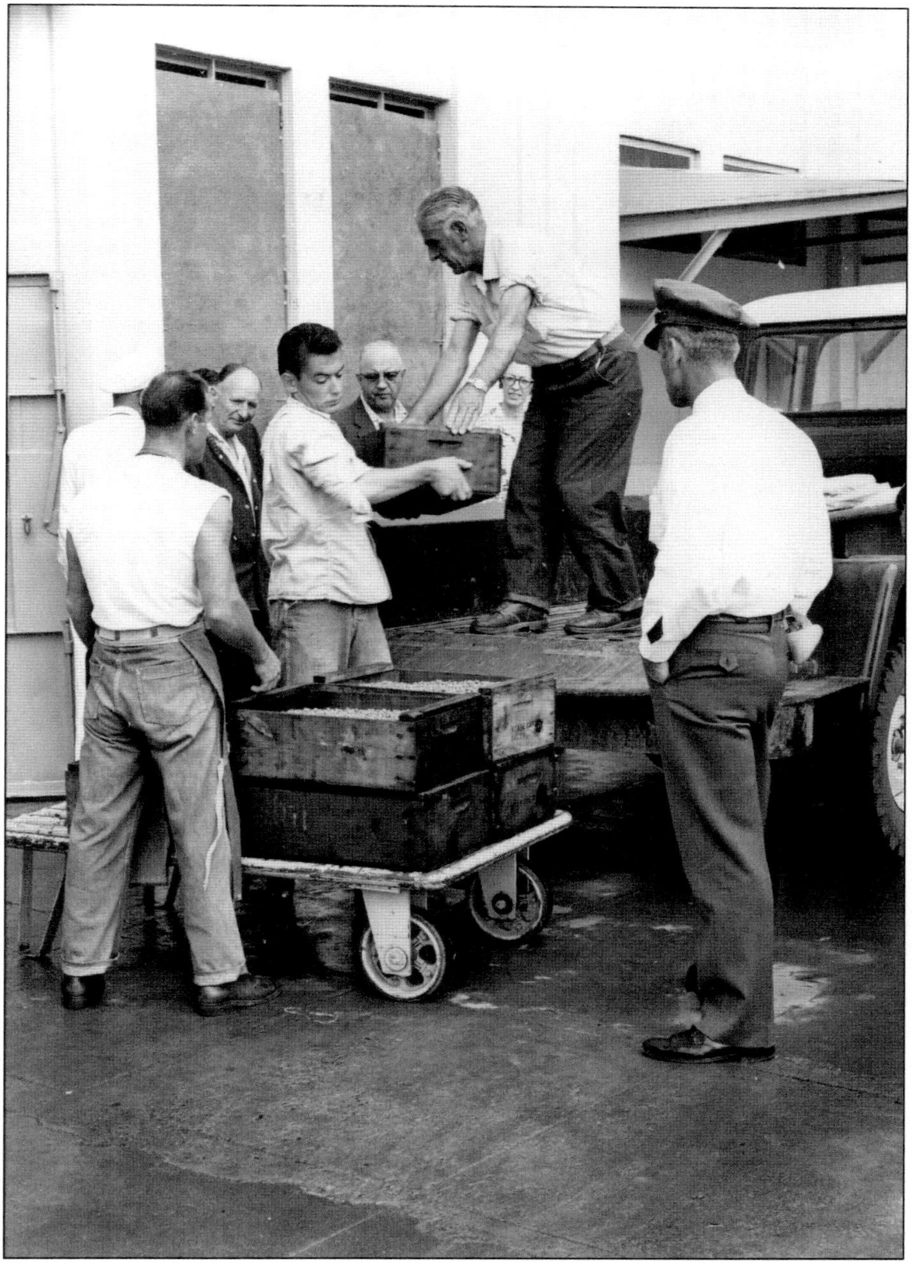

The prison had a fully functioning cannery from 1916 until the late 1960s and employed hundreds of inmates. Local produce was trucked into the prison from the Salem area and farms as far away as Eugene. The inmates sorted, washed, chopped, and canned all sorts of valley produce under the "Prison Packed" label. The vegetables were then packed into regular-, large-, and jumbo-sized cans and sent to the steam cookers, after which they were sealed and labeled. During the Great Depression, the canned food often supplied several soup kitchens in downtown Salem and was brought to state facilities, local schools, and food banks. The Army even requisitioned hundreds of tons of Prison Packed food for its base at Camp Adair, Oregon, outside of Corvallis. It was a source of pride for the inmates to know that the food they prepared fed children and handicapped people in the state's institutions and Army soldiers at the base getting ready to enter World War II.

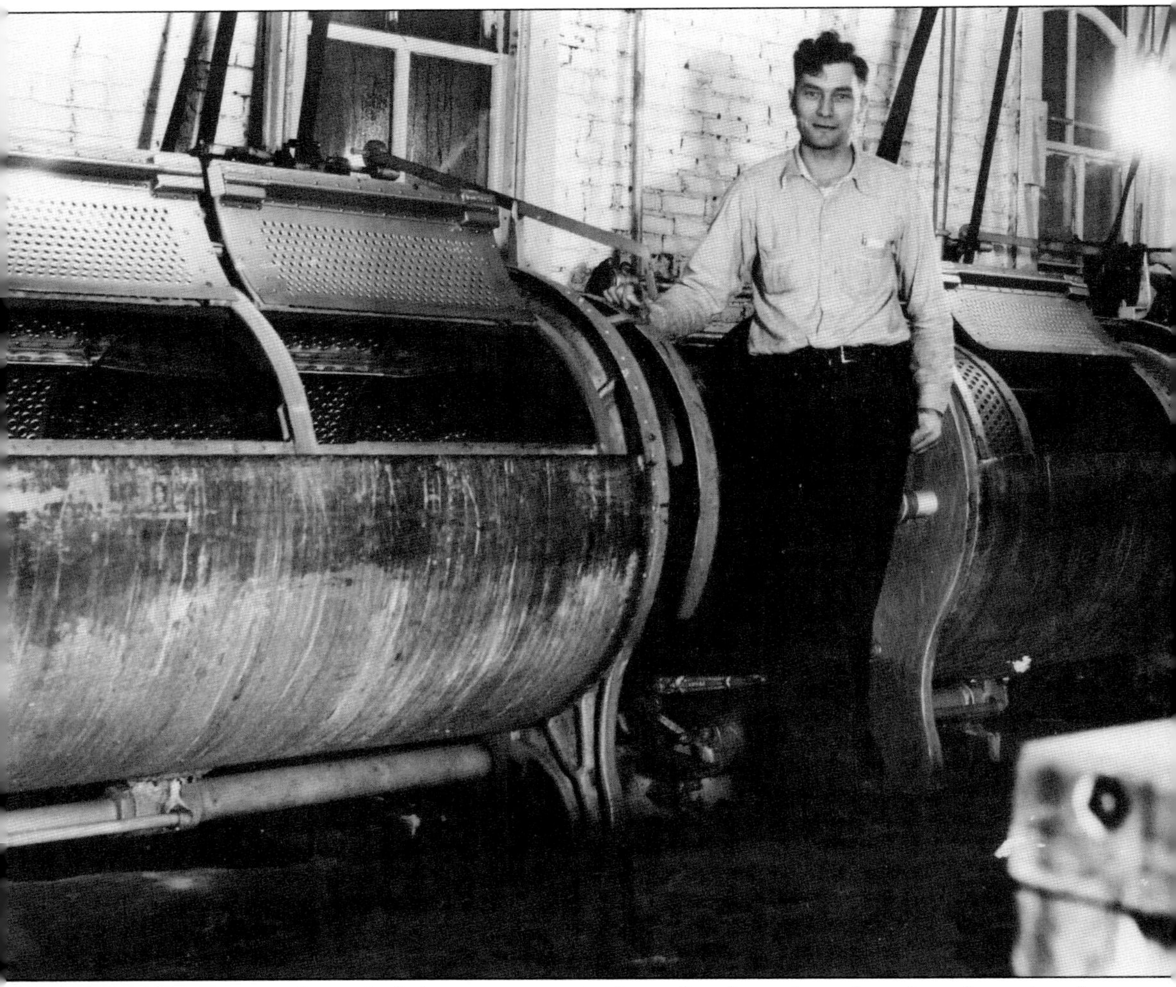

In 1929, prison jobs included assignments in the tailor shop, shoe shop, laundry, print shop, commissary department, culinary department, farm operations, and lime department, as well as work in the officers' quarters. On February 26, 1926, the lime plant was moved from Gold Hill to the penitentiary. As a state-owned operation, it provided lime to farmers at minimal cost. Farmers paid $4 a ton instead of $5. A new laundry was built at OSP in 1952 at a cost of $44,000. The prison laundry facility began processing the state hospital's laundry five years later. The 125 convicts worked two eight-hour shifts to process 100,000 pounds a month. By 1958, it was cleaning 450,000 pounds of dry wash a month, 75 percent of which was for the state mental hospital. The dry-cleaning shop was turned over to the Industries Program.

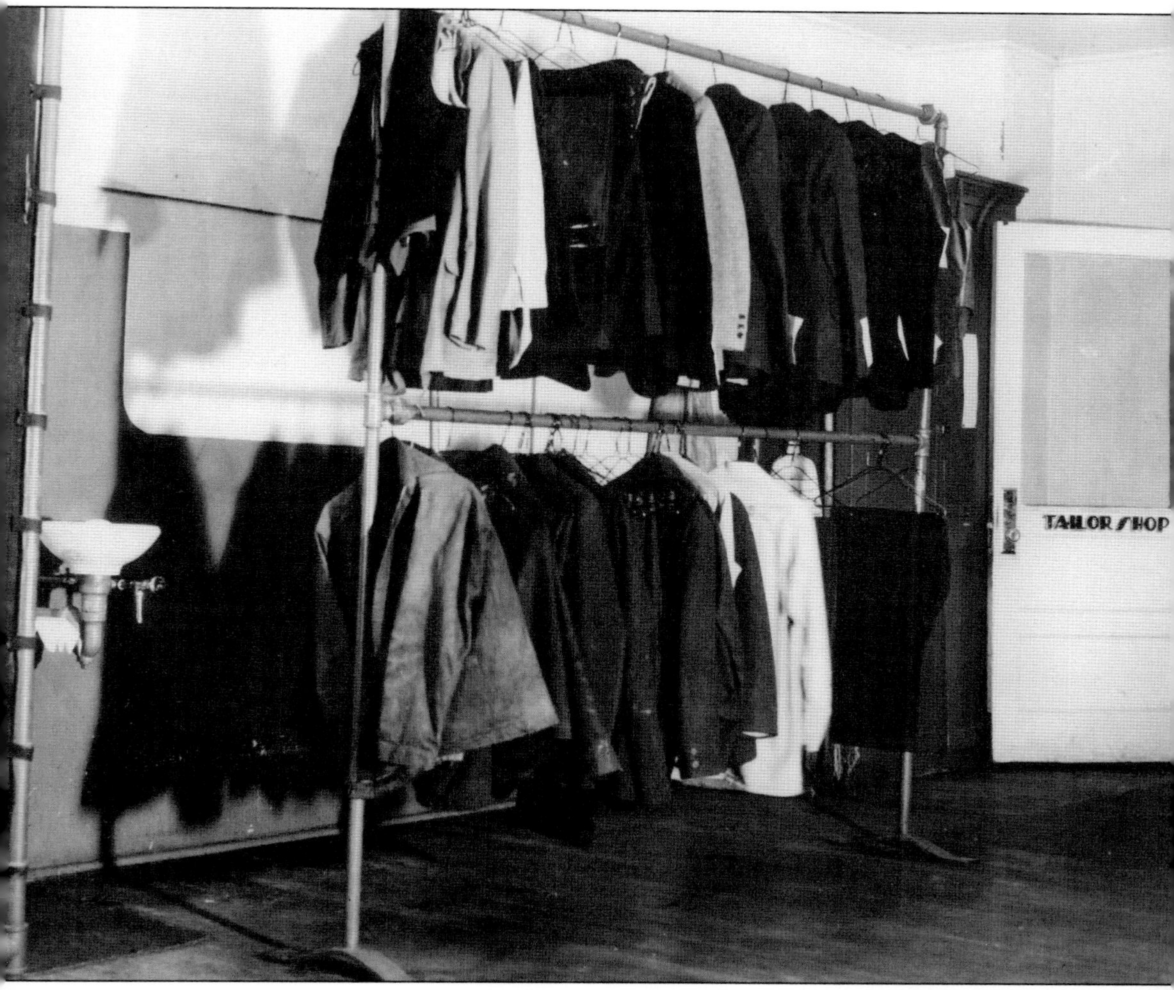

This photograph shows a variety of clothing provided to inmates when they left OSP. Between 1909 and 1910, the tailor shop used 244 yards of cadet gray suiting for prisoners' clothing. In 1956, the shop employed 25 inmates and produced 31,787 items of clothing such as shirts, blue jeans, and jackets. It made denim uniforms for the men in the prison and other state institutions. In 1958, the shop began making bib-type overalls, khaki shirts, and trousers. In addition, the shop made laundry bags, linen hampers, scuffs, oven mitts, warning flags, and mattress covers.

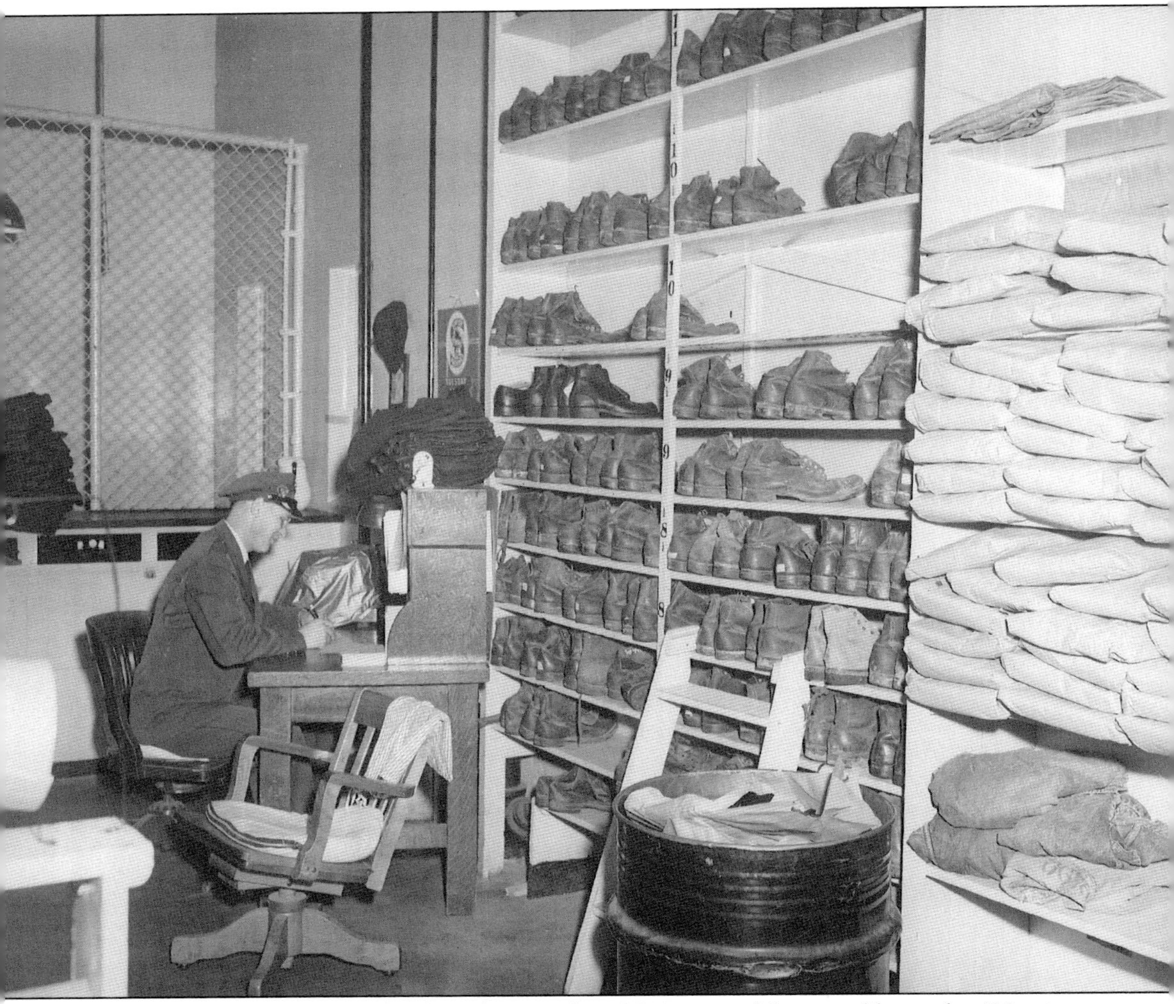

Between 1909 and 1910, the shoe shop produced 311 pairs of shoes and boots for 420 prisoners. The 1911 biennial report was extremely detailed and itemized such items as thread, snaps, eyelets, and tacks used during the past two years. The shop used 2,330 pounds of leather soles for repairs. After the Oregon State Correctional Institution was opened in 1959, demand for shoe repairs increased. After 1958, the shop provided many specialty items, including restraining equipment, gun cases, tree-planting bass, and other canvas and leather items. In addition, the manufacturing and repairing of briefcases were added to the work done in the shoe shop. By 1960, the shop was also repairing all kinds of athletic equipment. The shop was transferred to the Oregon Correctional Institution in November 1961. (Courtesy of OSA.)

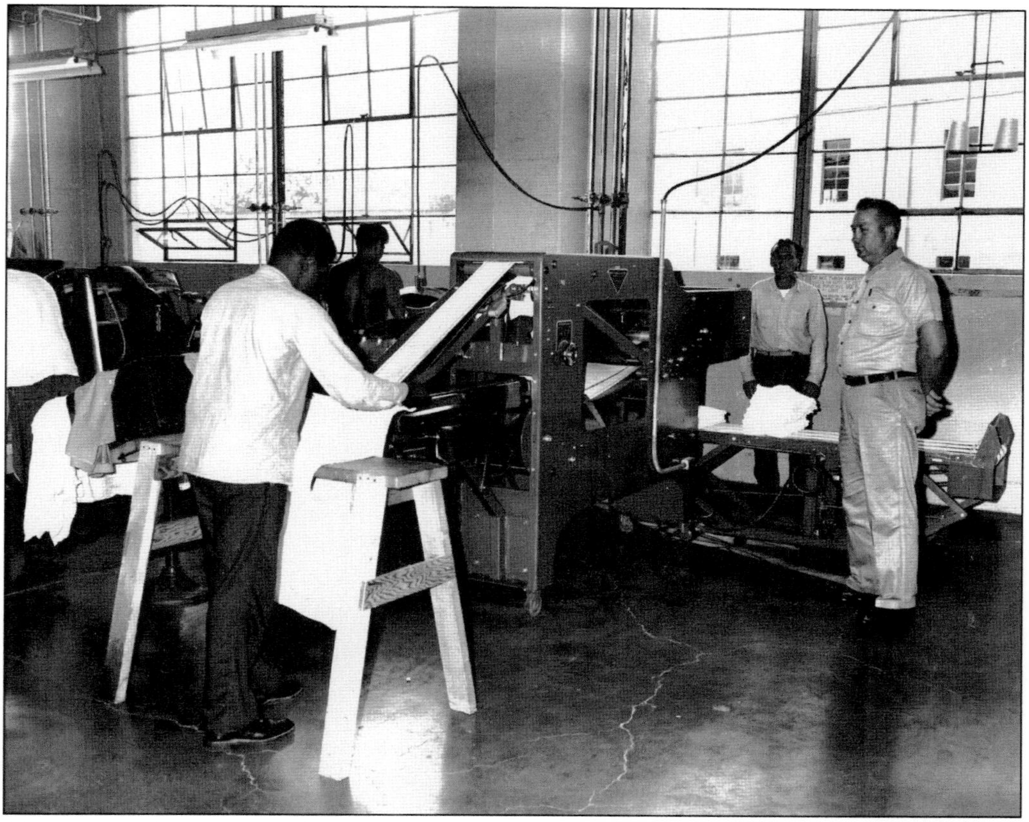

The men in this photograph are working in the laundry, ironing clothing and other articles worn and used at the mental hospital and the prison. A corrections officer watches intently, and another inmate prepares to fold the articles coming out of the machine. The sign on the wall states, "Do not throw cigarette butts or matches out the windows—use butt cans—If you follow this all windows will be shut."

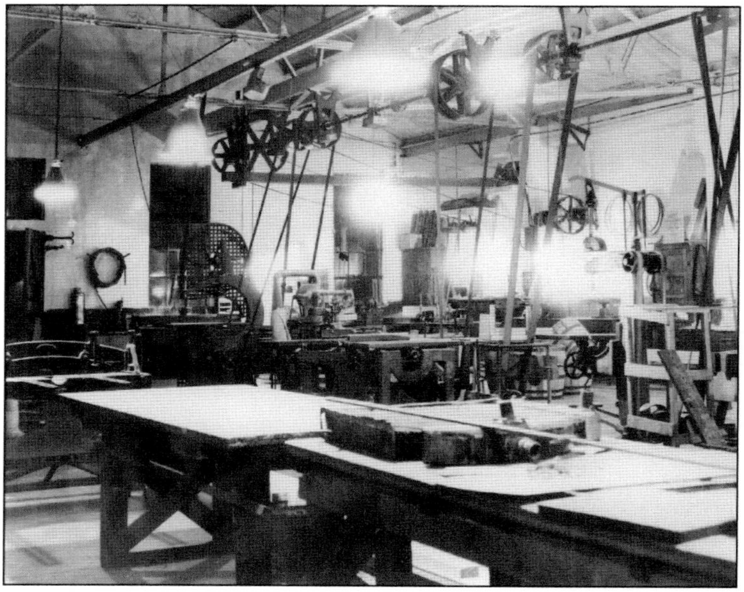

The prison machine shop repaired everything mechanical in the prison. It was a "working city," and machinists needed to fix engines, steam joints, food cauldrons, light fixtures, and 100-year-old plumbing and electrical fixtures. Civilian master machinists, electricians, and plumbers were hired to direct the inmate crews.

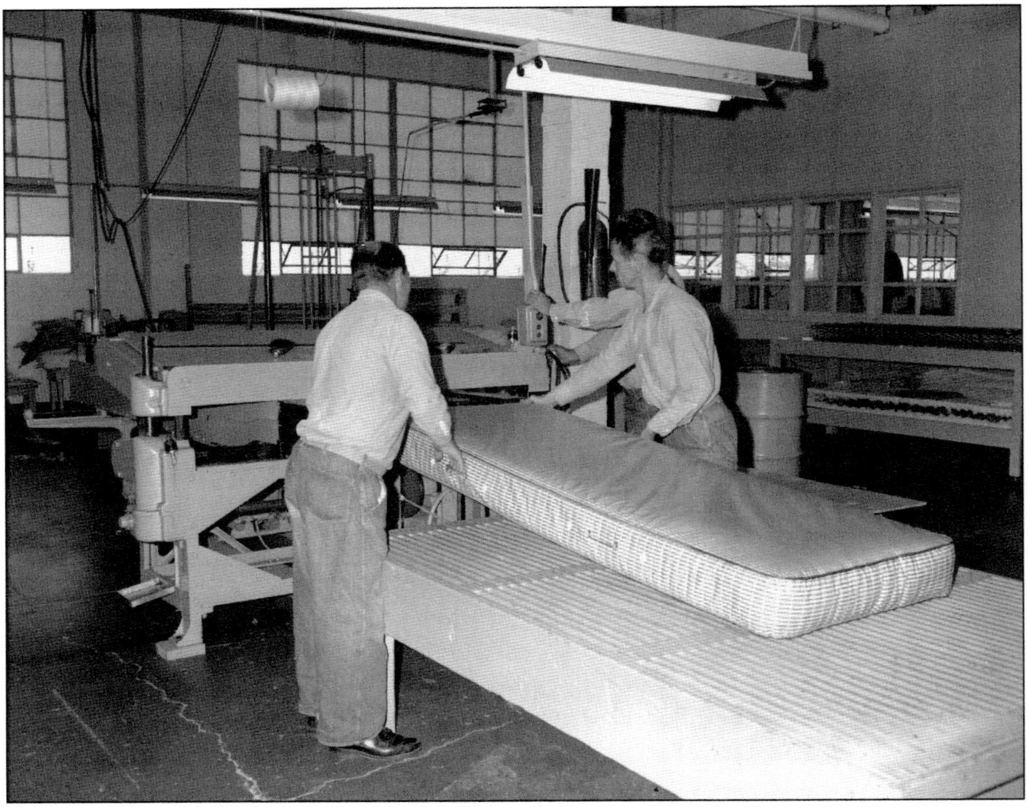

The first mattress factory was established in 1953, after the flax industry was closed. It manufactured and renovated both innerspring and cotton felt mattresses. The prison stopped making mattresses in 1958. The 1967 furniture factory employed 100 men, producing fancy chrome and Naugahyde–covered government furniture. About 400 men were employed in printing, sign making, metalworking, and garment making.

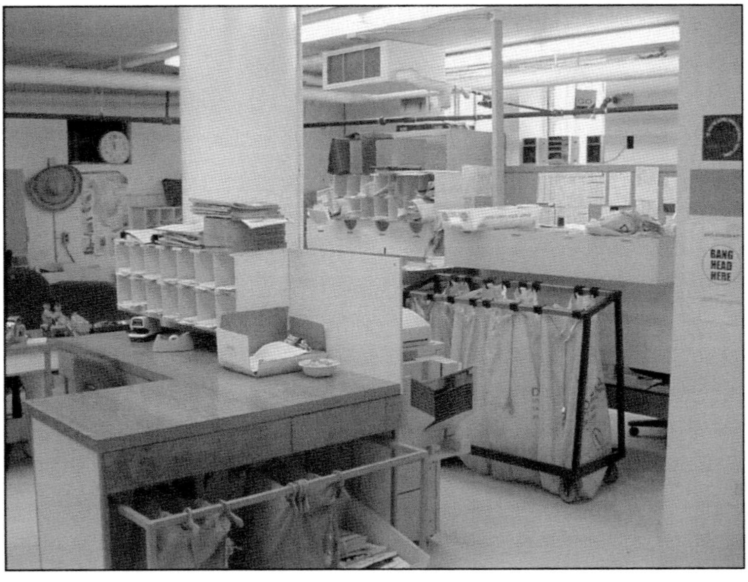

Receiving mail was an important part of every convict's life inside OSP. Even those who were illiterate enjoyed hearing from their loved ones. Between 1930 and 1932, there were 23 men and one woman who were illiterate, as well as 613 men and 27 women who had grade-school educations.

Warden Clarence Gladden increased the number of jobs available to inmates by expanding the furniture factory. In 1958, the furniture factory replaced the flax plant, a mattress plant, a laundry facility, a tailor shop, a sheet metal and machine shop, and a large cannery. As of 1958, convicts could earn between 20¢ and $1 a day, plus get two days of good time credit a month toward release.

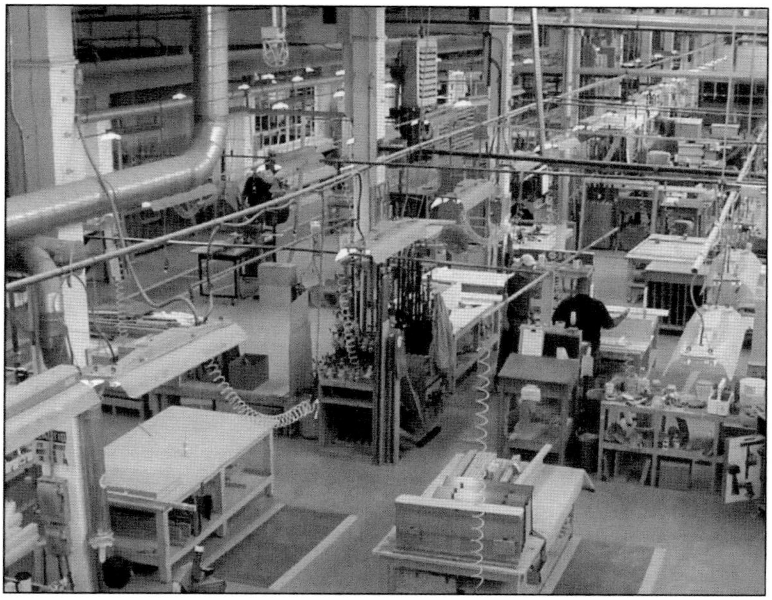

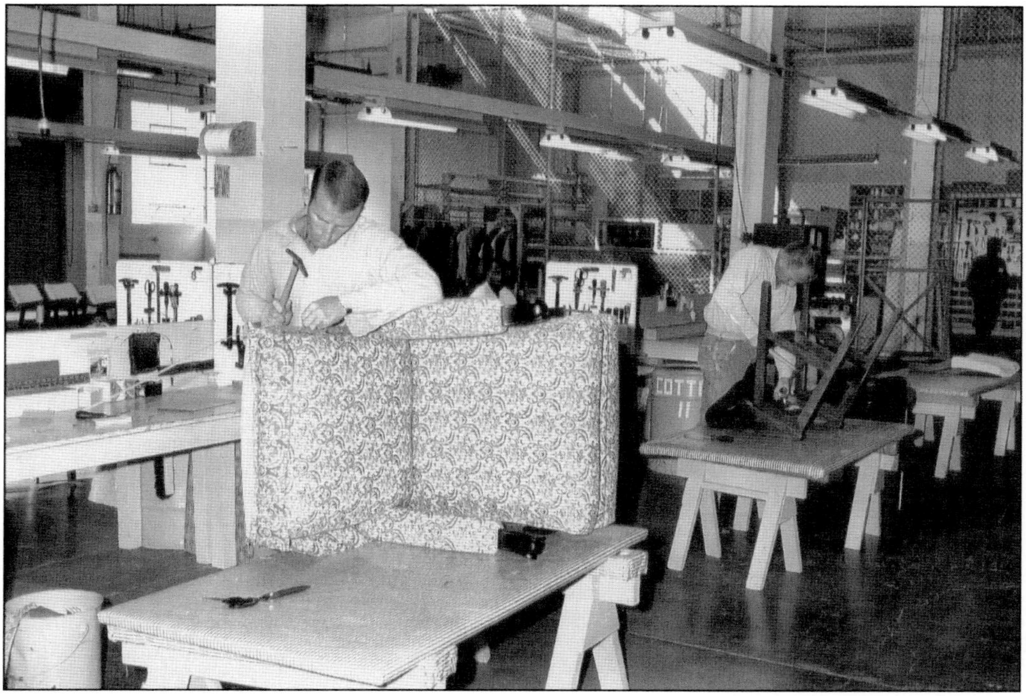

The 1960 furniture factory was equipped to repair, refinish, and upholster all types of office and institutional furniture. It was not meant to produce a great profit but only to pay for itself and to teach 130 inmates a useful trade. Inmates earned 50¢ a day and two days a month meritorious good time off their sentences.

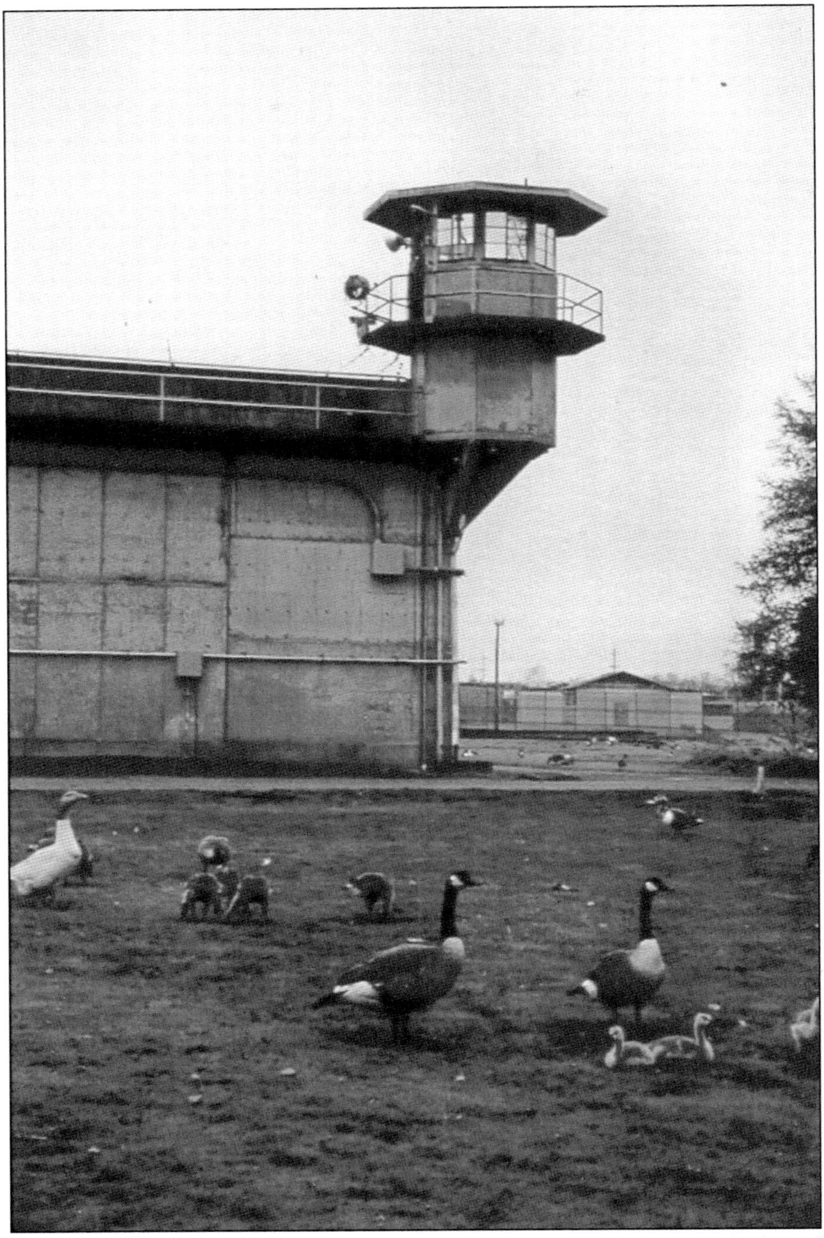

From the outside, the walls surrounding the Oregon State Penitentiary give little indication of the activities going on inside. Until 1930, guards worked every day, including Sundays. At that time, changes were made allowing each employee two days off per month. In 1933, warden J.W. Lewis wrote the prison authorities and suggested that each employee be given at least one day off each week. By the end of 1959, employee salaries were costing the state $11.33 per inmate per month, a large increase from two years earlier, when that figure was only $5.25 per inmate per month. The increase was primarily due to rising salary costs. In 1975, the prison produced davenports, mattresses, chairs, and various kinds of tables for state agencies and institutions. It also made thousands of pallets for the state liquor commission. Over 350 desks a year were built for state offices. In addition, there was an enormous backlog of special orders for a variety of state buildings.

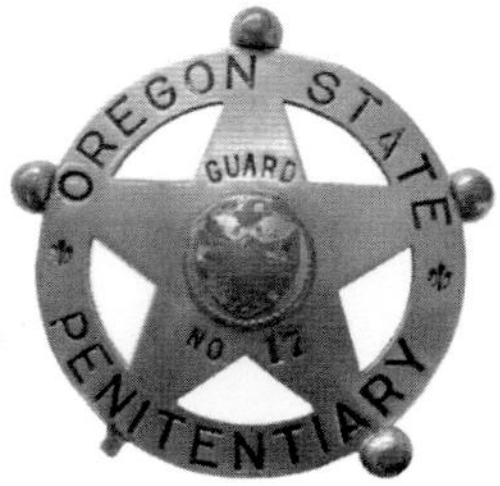

Six

Executions

The Oregon State Penitentiary is the only maximum-security prison in Oregon. Before 1904, county sheriffs were in charge of all executions. For more information on those executions, please see *Necktie Parties: History of Legal Executions in Oregon, 1851–1905*, written by the coauthor of this book, Diane L. Goeres-Gardner. In 1904, the law was changed, requiring that all executions be done in the penitentiary. Between 1904 and 1931, a total of 41 men were hanged in the OSP. Prior to that, all hangings took place in the county where the murder took place.

The youngest man executed was Frank Seymour, age 19, and the oldest was L.W. Peare, age 70. On December 19, 1912, four men were hanged on the same day. Between April 1, 1903, and May 6, 1912, warden C.W. James held 15 hangings in the prison. Warden Berton K. Lawson supervised nine hangings during his tenure, from October 1, 1912, to March 8, 1915. Capital punishment was voted out between 1914 and 1920, and it was again discontinued between 1964 and 1984.

The first 42 executions in the penitentiary were by hanging. In 1938, Oregon installed a modern gas chamber in which 18 men died. Warden George Alexander supervised 17 executions in the gas chamber during his tenure, from December 1938 to April 1953. The last two executions, Douglas Wright, in 1996, and Harry Moore, in 1997, were killed by lethal injection. Between 1904 and 1994, out of the 115 people who have been sentenced to death in Oregon, only 58 have actually been executed. Capital punishment is still legal in Oregon. At the time of this writing, in 2013, there are 22 men waiting on death row in OSP.

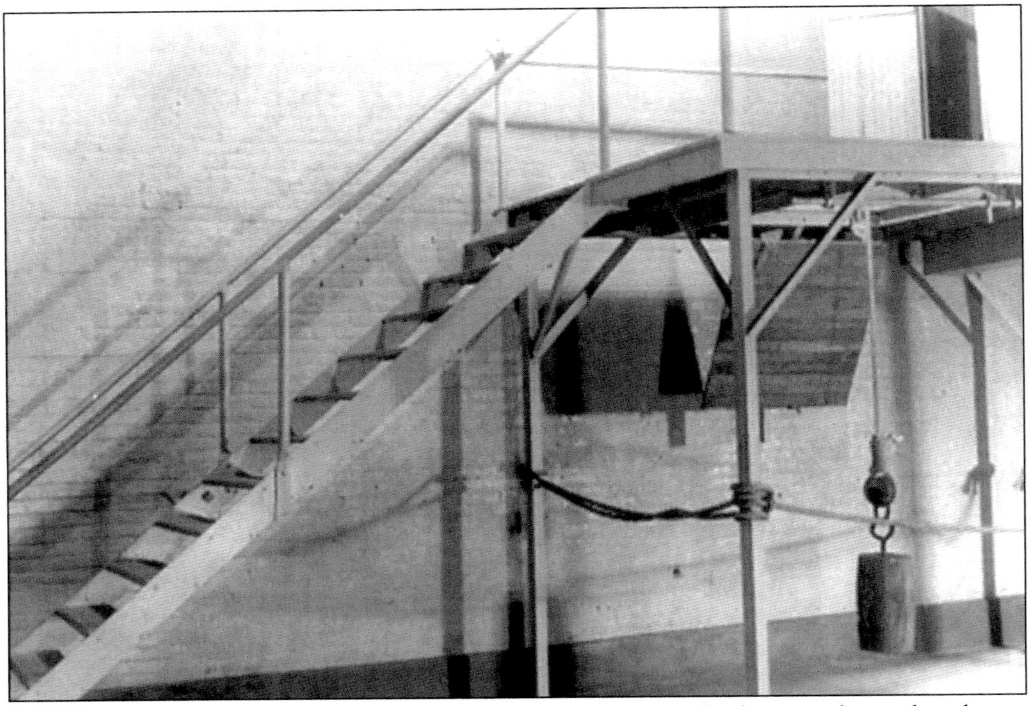

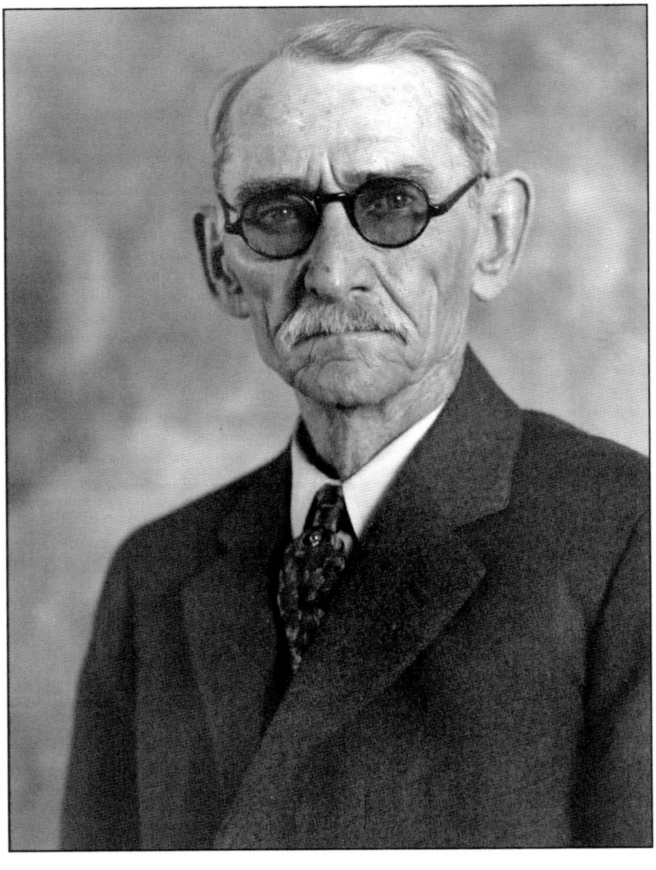

The first man hanged in the Oregon State Penitentiary was Harry Egbert, age 27, on January 29, 1904. Before his execution, he gave his personal guard, Warren Cyrus, a silver ring. Over the next 26 years, another 39 men were hanged. The last was James Kinglsey, age 25, on January 30, 1931. Kingsley went to his death wearing a new suit in front of 75 witnesses. The manila rope had seven turns.

William E. "Daddy" Lamb was the official Oregon hangman for 16 years while serving as a prison guard. During his tenure, he officiated at 14 hangings. After adjusting the black cap and noose, he would wave his hand above the partition and three guards would cut the ropes, releasing the trap. Only the hanging of Isaac Harrell, on September 9, 1910, resulted in cutting the convict's neck. (Courtesy of OSA.)

OREGON STATE PENITENTIARY

SALEM, OREGON

$1,000 REWARD

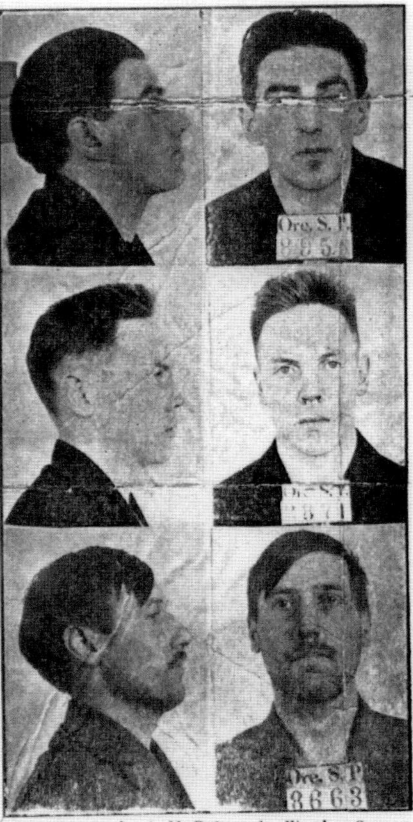

For the arrest, detention and advice of each of the following escapes:

No. 8956 JAMES WILLOS, alias Walter Burns, received April 13, 1924, from Umatilla County for 7 years on a burglary charge. Age, 27; height, 5 ft 4¼ in; weight, 141; complexion, dark; eyes, grey-brown; hair, dark brown; build, short and chunky. Served in San Quentin as Walter Burns, No. 30307. Has tattoo of I on left upper arm. Tattoo of ship, eagle and flag on left forearm; tattoo of anchor back of left hand between thumb and index finger; Tattoo dots back left hand; round shouldered.

PRINTS: 25 IM 17 / 28 I 21

No. 8871 TOM MURRAY, received December 31, 1923, from Lane Co. under two sentences of 10 years each, on charges of larceny and assault with a dangerous weapon. Age, 21; height, 5 ft. 9½ ins.; weight, 157; complexion, light; eyes, slate blue; build, medium; hair, light brown. Served in San Quentin as Joe Johnson, No. 34891. Tattoo of cross on left upper arm; ragged scar inside second joint right middle finger. Is reported to be shot in hand.

PRINTS: 31 IM 18 / 28 OM 19

No. 8663 ELLSWORTH KELLEY, received January 20, 1923, from Josephine Co. for a term of 20 years for aiding prisoners to escape. Age 28; height, 5 ft. 7 in.; weight, 150 lbs.; complexion, medium; eyes, blue; hair, dark brown; build, muscular. Served prior term as No. 7331. Has large V-shaped scar on right forearm.

PRINTS: 1 R II / 1 Rr II 12

Arrest and wire A. M. Dalrymple, Warden Oregon State Penitentiary, Salem, Oregon.

PROCLAMATION

On Wednesday evening, August 12 at about 6 o'clock P. M., four prisoners, namely: Bert Jones, James Willos, Tom Murray and Ellsworth Kelley, escaped from the State Penitentiary at Salem, Oregon, murdering J. M. Holman and John Sweeney, guards, and seriously wounding Lute Savage, guard. Bert Jones, one of the escaping convicts, was killed by John Davidson, a guard.

The murder of these two faithful guards was an atrocious crime, and I feel that every official in the state of Oregon should make every possible effort to effect the capture of these escaped convicts and return them to the Oregon State Penitentiary for punishment as provided by law.

NOW, THEREFORE, I, Walter M. Pierce, Governor of the State of Oregon, by virtue of the authority in me vested, do hereby proclaim that I shall recommend to the next succeeding legislature of the State of Oregon that a reward of $1,000.00 be paid by the State of Oregon to the person or persons instrumental in the apprehension and return of each of said convicts, James Willos, Tom Murray and Ellsworth Kelley, dead or alive.

IN TESTIMONY WHEREOF, I have hereunto set my hand and caused the seal of the State of Oregon to be hereunto affixed this 13th day of August, 1925.

WALTER M. PIERCE,
Governor of Oregon.

On August 12, 1925, four convicts escaped over the roof of the cellblock. They first assaulted a guard and grabbed weapons. Three of the convicts, James Willos, Tom Murray, and Ellsworth Kelley, escaped, killing three guards in the process: J.M. Holman, J.L. Sweeney, and Lute Savage. Bert "Oregon" Jones was killed during the escape by guard John Davidson. The escapees eluded the posse for 10 days until they were captured in Washington. (Courtesy of OSA.)

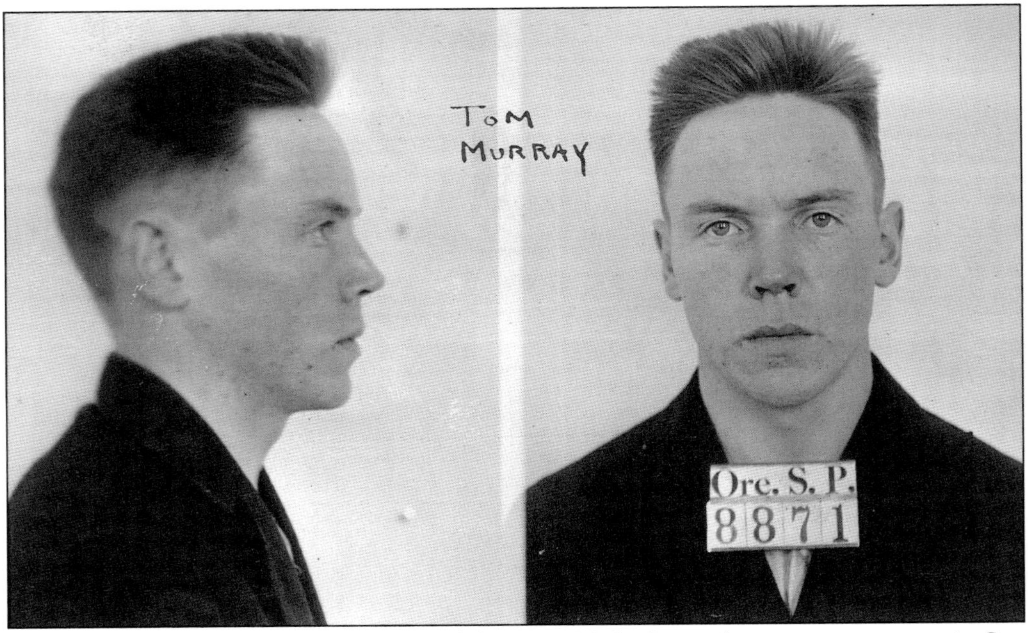

Tom Murray, age 20, was the ringleader of the gang. He had served a previous sentence in San Quentin and was sent to OSP on December 31, 1923. He was reputed to be a crack shot. Murray and Kelly had escaped from OSP before, in March 1924. After being recaptured, Murray was sentenced to hang on December 18; instead, he committed suicide by hanging himself. (Courtesy of OSA.)

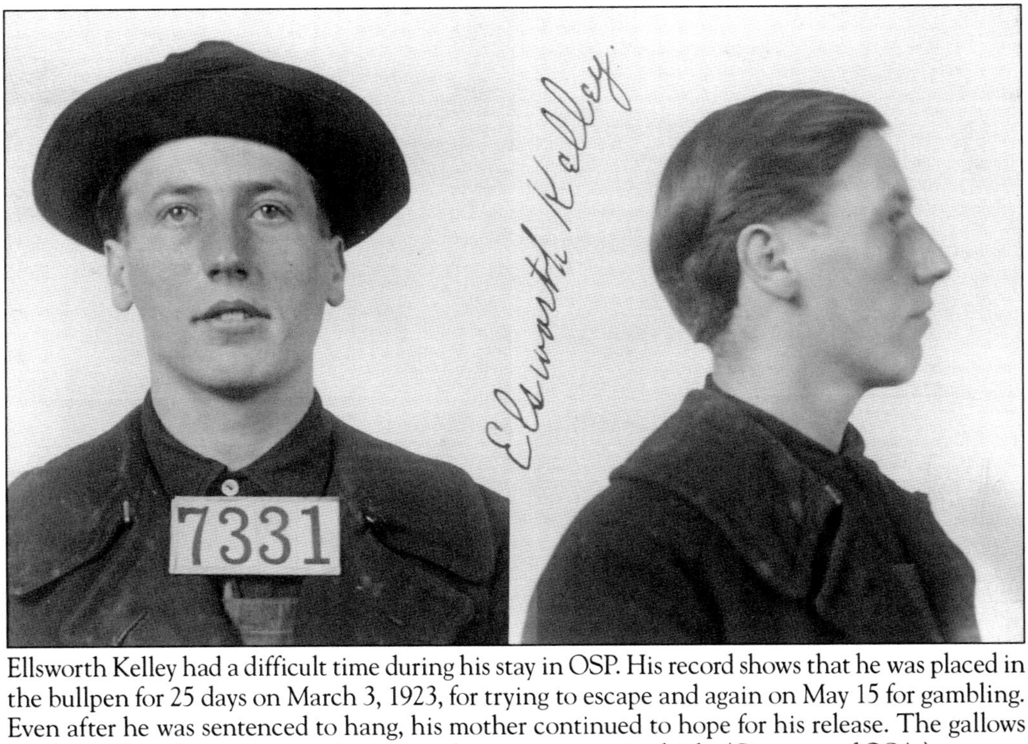

Ellsworth Kelley had a difficult time during his stay in OSP. His record shows that he was placed in the bullpen for 25 days on March 3, 1923, for trying to escape and again on May 15 for gambling. Even after he was sentenced to hang, his mother continued to hope for his release. The gallows was located in the south wing in a room that was two stories high. (Courtesy of OSA.)

OREGON STATE PENITENTIARY
H. W. MEYERS, SUPT. JAS. LEWIS, WARDEN

SALEM, OREGON
AUGUST 4, 1927

MR. I. H. Van Winkle, Attorney General

THIS IS AN INVITATION FOR YOU TO WITNESS
THE EXECUTION ACCORDING TO LAW OF

JAMES WILLOS AND ELLSWORTH KELLEY

FRIDAY, THE 19TH DAY OF AUGUST, 1927

BEGINNING AT 8:30 A. M. IN THE OREGON STATE PENITENTIARY

H. W. Meyers
SUPERINTENDENT

NOT TRANSFERABLE—PRESENT THIS CARD FOR ADMITTANCE

JAMES WILLOS, RECEIVED FROM UMATILLA COUNTY, APRIL 13, 1924, FOR A TERM OF SEVEN YEARS, ON A CHARGE OF BURGLARY.

ELLSWORTH KELLEY, RECEIVED FROM JOSEPHINE COUNTY, JANUARY 20, 1923, FOR A TERM OF 20 YEARS, ON A CHARGE OF AIDING PRISONERS TO ESCAPE FROM LEGAL CONFINEMENT.

WHILE MAKING AN ESCAPE AUGUST 12, 1925, JOHN L. SWEENEY AND J. M. HOLMAN, PRISON GUARDS WERE MURDERED. WILLOS AND KELLEY WERE TRIED AND CONVICTED ON THE SWEENEY CASE. THEY TOOK AN APPEAL TO THE STATE SUPREME COURT, WHICH AFFIRMED FORMER SENTENCE. APPEAL THEN TAKEN TO U. S. SUPREME COURT. CASE BEING DISMISSED FOR WANT OF JURISDICTION. WERE RE-SENTENCED ON JULY 15, 1927, TO BE EXECUTED ON ABOVE DATE.

In a separate trial, Ellsworth Kelley and James Willos were convicted of first-degree murder in the deaths of prison guard John Sweeney and sentenced to hang. The trial took place in October 1925. After an appeal to the Oregon Supreme Court, they were sentenced to hang together on August 19, 1927. After another appeal, the hanging finally took place on April 20, 1928. (Courtesy of OSA.)

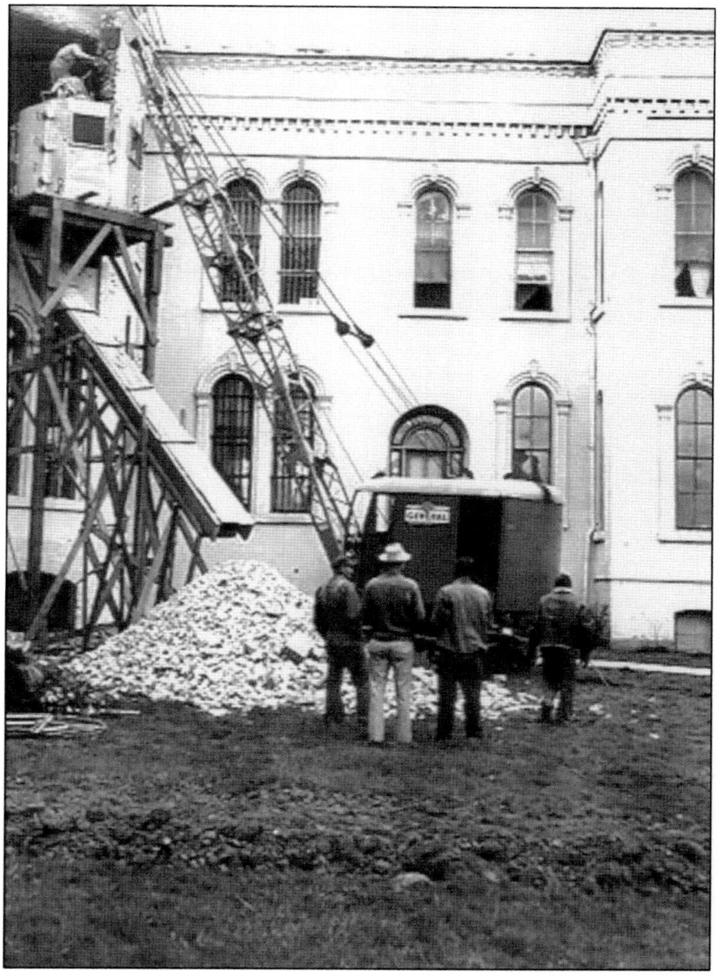

The Oregon Legislature voted to use the gas chamber for executions in 1936. A room was constructed at a cost of $2,000 on the second floor of the main prison building. The chamber was purchased from the Eaton Metal Products Company of Denver for $3,800 and transported by train to the prison in December 1937.

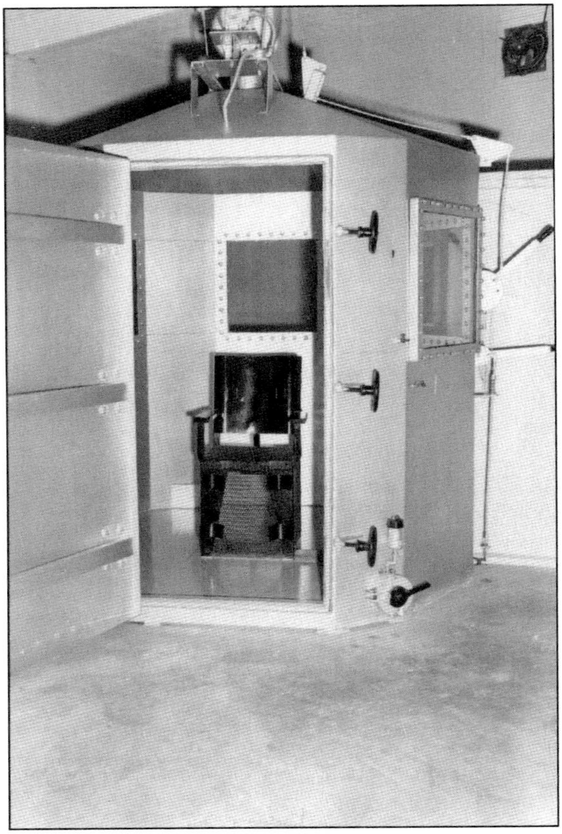

Between June 1939 and August 1962, there were 18 men executed in the gas chamber. The first execution was of Leroy McCarthy on June 20, 1939. The youngest man was John Soto, age 17, on March 20, 1942, and the oldest was William Wallace, age 54, on February 26, 1943. On January 9, 1953, another double execution took place in the chamber.

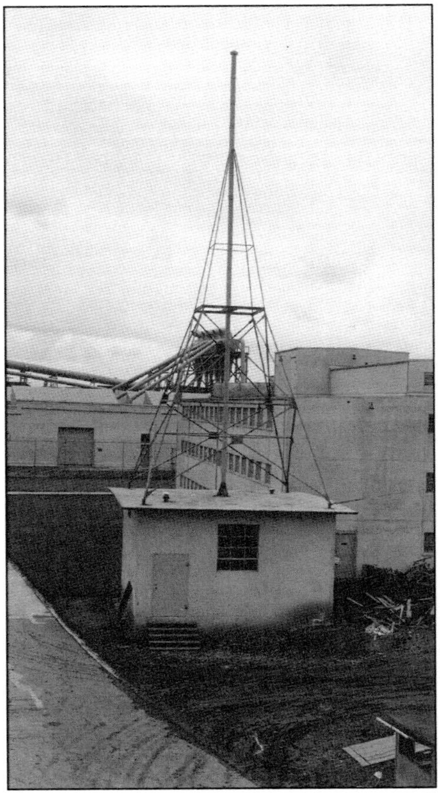

The gas chamber was moved out of the main prison building in 1952. This photograph of the death house was taken in 1968. The tall tower on the small building with one window supported the exhaust from the gas chamber after the execution was finished. It needed to be tall to make sure the fumes blew away. The building only had one door. (Courtesy of OSA.)

OREGON STATE PENITENTIARY
GEO. ALEXANDER, SUPERINTENDENT
V. J. O'MALLEY, WARDEN

SALEM, OREGON
Jan. 2, 1953

MR. ....

THIS IS AN INVITATION FOR YOU TO WITNESS
THE EXECUTION ACCORDING TO LAW OF

Morris Leland and Frank Oliver Payne

FRIDAY, THE 9TH DAY OF JANUARY, 1953
BEGINNING AT 12:15 A. M. IN THE OREGON STATE PENITENTIARY

SUPERINTENDENT

NOT TRANSFERABLE—PRESENT THIS CARD FOR ADMITTANCE

Morris Leland for the murder of Thelma Taylor, 15-year old high school girl at Portland, Ore., Aug. 6th, 1949, and Frank O. Payne for the murder of H. Nathan Butler, Portland grocer, Jan. 9, 1951, in a robbery attempt.

Invitations to executions have been used in Oregon since about 1870, when the first stockades were built to hide the execution. Authorities continued to issue invitations through 1960. This invitation notes the execution of Morris Leland and Frank Payne. Leland was executed one hour before Payne in front of 80 people. A light lunch was served afterward in the guards' quarters.

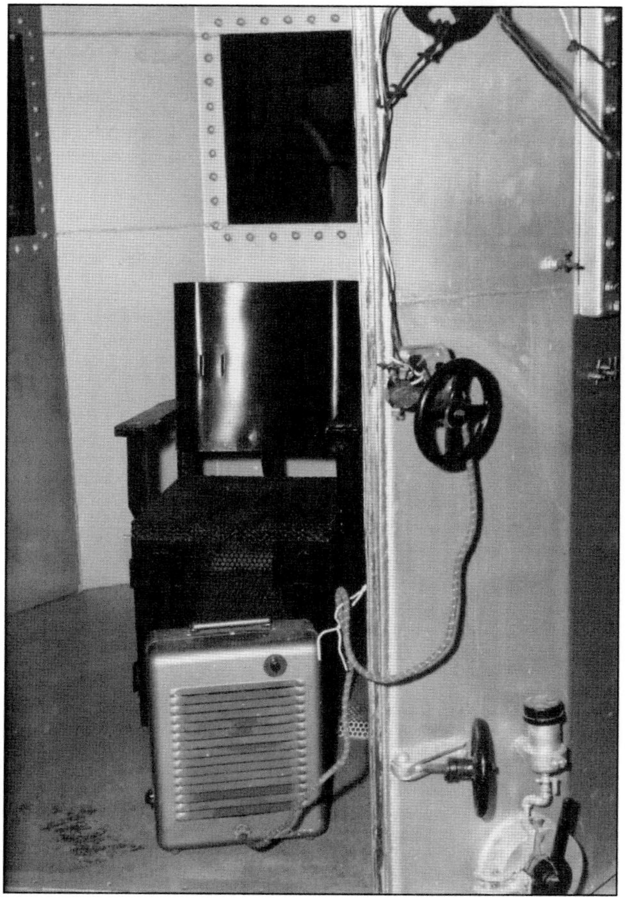

This photograph was taken just before a double execution on January 9, 1953. Frank Payne, age 52, and Morris Leland, age 22, were both executed that day. Because the building was so rarely used and the condemned were lightly attired, warden Virgil O'Malley ordered the chamber to be warmed before the executions. (Courtesy of OSA.)

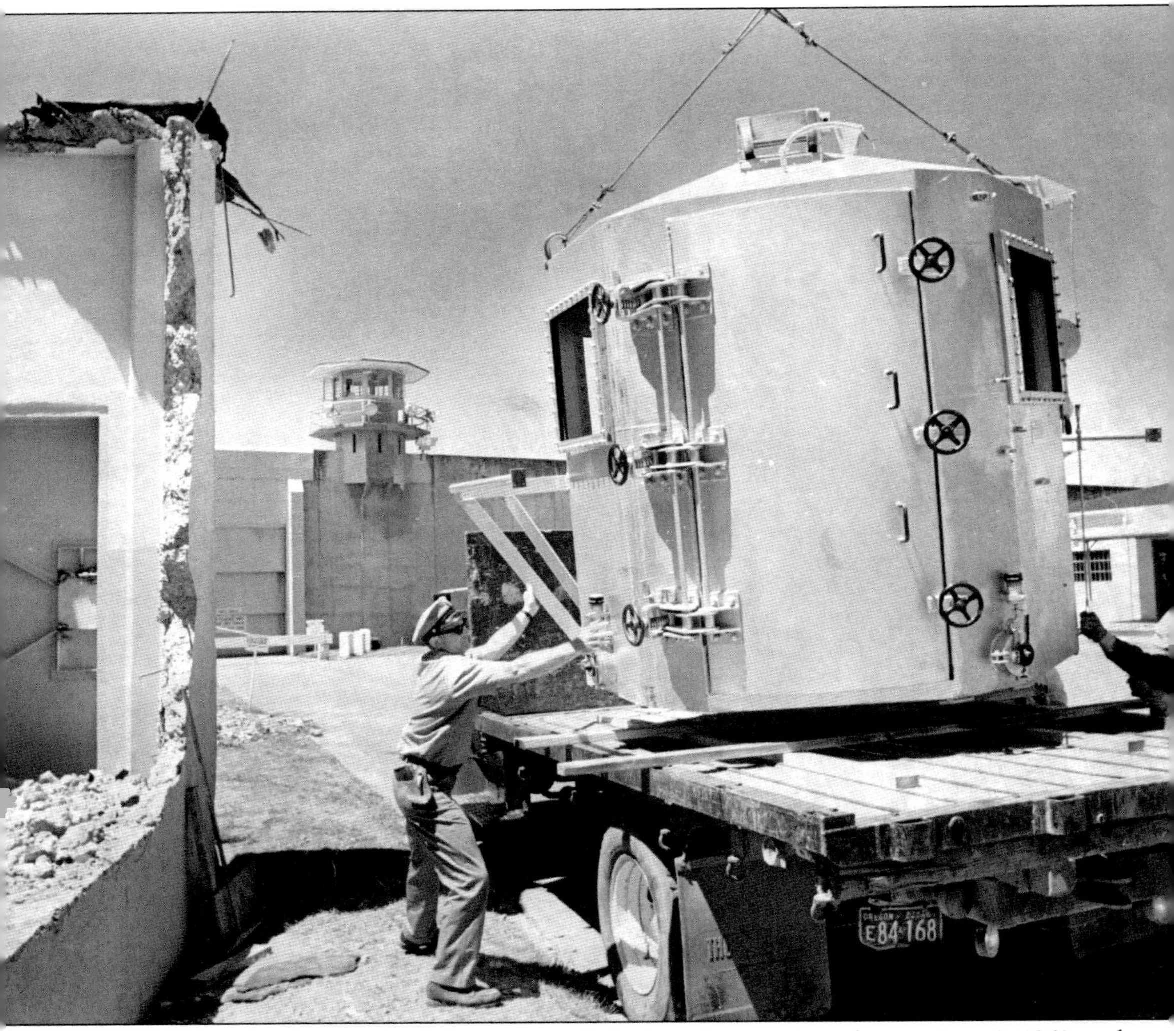

The old gas chamber was hauled away on a flatbed truck to a prison shop on June 2, 1969, and cut up for scrap after the state repealed capital punishment. Space formerly used by the death house was converted into a maximum-security exercise yard. Prison officials refused all requests from outside parties to purchase the chamber. Lethal injection was approved in April 1979 after voters reinstated capital punishment in November 1978. Executions were then done by intravenous injection of ultra-short-acting barbiturates, replacing the gas chamber. This new form of lethal injection has been used twice in Oregon: once on September 6, 1996, and again on May 16, 1997. (Courtesy of SJ.)

Seven

The Many Faces of OSP

Besides prisoners, there were many other people involved in OSP affairs. Occasionally, a prisoner became famous for writing a book, as Bunco Kelly did. The women's section of OSP was rarely mentioned in official prison reports or in newspaper articles. Even though women had been incarcerated at OSP since 1851, when Charity Lamb was convicted of murder, OSP did not hire a matron until 1900. Women were kept in the top two floors of the administration building until 1965, when the first women's prison was built next door to OSP. Originally designed to hold 40 prisoners, it was hastily redrawn to hold twice that number.

Guards and other employees were necessary and important to efficient penitentiary operations. After 1968, they were called corrections officers instead of prison guards, highlighting the new emphasis placed on rehabilitation, vocational training, and education. Guards wore their own clothing to work for the first 50 years of OSP operations, until 1925. Over the next 80 years, uniforms changed to accommodate fashion, usefulness, and necessity.

Training for employees became a required component of every job at the prison. The purpose of the prison was first to incarcerate the men convicted of breaking the law and second to provide some meaningful and productive activities leading to rehabilitation. This required a variety of people, including corrections officers, counselors, chaplains, and teachers. This chapter illustrates the variety of inmates and staff that have lived and worked inside OSP.

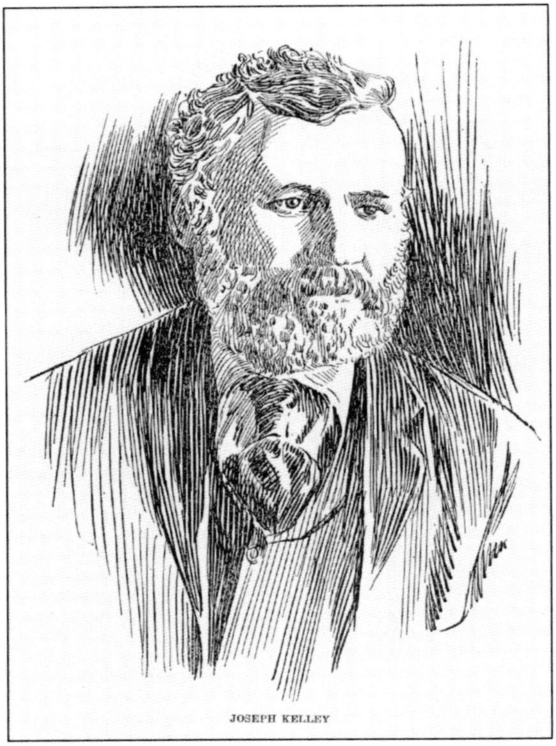

Joseph "Bunco" Kelly was a famous inmate at OSP. He was convicted of second-degree murder in September 1894. His major occupation at that time was shanghaiing men for the sailing ships that stopped in Portland on their way to the Orient. He was pardoned on July 21, 1907. After his release, he wrote and published a book, *Thirteen Years in the Oregon State Penitentiary*. (Courtesy of OSL.)

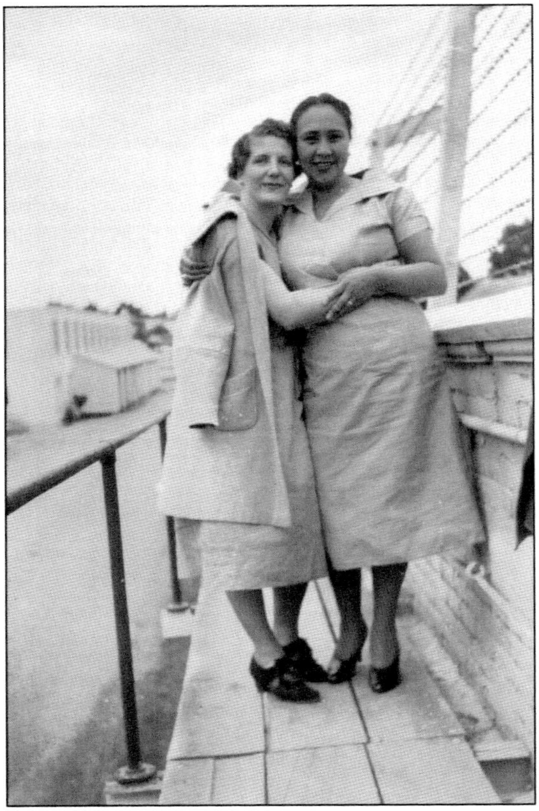

Prior to 1900, there was no matron employed to supervise the female prisoners, who were kept in solitary confinement. After 1900, women were housed in a large room with light and heat during the day and in single cells at night. In 1930, the women's quarters were moved from the second floor of the chapel, with compartments made of wooden partitions, to rooms on the second floor of the new administration building. (Courtesy of OSA.)

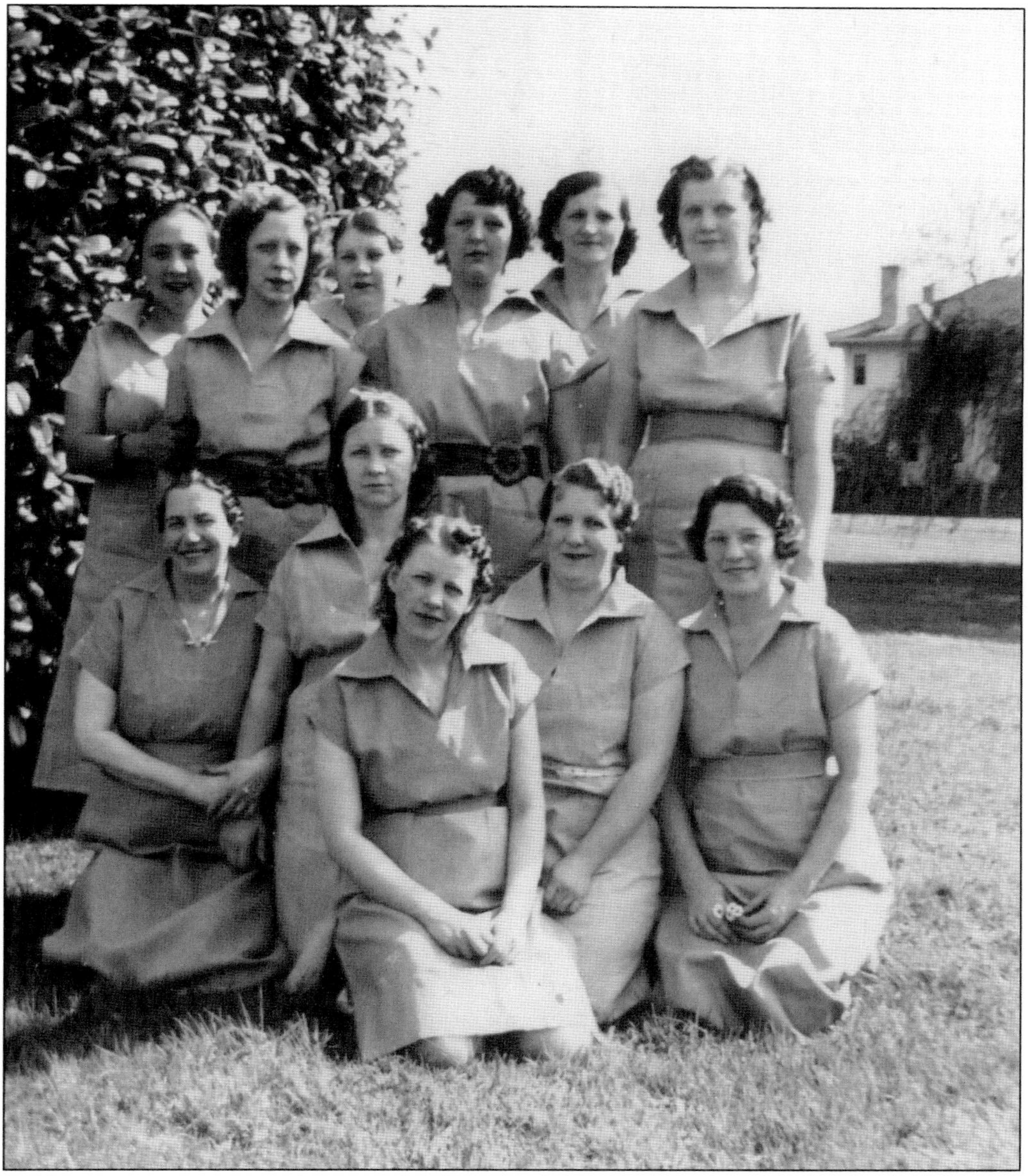

In 1930, a new four-story administration building was erected, with the second and third floors allocated for women prisoners. The reinforced-concrete building was 40 feet by 100 feet and cost about $40,000 to build using prison labor. The deputy warden and his wife, who became the matron, lived on the second floor. It also held the women's work area, dining room, kitchen, and laundry. The third floor held the assistant matron's quarters and the sleeping rooms for the women, with separate baths and a surgery. The 1930 biennial report itemized the 27 females separately from the 884 males. Of the 27 women, 14 were under age 30. Two were African American, one was Native American, and 24 were white. Nine were housewives, seven were waitresses, and four were factory workers. The prison's female population continued to increase until a women's prison was built in 1965. (Courtesy of OSA.)

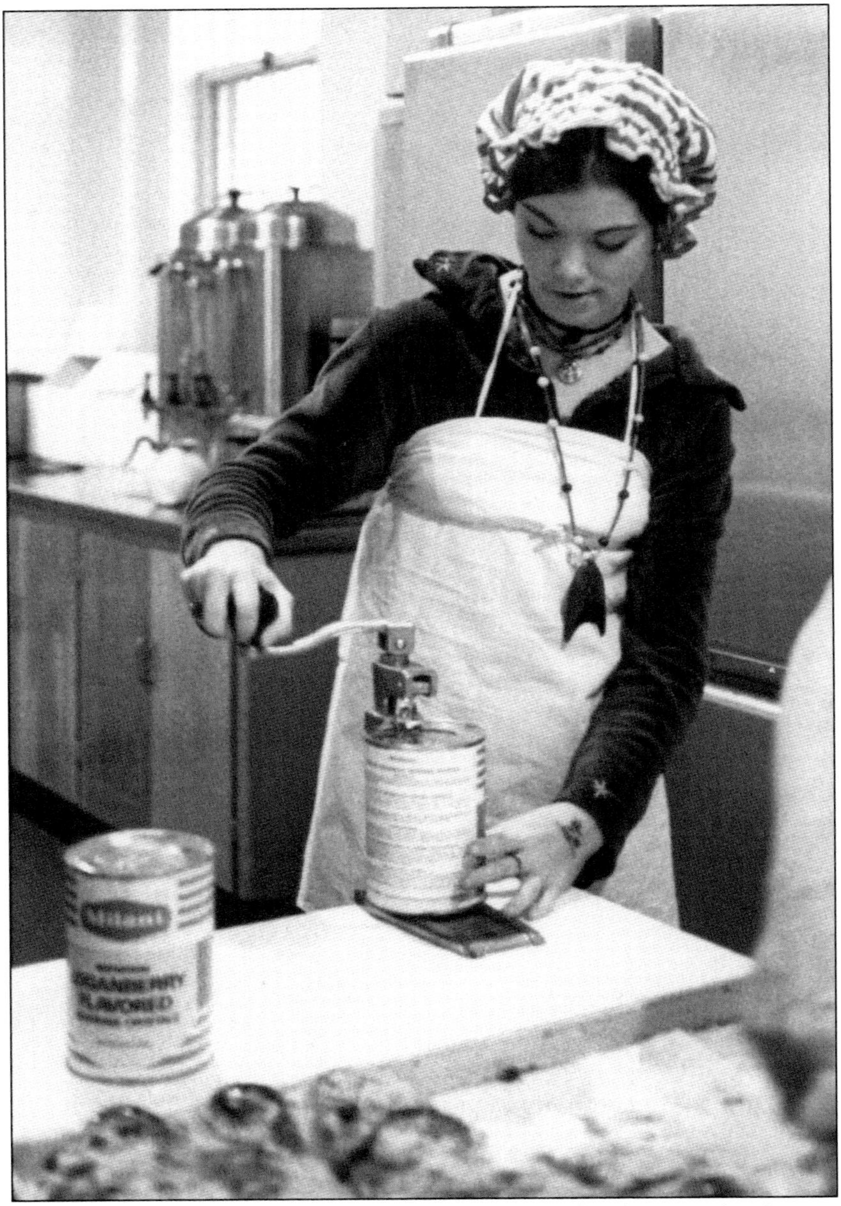

The first matron, hired in 1900, received $30 a month. Typically, she was related to some prison official. Mrs. James, the matron in 1905, was the warden's daughter. That year, Frankie Woolridge, a black woman, was segregated from white prisoners. The six women incarcerated in 1914 worked for the state library, cataloging 4,000 volumes of books. The women embossed, stamped, and cut the pages of the books and pasted the pockets for cards in the back. In 1929, OSP stopped housing federal women convicts and lost the $40 a month the government paid for each prisoner. These women were now sent to Alderson, West Virginia, to a Federal Industrial Institution for Women. The 19 females incarcerated in 1929 were allowed to write one letter a week. By 1948, there were 28 women incarcerated in the prison. One or two women trusties cooked meals for the OSP staff under close supervision. Female trusties were also assigned to housecleaning duties for the superintendent and warden. This girl worked in the guards' kitchen preparing food. (Courtesy of OSA.)

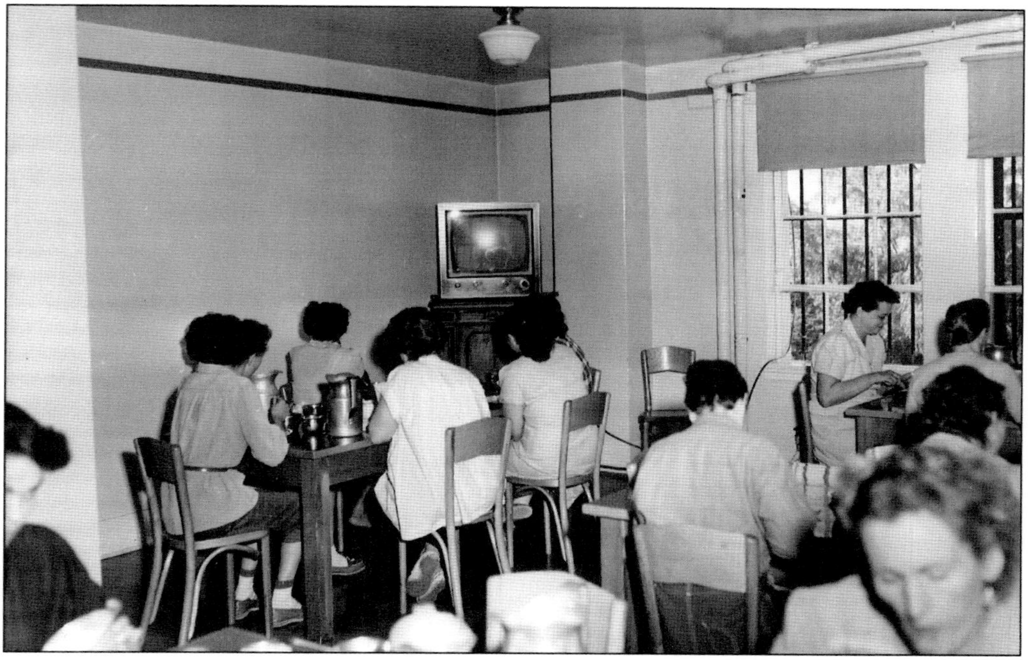

The women's quarters were capable of holding 40 inmates, and by 1954 there were 28 women incarcerated in OSP. All had work assignments except when they were ill. About half of the women translated books into Braille. Recreation included television and radio in this small recreation room. Classes in practical nursing were popular, as they allowed participants to work in the state hospital. (Courtesy of OSA.)

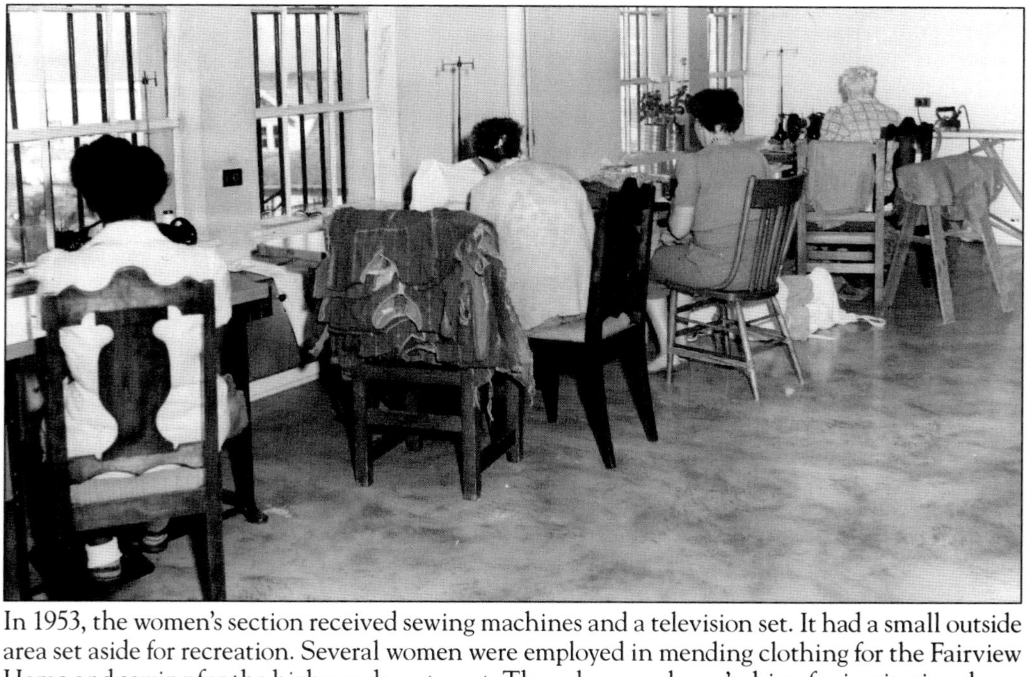

In 1953, the women's section received sewing machines and a television set. It had a small outside area set aside for recreation. Several women were employed in mending clothing for the Fairview Home and sewing for the highway department. They also sewed men's shirts for institutional use. Nine were enrolled in correspondence courses, and 21 were enrolled in basic education courses. (Courtesy of OSA.)

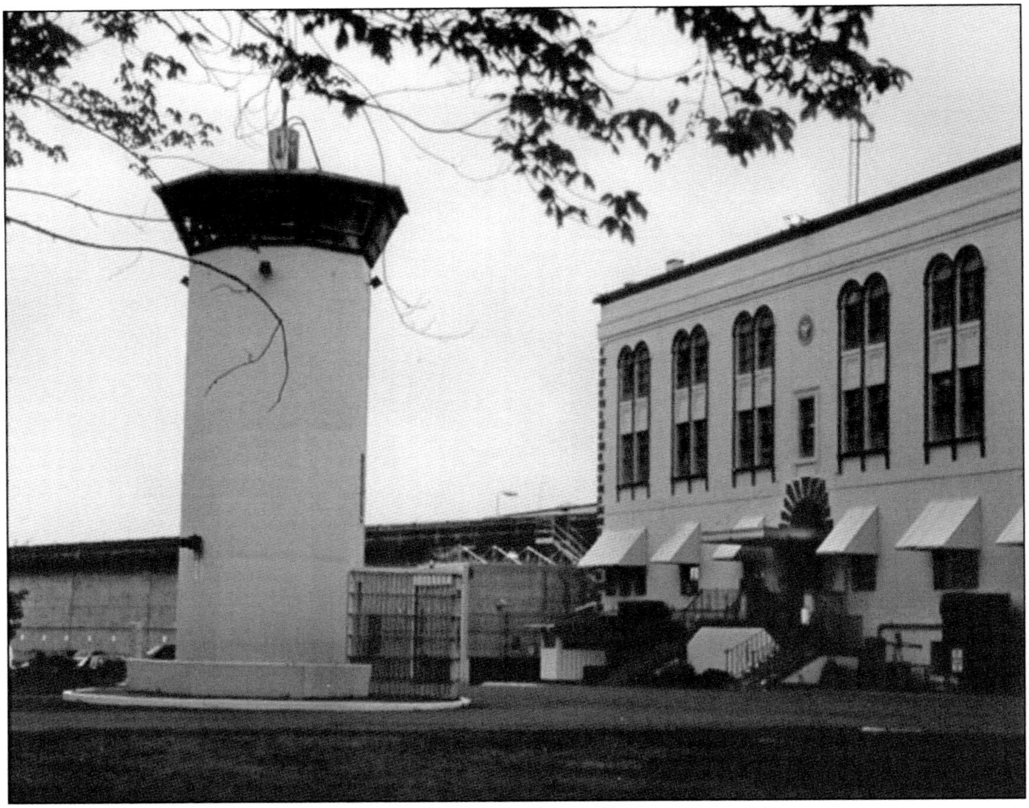

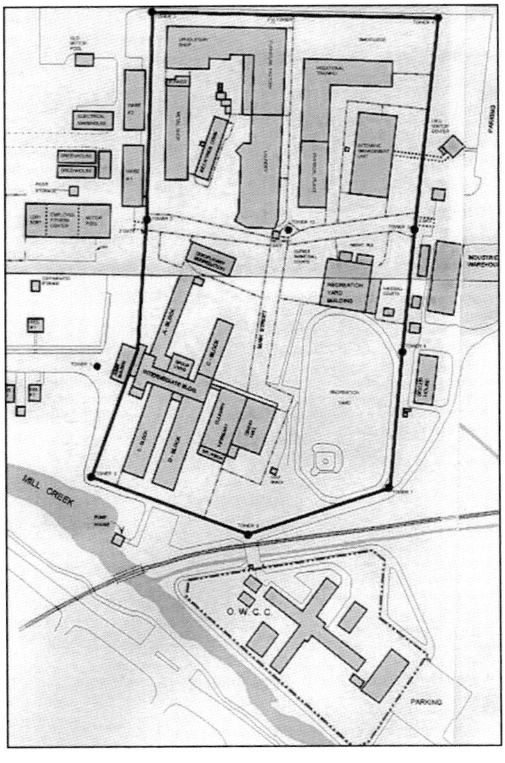

By 1958, there were 38 women prisoners who were housed in the top two floors of the administration building. The circular building in front was the prison arsenal and designated as tower no. 1. Outside contractors built it in 1954 to hold the prison's guns and riot gear. The flagpole was erected in 2001.

This architectural drawing shows the new Oregon Women's Correctional Center (in the lower-right corner) in relationship to the Oregon State Penitentiary. A 12-foot-high fence topped with rolling concertina wire surrounded the building. This facility housed up to 193 inmates until 2001, when all women were transferred to the Coffee Creek Correctional Facility.

Paul F. Bobou was a guard at OSP in 1910. Guards worked 12 hours a day and had target practice every Thursday. They wore their own clothes until 1925, when distinctive uniforms were designed and manufactured in the prison so they could be more easily distinguished from prisoners. In 1878, guards received $50 a month and were given room and board. By 1940, probationary guards received only $90 a month. (Courtesy of OSA.)

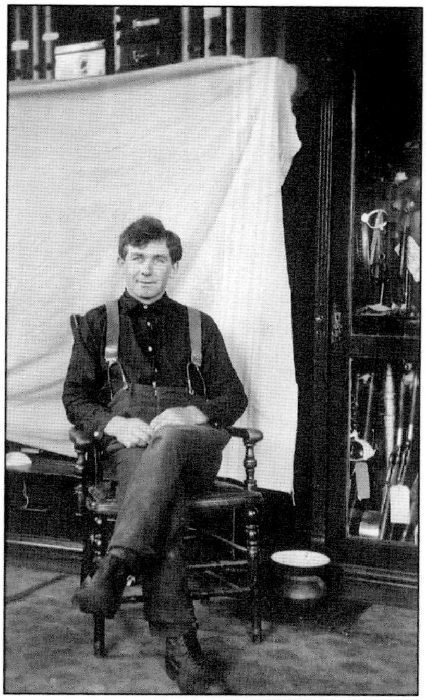

In 1904, the basement of the administration building was refurbished as a dining room and washroom for the guards. It was eventually enlarged to include a gathering place to muster the guards before each shift. The guards' work hours were reduced to eight hours a day in 1907.

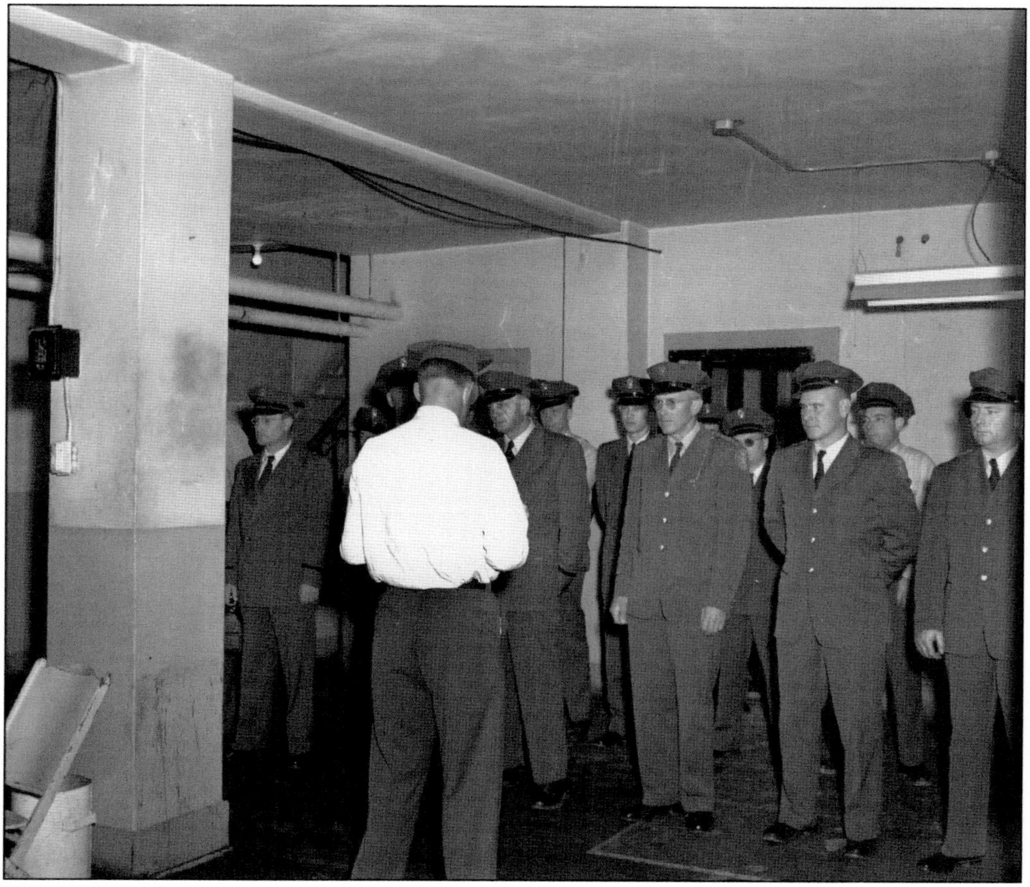

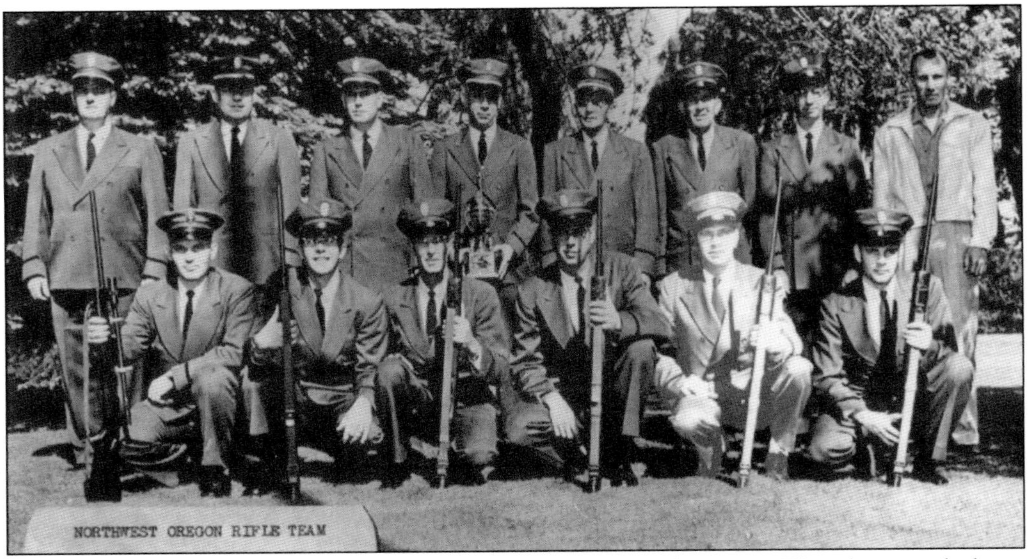

Weapons training was a large part of the correction officers' work routine. This photograph shows the 1961–1962 prison rifle team. Officers assigned to the towers on the wall were required to qualify every month with firearms. Officers assigned inside had to pass strict judo tests every 90 days or forfeit their pay raise. The prison team competed at local competitions and won many trophies.

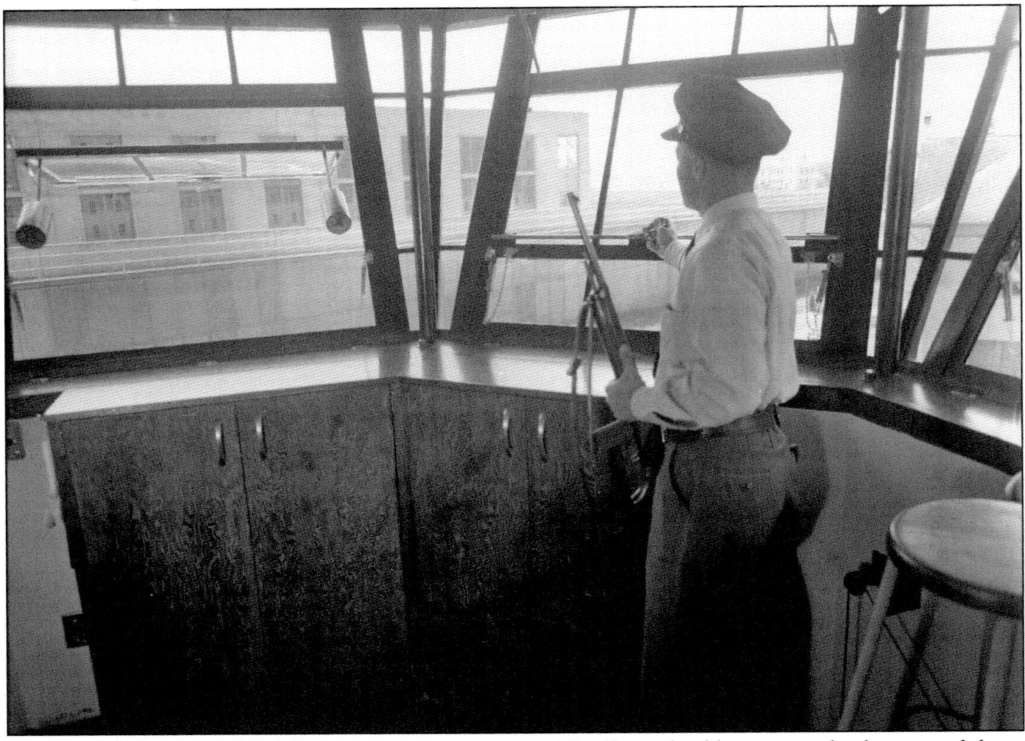

In 1952, while Virgil O'Malley was superintendent, 25 officers had been assaulted, some of them several times. This situation resulted in a 91 percent turnover in staff. This photograph, taken about 1960, shows a guard in the control tower looking toward the prison wall. The first female corrections officer, Debra Martin Dawes, was hired while Hoyt Cupp was warden. She later became a corrections department counselor.

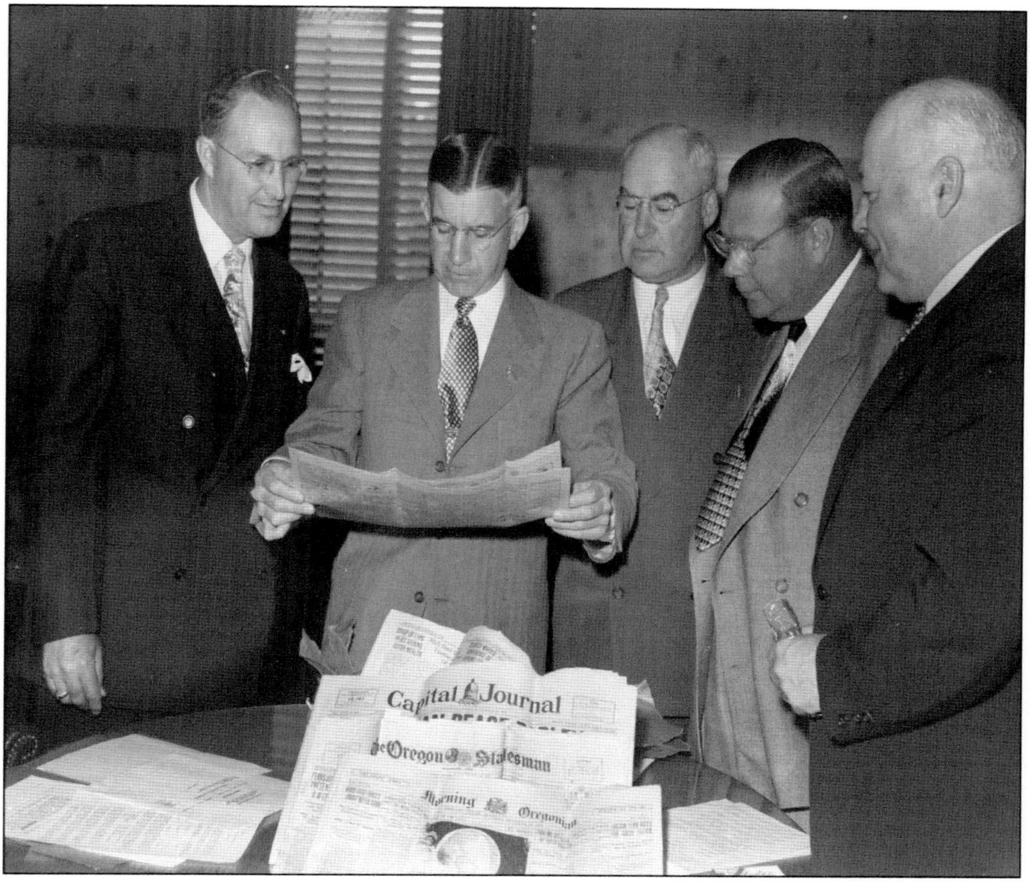

This cornerstone was laid in the walls of OSP on August 24, 1871. Gov. La Fayette Grover gave a speech at the celebration. It was opened on July 11, 1950. The officials pictured here are, from left to right, Earl Newbry, secretary of state; Douglas McKay, governor of Oregon; George Alexander, warden of the penitentiary; Walter Pearson, state treasurer; and Harry Dorman, director of budget. (Courtesy of SPL.)

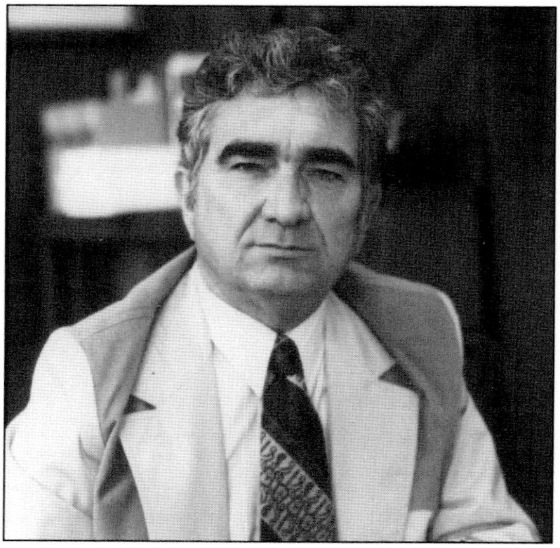

Hoyt C. Cupp was a proactive warden and was considered a benevolent dictator during his tenure from 1969 to 1984. He was commonly referred to as "the boss." He ran the prison with a personal touch, knew all the inmates, and had their respect. He believed that he could control the prison the same way he did his single-engine airplane: by being cautious and moderate, following the rules, and taking charge. (Courtesy of John Ritter.)

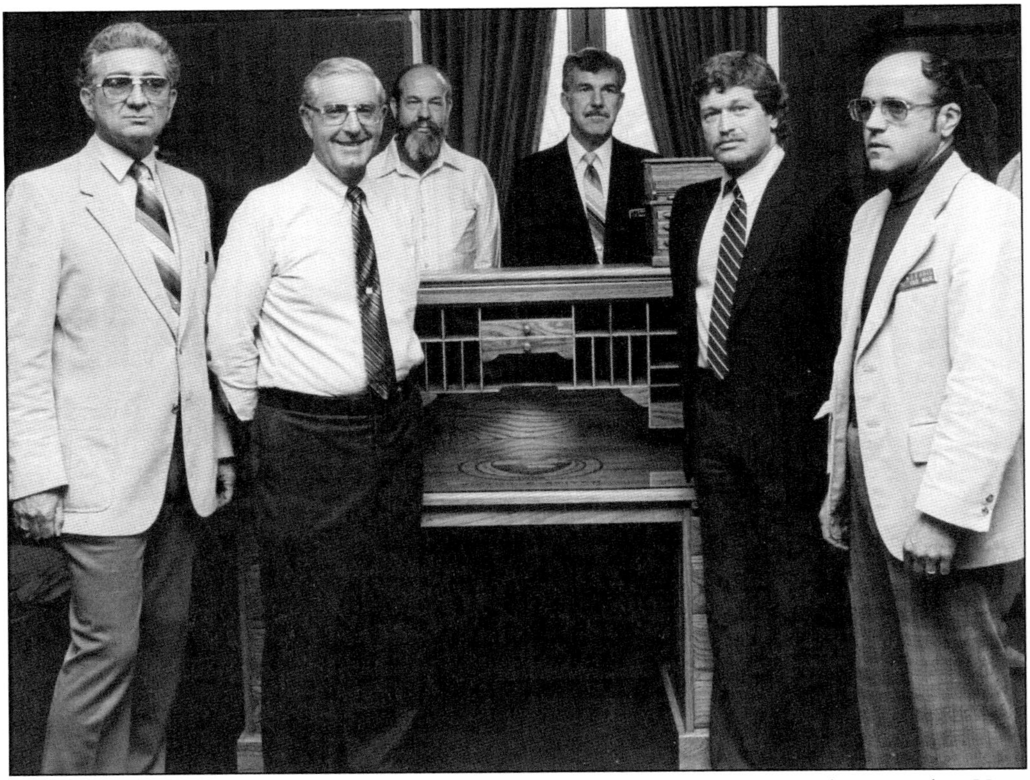

This desk was made by OSP inmate Homer Dennison, a master woodworker. Warden Hoyt Cupp allowed special accommodations to have Dennison attend the desk's presentation to Gov. Victor Atiyeh at the state capitol. Pictured here are, from left to right, Cupp, Governor Atiyeh, Dennison, assistant warden J.C. Keeney, executive assistant to the warden Larry Roach, and prison industries director Joe Fabus.

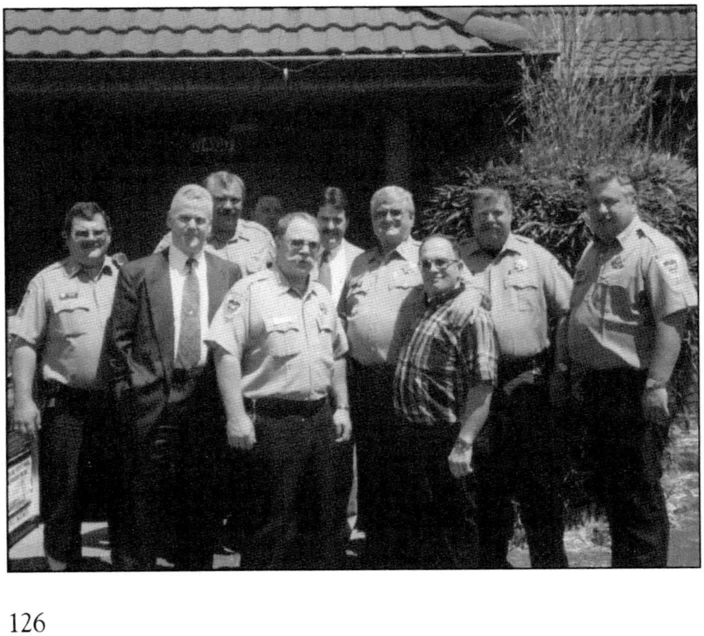

Keith Leavitt was one of the most-respected and well-known captains during the 22 years he worked at OSP. This photograph shows the men gathered to honor him at his retirement celebration. From left to right are Mike Humphries; Bill Hoefel, food services manager; Dave Heppner; unidentified; Gerry Fry; Mitch Morrow, deputy director of corrections; Keith Leavitt; John Ritter, education manager; James Ramsey; and Jeff Forbes. (Courtesy of John Ritter.)

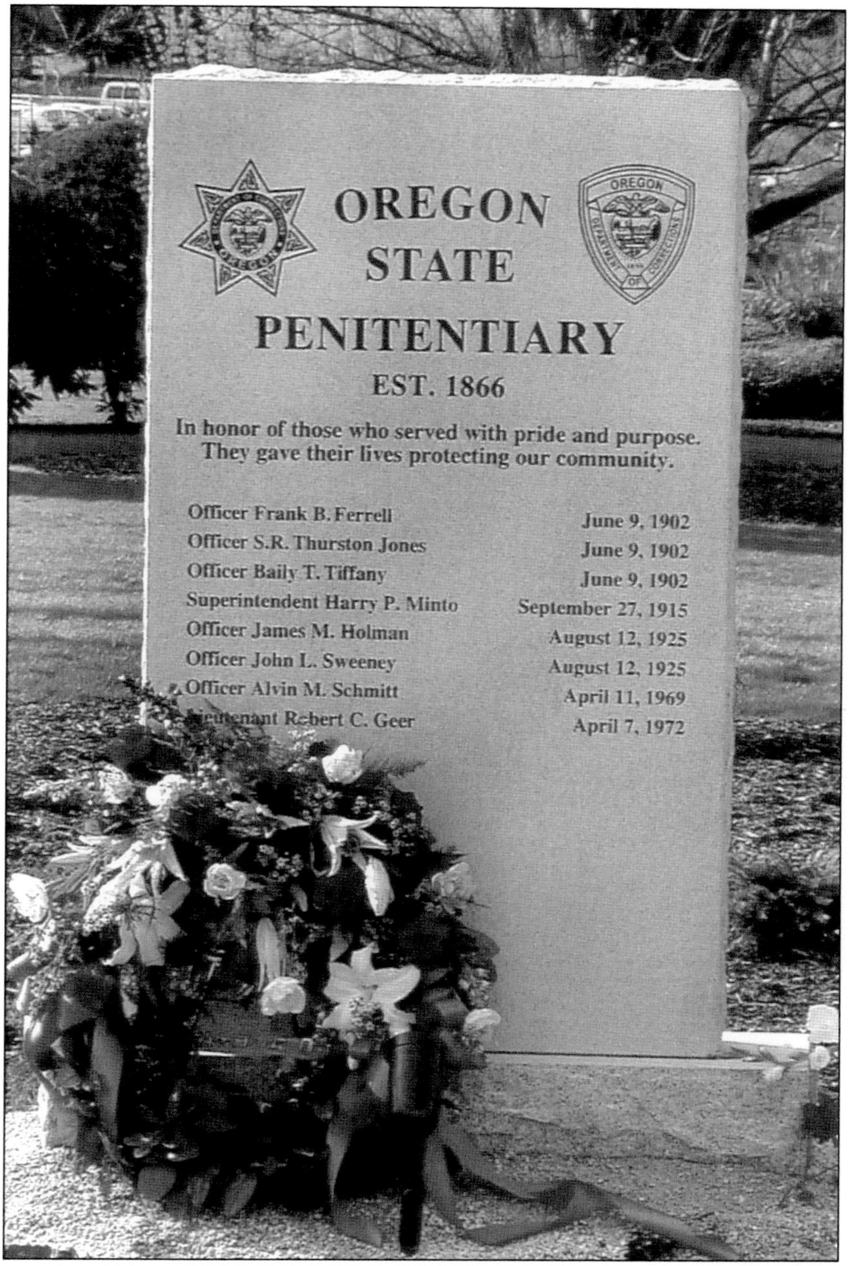

Cpl. Don Peterson researched and promoted this memorial honoring the forgotten heroes of the Oregon State Penitentiary. The dedication ceremony took place on March 27, 2000, on the prison's front lawn. The stone monument is five feet tall and three feet wide and includes the names of the eight prison employees killed since OSP opened. The memorial stands on the front lawn of the entrance to the penitentiary. Corporal Peterson stated, "It recognized the kind of sacrifice that's made on behalf of public safety by those people inside institutions over the course of many, many years." Superintendent Joan Palmateer supported and encouraged the project. One of the speakers was Randy Geer, the son of deceased corrections employee Robert Geer and a corrections department administrator himself. He worked at the penitentiary from 1983 until 1998, when he left to become operations coordinator of new prison construction.